D1446747

The Dialogical Self in Psychotherapy

The basic assumption of the 'dialogical self' is that there is no centralized 'headquarters' in the mind, but that the self is made up of a number of different 'characters'. Interpersonal relationships, from infancy onwards, become internalized – these internalized relationships then influence relationships during life. *The Dialogical Self in Psychotherapy* explores this concept. Divided into four clear parts, it covers:

- Theoretical and historical assumptions of the dialogical self from different angles: psychological, developmental and neurobiological
- The relationships between dialogical self therapy and the authors' own theoretical perspectives
- Treatment of clients suffering from severe disorders
- Method and research

The Dialogical Self in Psychotherapy gathers together psychotherapists from divergent origins to explore current thinking in the field: cognitive, constructivist, process-experiential, narrative, psychodynamic, psychodramatic, humanistic and cognitive analytic. This innovative book brings together inter- and intra-subjective dialogue and clearly demonstrates how they are incorporated into the therapeutic process.

Hubert J.M. Hermans is emeritus professor of psychology at the University of Nijmegen, The Netherlands.
Giancarlo Dimaggio is a psychiatrist and psychotherapist at the Terzo Centro di Psicoterapia Cognitiva, Rome.

The Dialogical Self in Psychotherapy

Edited by Hubert J.M. Hermans and Giancarlo Dimaggio

Brunner-Routledge
Taylor & Francis Group

HOVE AND NEW YORK

First published 2004 by Brunner-Routledge
27 Church Road, Hove, East Sussex BN3 2FA

Simultaneously published in the USA and Canada
by Brunner-Routledge
270 Madison Avenue, New York, NY 10016

Brunner-Routledge is an imprint of the Taylor & Francis Group

Typeset in Times by RefineCatch Ltd., Bungay, Suffolk
Printed and bound in Great Britain by MPG Books Ltd, Bodmin,
Cornwall
Paperback cover design by Sandra Heath

This publication has been produced with paper manufactured to
strict environmental standards and with pulp derived from
sustainable forests.

British Library Cataloguing in Publication Data
A catalogue record for this book is available from the British Library

Library of Congress Cataloging-in-Publication Data
The dialogical self in psychotherapy / edited by Hubert J.M. Hermans
and Giancarlo Dimaggio.
     p. cm.
   Includes bibliographical references and index.
   ISBN 1-58391-855-8 (hbk)
   1. Self.   2. Psychotherapy.   I. Hermans, H.J.M.   II. Dimaggio,
Giancarlo.   III. Title.

RC489.S43D53 2004
616.89'14—dc22   2004006436

ISBN 1-58391-855-8 (Hbk)

Contents

Illustrations

FIGURES

TABLES

Notes on Contributors

Dr Lynne Angus, Clinical Psychologist, is an Associate Professor of Clinical Psychology at York University and is president of the North American Chapter, Society for Psychotherapy Research. Dr Angus is the senior editor of the *Handbook of Narrative and Psychotherapy* (Sage 2004) and has published over 30 research articles and chapters relating to the contributions of narrative expression and metaphor to psychotherapy outcomes. She is the originator of the Narrative Processes Coding System (NPCS) which was co-developed with Heidi Levitt PhD and Karen Hardtke M.A. The NPCS has been translated into Portuguese, Spanish, Finnish and German and is currently being used in several international psychotherapy research initiatives. Her therapeutic practice and ongoing research programme are centrally concerned with understanding the role of client narrative expression in experiences of significant self change in psychotherapy.

Michael Barkham is Professor of Clinical and Counselling Psychology and Director of the Psychological Therapies Research Centre at the University of Leeds. He is also a Visiting Professor at the Universities of Sheffield and Northumbria at Newcastle.

Marie-Cécile Bertau, PhD, studied psycholinguistics, pedagogy, phonetics, and philosophy at the University of Munich. Her PhD dissertation was on metaphors and Western ways of conceiving language. She is Lecturer at the Institute of Psycholinguistics, University of Munich and in addition, undertakes consulting work for the Federal Ministry for Families', Senior Citizens', Women's and Youth Affairs. She is also involved in research in the ontogenesis of cognition from communication.

Philip M. Bromberg, PhD, is Training and Supervising Analyst, William Alanson White Psychoanalytic Institute; Clinical Professor of Psychology, New York University Postdoctoral Program in Psychotherapy and Psychoanalysis; Associate Editor, *Psychoanalytic Dialogues* and *Contemporary Psychoanalysis*; Editorial Board Member, *Psychoanalytic Inquiry* and *The Journal of the American Academy of Psychoanalysis*; Author, *Standing in the Spaces: Essays on Clinical Process Trauma, and Dissociation* (The Analytic Press, 1998).

Dr Marla Buchanan-Arvay is an Associate Professor in the Department of Educational and Counselling Psychology and Special Education at the University of British Columbia in Vancouver, BC, Canada. She teaches in the Graduate Program in Counselling Psychology with special concentration in qualitative research methods and clinical supervision of counsellors in training. Her research is in the field of trauma with a particular focus on secondary traumatic stress among health care professionals.

Antonino Carcione, MD, Psychiatrist and Psychotherapist, Member of Terzo Centro di Psicoterapia Cognitiva, trains students at the Società Italiana di Terapia Cognitiva e Comportamentale and the School for Specialization in Psychotherapy – Associazione di Psicologia Cognitiva (APC). He is author of various articles in national and international journals about psychotherapeutic process and personality disorders and Editor of the journal *Cognitivismo Clinico*.

Dario Catania, MD, is a Psychiatrist and Psychotherapist in a public Department of Mental Health in Rome. His main interest is the role of narrative in psychotherapy. He is member of Terzo Centro di Psicoterapia Cognitiva and author of various articles in national and international journals about clinical psychiatry and psychotherapy.

Mick Cooper, PhD is a Senior Lecturer in Counselling at the University of Strathclyde, and a UKCP-registered psychotherapist, whose practice combines elements of existential and person-centred approaches to therapy. Mick is co-editor of *The Plural Self* with John Rowan (Sage 1999), author of *Existential Therapies* (Sage 2003), and has written several papers and chapters on self-pluralistic, person-centred and existential approaches to therapy.

Let Dillen is Master of Science in clinical psychology. She is currently employed as a researcher of the Fund of Scientific Research-Flanders at the University of Ghent (Belgium), Department of Developmental, Personality and Social Psychology, where she investigates complicated grief in childhood and adolescence.

Giancarlo Dimaggio, MD, Psychiatrist and Psychotherapist has written papers about the narrative/dialogical processes in psychotherapy and about pathology and treatment of personality disorders in *Psychotherapy Research, Psychology and Psychotherapy, Journal of Constructivist Psychology, Journal of Psychotherapy Integration, Clinical Psychology and Psychotherapy*. He's a member of the editorial board of the *Journal of Constructivistic Psychology*. In Italy he's co-editor of the book *I disturbi di personalità. Modelli e trattamento* (Personality Disorders. Models and treatment).

Meredith J. Glick is a doctoral student in Clinical Psychology at Miami University in Oxford, Ohio, USA. Her research interests include using the Assimilation Model to study psychotherapy process and outcome, internal multiplicity, and clients' perceptions of change in psychotherapy. She enjoys playing the French horn in her spare time.

Michael A. Gray is a doctoral student in clinical psychology at Miami University in Oxford, Ohio USA. His research focuses on the treatment of anxiety disorders, in particular focusing upon how anxious persons acknowledge and work through problematic experiences in psychotherapy. His clinical work is chiefly with adult and adolescent clients with severe mental illness, including personality disorder, panic disorder, and post-traumatic stress disorder.

Leslie S. Greenberg is professor of clinical psychology at York University in Toronto, Ontario, Canada. He is one of the originators of Process-Experiential therapy and has made substantial contributions to the understanding of emotional processes in psychotherapy. Furthermore, he and Pascual-Leone have developed the dialectical-constructivist model of the construction of the self.

Denis Helskens is student at the University of Ghent (Belgium) and will soon graduate as Master of Science in clinical psychology (foreseen from July or September 2004 on).

Hubert J. M. Hermans is emeritus-professor of psychology at the University of Nijmegen, The Netherlands. He developed a valuation theory and a self-confrontation method. His most recent work is on the multivoicedness and dialogicality of the self. He is 'First International Associate' of the Society for Personology and President of the International Society for Dialogical Science (ISDS). Address: Hubert J.M. Hermans, Department of Psychology, University of Nijmegen, P.O. Box 9104, 6500 HE, Nijmegen, The Netherlands. E-mail: HHermans@psych.kun.nl. Homepage: www.dialogicalself.info

Els Hermans-Jansen originally worked with adolescent boys and girls with serious behavioural problems. After finishing her studies at the University of Nijmegen, she became qualified in several psychotherapeutic and counselling techniques. She is acknowledged as a psychotherapist by the Ministry of Welfare in the Netherlands. She works in a private practice in Berg and Dal where she has applied, in cooperation with Hubert Hermans, ideas around valuation theory, self-confrontation and dialogical self, with a large variety of clients. She co-authored *Self-Narratives: The construction of meaning in psychotherapy* (New York: Guilford).

Mikael Leiman is a Docent of Psychotherapy and Psychotherapy research at the University of Joensuu, Finland. He has been involved in bringing cognitive analytic therapy to Finland and contributed to the dialogical turn of its conceptual basis. His current interests concern very brief dialogical interventions in primary health care and vocational counselling.

Marc D. Lewis is a Professor at the University of Toronto. His publications include theoretical work on dynamic systems modelling of cognition-emotion and personality development, as well as empirical work on infant and child emotional development. With Isabela Granic he edited *Emotion, Development, and Self-Organization: Dynamic Systems Approaches to Emotional Development* (Cambridge 2000). An in-press paper in *Behavioral and Brain Sciences* extends this perspective to the neurobiology of emotion.

John T Lysaker PhD is an Associate Professor of Philosophy at the University of Oregon in Eugene Oregon, USA. He has active interests in studies of Emerson, deconstruction and the Frankfort School Critical Theory, schizophrenia, and the dialogical self

Paul Lysaker PhD is a staff psychologist at the Roudebush VA Medical Center and an Assistant Professor of Clinical Psychology Department of Psychiatry, Indiana University School of Medicine, Indianapolis, USA. He has active research interests in psychotherapy and rehabilitation interventions for schizophrenia.

Hannah Mackay has a BA(Hons) Psychology from the University of Sheffield (UK), and a PhD in psychotherapy research from the University of Leeds (UK). She is currently working as a shiatsu practitioner and is involved in researching complementary and alternative medicine.

John McLeod is Professor of Counselling at University of Abertay Dundee, in Scotland. He is interested in understanding the role of narrative in psychotherapy process, and is author of *Narrative and Psychotherapy* (Sage 1997) and co-editor (with Lynne Angus) of the *Handbook of Narrative and Psychotherapy* (Sage 2004).

Robert A. Neimeyer, PhD, holds a Dunavant University Professorship in the Department of Psychology, University of Memphis, in Memphis, Tennessee, USA, where he also maintains an active private practice. He has published or edited 18 books, including *Constructivism in Psychotherapy*, *Constructions of Disorder*, and *Meaning Reconstruction and the Experience of Loss*. The author of over 200 articles and book chapters, he is currently most interested in developing a narrative and constructivist framework for psychotherapy, with special relevance to loss and grief. He is the Co-Editor of the *Journal of Constructivist Psychology*.

Giuseppe Nicolò, MD, Psychiatrist and Psychotherapist, is a Member of Terzo Centro di Psicoterapia Cognitiva in Rome. He trains students at the Società Italiana di Terapia Cognitiva e Comportamentale and at the School for Specialization in Psychotherapy – Associazione di Psicologia Cognitiva (APC). He directs the training school Scuola di Psicoterapia Cognitiva (SPC) in Reggio Calabria. He is secretary of the Italian chapter of Society for Psychotherapy Research. He is author of various articles in national and international journals about psychotherapeutic process and personality disorders.

Katerine Osatuke is a doctoral student in clinical psychology at Miami University in Oxford, Ohio, USA. Her research focuses on empirically describing multiple internal parts within people, and in particular examining how they are expressed in sounds of clients' speech in therapy. Her clinical work is mainly with patients who have a borderline personality disorder or severe trauma history.

Michele Procacci, MD, Psychiatrist and Psychotherapist, is a Member of Terzo Centro di Psicoterapia Cognitiva. He trains students at the Società Italiana di Terapia Cognitiva e Comportamentale and at the School for Specialization in Psychotherapy–Associazione di Psicologia Cognitiva (APC), and is Professor in Psychopathology at the University of Naples, Faculty of Psychology. He is author of various articles in national and international journals about psychotherapeutic process and personality disorders.

Giampaolo Salvatore, MD, Psychiatrist and Psychotherapist, teaches Psychological Physiology at the Pontificia Università Ateneo Salesiano in Rome. His main interests are the neurobiological basis of narrative mental processes and the role of narrative in psychotherapy. He is member of Terzo Centro di Psicoterapia Cognitiva and author of various articles in national and international journals about clinical psychiatry and psychopathology and psychotherapy of personality disorders.

Antonio Semerari, MD, is a psychiatrist and psychotherapist who teaches at the Specialist School, Associazione di Psicologia Cognitiva, of Rome. Since 1995, he has directed the research group of Terzo Centro di Psiocterapia Cognitiva, in Rome, which specializes in the treatment of personality disorders. The research group's main interests involve the analysis of metarepresentative functions, variations of mental states, and the analysis of narrative forms in the psychotherapeutic process. He is author or editor of several books.

Mariska Siongers is a student at the University of Ghent (Belgium) and will soon graduate as Master of Science in clinical psychology (foreseen from July or September 2004 on).

William B. Stiles is a professor of psychology at Miami University in Oxford, Ohio, USA. He received his PhD from UCLA in 1972. He is the author of *Describing Talk: A Taxonomy of Verbal Response Modes*. He is a past president of the Society for Psychotherapy Research, and former North American editor of *Psychotherapy Research*.

Rebecca Todd is a doctoral candidate in Developmental Science at the University of Toronto. Her research interests include cognition-emotion interactions and the study of neural processes associated with intersubjectivity and dyadic interactions. Prior to beginning her doctoral studies, she was a choreographer and arts writer with a focus on fostering dialogue between art and science.

Leni M. F. Verhofstadt-Denève is Professor in Theoretical and Clinical Developmental Psychology at Ghent University (Belgium). She is a Member of the Belgian Royal Academy of Science and has several national and international publications on (1) long-term follow-up research from adolescence into adulthood and (2) theory and practice on Clinical-therapeutic action and drama strategies. She is trained in clinical psycho-drama by Dean and Doreen Elefthery and is Certified Practitioner (CP) and Trainer Educator Practitioner (TEP) from the Netherlands-Belgian psychodrama board.

William J. Whelton is an assistant professor in counselling psychology at the University of Alberta in Edmonton, Alberta, Canada. His work has focused on the nature and variety of self-critical and self-resilient voices within the self and on the role of emotion in the construction of the self.

The dialogical self in psychotherapy

Introduction

Hubert J.M. Hermans and Giancarlo Dimaggio

This book is generated by the theoretical marriage of two concepts, self and dialogue, representing different traditions in the history of human thought. After centuries of philosophical discussions about the human soul, William James (1890) was one of the main thinkers who proposed a conception of the self that would have an enormous impact on theory and research in American psychology of the twentieth century. In the period that American psychologists, inspired by James, Mead and other theorists, were giving shape to a 'psychology of the self', there emerged in Russia a dialogical school inspired by the literary scientist Mikhail Bakhtin (1973, 1981), who presented a fine-grained analysis of the human capacity for communication and interchange. The 'dialogical self' brings these two concepts, self and dialogue, together in such a way that a fertile field of theory, research and practice is disclosed.

Self-narratives as spatially structured and multivoiced

One of the developments, influenced by the American psychology of the self, is the narrative approach dealing with the various ways in which people tell stories about themselves and the world (e.g. Bruner 1986; Sarbin 1986). Narrative psychologists posed a question which is of immediate significance for psychotherapists working with the stories of their clients: how do clients organize their self-narratives and how do they reorganize it over time (Angus and McLeod 2004)?

It is one of the premises of the dialogical self that self-narratives are not only temporally but also spatially structured. The person who is telling a story is doing so from a particular position in space and time (Hermans and Kempen 1993). When the storyteller is positioned, there is always another position, in the environment or in the self, involved. The spatial organization of self-narratives has a far-reaching implication: when a narrative is told, there is not simply one story with a beginning, middle and ending, that is 'owned' by the teller of the story and can be, as a ready-made chapter of a book, communicated to another person. Rather, a self-narrative is continuously structured and restructured by two or more voiced positions that in their dialogical interchange endorse, revise, restructure and develop any existing story. Both teller and listener of a story are positioned in a space and between the several positions a field of tension is stretched in which any temporally organized story is constantly challenged by spatially opposed interlocutors. Before the story reaches a final ending, it has taken another direction or turn under the influence of voices co-constructing new or alternative stories as part of the polyphony of the mind. In everyday life we can see that people tell different stories, about themselves and the world, or give different versions of the 'same' story, dependent on the interests, expectations, questions and responses on the part of the audience. The person even functions as his or her own audience in any narrative construction (Baldwin and Holmes 1987).

Given the intrinsic interwovenness of internal and external dialogues, the self does not function as a 'container' of cognition, thought and emotion, centralized in itself. It does not operate as a unified agency in a multivoiced environment. Rather, the self is multivoiced because the multiplicity of voices is also in the self and their mutual relationships characterize the self as a 'society of mind'.

As a multivoiced and dialogical process, the self is made up of various positions, voices or characters, each of them functioning as a partly independent agency that generates specific memories, thoughts and stories. Each character can temporarily take over the control of actions as the principal actor in a client's mind. From this theoretical perspective, there is no centralized, controlling headquarters ordering when other characters make their appearance. Rather, they alternate with each other, with the dominant character being identified by the subject as I (for review of the multiplicity of self and identity, see Rowan and Cooper 1999).

Since the 1980s psychopathologists have acknowledged the multivoicedness of the self (see Putnam 1989). In the well-known disorder 'multiple personality' (more recently known as 'dissociative identity disorder'), multiple I-positions manifest themselves in dramatic ways. Although in some cases one 'alter' may be co-conscious with another one and different parts of the self can even communicate with each other (Barresi 1994), the dialogical interaction between the several parts and the flexibility to move from one part to another is severely constrained. Generally speaking, there is little cooperation and interaction among the several alters and the accessibility of significant parts of the self may be seriously reduced. In one I-position the person is doing or saying things that are often beyond the control of the person in the other position. Moreover, some positions, usually the 'bad' ones, are not well integrated in the organization of the self. In Ellenberger's (1970) words:

> An individual suddenly seems to lose his identity to become another person. His physiognomy changes and shows a striking resemblance to

the individual of whom he is, supposedly, the incarnation. With an altered voice, he pronounces words corresponding to the personality of the new individual.

(Ellenberger 1970: 13)

In other words, multiple personality, as an abnormal phenomenon, seems to be the pathological side of a healthy functioning dialogical self (see Bromberg, Chapter 9 in this volume, for the difference between healthy and dysfunctional dissociation).

In the conceptual framework of the dialogical self others are not simply 'external', but rather possess a double position: both internal and external. In fact, from infancy onwards, interpersonal relationships become part of the self and significant others become characters in one's inner scenario (see Bertau, Chapter 2 in this volume). Based on these interpersonal relationships these memory patterns influence relationships during life. A loop thus gets formed in which others are incorporated into the self and the self orchestrates the relationship of a subject with others. As a result, the self is truly immersed in a world of relationships (see Verhofstadt-Denève, Dillen, Helskens and Siongers, Chapter 10 in this volume).

The psychotherapeutic models presented in this book take the multivoicedness and the dialogical dimension into account. The therapist has a chance to become a new position in the client's mental scenario, facilitating and changing the organization of the client's self. If the therapist reaches this position, often a privileged one, he or she is committed to modify the dysfunctional elements in this scenario, while remaining aware that he or she is involved personally in the relationship with the client (see Semerari, Carcione, Dimaggio, Nicolò and Procacci, Chapter 14 in this volume). A client enters a therapist's scenario too, arousing emotional reactions and dialogues that are either a benefit or a hindrance to the therapeutic process.

Implications of a dialogical view for dysfunctions in the self

In line with the preceding considerations, this present book has two central features which directly pertain to the psychotherapy of clinical dysfunctions. First, it offers a conceptual framework that finds its basis in normal functioning. Dysfunctions are not considered as phenomena in themselves and the self is not reduced to its malfunctioning aspects. Instead, clients are treated on the basis of the question of how the dysfunctional elements in the self may be changed as part of a broader organized position repertoire. This view takes its starting point not in the question of how dysfunctions may be *reduced* but what can be *added* to the repertoire, so that its self-healing capacities are strengthened and developed. Acknowledgement of the multiplicity of the self enables therapist and client to make a distinction between functional and dysfunctional parts of the self and to protect the former ones from the generalizing influence of the latter. Moreover, the functional parts of the self may provide productive forces that facilitate the modification of the dysfunctional parts of the self and allow their inclusion as components of larger, more adaptive coalitions (see Hermans and Hermans-Jansen, Chapter 8 in this volume).

The second central feature of this book is that dysfunctions are studied and treated as parts of a self that is located on the interface of intra- and interpersonal relationships. Studying and treating the two realms in their interconnection, results in a model that acknowledges the therapist as an important, temporary position in the client's self and allows the client to play a meaningful role as part of the multiplicity of the psychotherapist's self (see Dimaggio, Salvatore and Catania, Chapter 12 in this volume). A dialogical perspective enables the client to meet the therapist as a source of new ideas and understandings and to use this perspective to deal with the problems in the contact with significant others in the social environment. From the perspective of the dialogical self, changes on the intra-mental plane are systematically related to changes on the inter-mental plane.

In order to demonstrate how these intra- and inter-mental processes take place in the context of psychotherapy, all authors of the therapeutic chapters (Parts 2 and 3) have presented cases of actual clients. The cases demonstrate, in various ways, that intra- and interpersonal processes are intimately intertwined.

The dialogical self as linking different therapeutic traditions

One of the purposes of this book is to explore to what extent dialogical self theory can serve as a conceptual framework in which different psychotherapeutic schools can meet. Contributions from different psychotherapeutic traditions are brought together in order to create a platform where therapists from divergent origin can discuss their commonalities, differences, agreements and disagreements.

Authors from different orientations are represented in this book: *cognitive* (Stiles, Osatuke, Glick and Mackay; Osatuke, Gray, Glick, Stiles and Barkham; Semerari, Carcione, Dimaggio, Nicolò and Procacci), *constructivist* (Neimeyer and Arvay), *process-experiential* (Whelton and Greenberg), *narrative* (Angus and McLeod; Dimaggio, Salvatore and Catania; Hermans and Hermans-Jansen; Lysaker and Lysaker), *psychodynamic* (Bromberg), *psychodramatic* (Verhofstadt-Denève, Dillen, Helskens and Siongers), *humanistic* (Cooper) and *cognitive-analytic* (Leiman). The authors describe the ways in which they treat clients with proper attention to their multivoicedness, dialogical relationships, and the organization and reorganization of the clients' selves.

When we (the editors of this book) participated in the First and Second International Conferences on the Dialogical Self, we discovered that psychotherapists from divergent origins often expressed ideas which were strikingly similar despite the conceptual differences of their schools. We decided to invite representatives of the different traditions to meet on a 'dialogical platform', in order to explore the crossways and commonalities between the several schools. We suspected that, given the common theoretical framework of the dialogical self, it would be possible to explore new linkages and perhaps new phenomena on the interface of the various approaches.

The search for commonalities between several therapeutic schools was a central issue at a plenary panel presented at the Society for Psychotherapy Research meeting in Geilo, Norway in 1997. The organizer and the members of the panel were impressed by the explanatory power of the notion of multiple voices in different clinical and psychotherapeutic traditions. This led to a special issue on the subject in the *Journal of Psychotherapy Integration* in which several contributions of the panel discussion were published, together with a virtual discussion (Elliott and Greenberg 1997; Fonagy 1997; Hermans 1997; Smith-Benjamin 1997; Stiles 1997). This book expands on this initiative by continuing the discussion on multivoicedness and dialogue in relation to adaptive and maladaptive functioning.

Here we touch on a difference with earlier traditions, like transactionial analysis and Gestalt, which focused on the multiplicity of the self. Often these approaches developed as separate schools having a minimum of communication with other schools despite their often implicit commonalities in theory and practice. This book explicitly aims to facilitate the contact between these approaches and provides a conceptual framework that addresses some of their major interests.

Connection between the dialogical self and brain research

The connection with developments in brain research is another topic in which dialogical self theory goes beyond existing approaches which focus on multivoicedness and dialogicality in psychotherapy. Recent developments in psychobiological research have resulted in the insight that the production of verbal thoughts is associated with an activation of the left inferior frontal region (McGuire et al. 1996a) and that ischaemic lesions to this part of the brain can cause a total loss of the ability to produce inner speech (Levine et al. 1982).

The representation of verbal thoughts expressed by someone else in one's own mental space (see Semerari and colleagues, Chapter 14 in this volume) requires not only the activation of the left inferior frontal region, but also the participation of certain other parts of the brain: the supplementary motor area, the left temporal cortex and the left premotor cortex. These centres are considered responsible for the monitoring of inner speech (McGuire et al. 1996b). This monitory activity is directly relevant to the dialogical self because with this activity one is able to identify any verbal thought or internal dialogue, that gets represented in one's mental space.

One of the researchers interested in the relationship between the dialogical self and the functioning of the brain is Schore (1994). He argues that complex functional brain systems are not ready-made at birth and do not arise spontaneously in development, but are formed in the process of social contact between child and caregivers and between the child and itself. Schore is particularly interested in the early postnatal growth of the orbitofrontal area. As a result of the social interactions between caregivers and child, hormonal and neurohormonal responses are triggered leading to physiological alterations which are registered within specific areas in the infant's brain. Through 'reflected appraisals' in non-verbal, prelinguistic dialogues with the child, the caregiver selects and influences, by her intonations, facial expressions, sounds and touching, specific emotional states which the emerging self can experience (see Bertau, Chapter 2 in this volume, for developmental issues, and Osatuke and colleagues' Chapter 15 for the distinction between content and sound of the clients' utterances). In responding to the child's emotional states, the caregiver facilitates transitions from one state to another, for example, from a high level of anxiety to relaxation. Given the pervasive influence of adult–child interactions on the maturation of the brain, Schore refers to the ability of the dialogical self to occupy a 'multiplicity of positions' and to the capacity to adaptively switch between psychobiological states that are coloured by different affects (Schore 1994: 495). Developing a dialogical self, the child is increasingly able to transcend his or her immediate state (e.g. distress) and to enhance 'self-solace' capacities, that is, the child is also able to make the transition between the two states when the mother is not present (see also Wilson and Weinstein 1992). As Schore (1994: 373–385) argues, this capacity to make transitions from negative to positive states of mind is seriously reduced in forms of insecure attachment.

Another researcher interested in the 'dialogical brain' is Lewis (2002; see also Lewis and Todd, Chapter 3 in this volume). He proposes a model of the brain which is based on recent neuroscientific evidence and examines to what extent this evidence is compatible with dialogical self theory. He concludes that in our daily lives we are involved in a dialogical relation with an anticipated, almost heard, other from the perspective of a familiar and rather continuous I-position. The orbitofrontal cortex, in its linkage to the subcortical limbic system, produces an affectively charged, gist-like sense of an interpersonal respondent, which is based on stabilized expectancies from many past interactions. Such interactions begin with attachment figures who produce gist-like images as fundamental arbitrators of emotion regulation. Lewis proposes a model in which relatively stable, emotionally charged, sublingual monologues put limits on the linguistic, dialogical processes. (For the central role of emotions in the functioning of the self, see also Angus and McLeod (Chapter 5); Bromberg (Chapter 9); Dimaggio et al. (Chapter 12); Hermans and Hermans-Jansen (Chapter 8); Osatuke et al. (Chapter 15); Stiles et al. (Chapter 6); and Whelton and Greenberg (Chapter 7) in this volume.)

Cross-fertilization among different contributions: the case of self-criticism

One of the advantages of an interdisciplinary approach is the possibility of cross-fertilization between the several contributions. We give only one example, the phenomenon of self-criticism that crops up in different chapters.

In her developmental contribution to this issue, Bertau describes how learning through the other is possible because of the ability to engage with the other in 'joint attention'. Prior to 9 months, the infant is only able to engage with an object *or* with a person. When interacting with a person, the object is not the focus of the interaction. After 9 months, however, a radical change takes place when the object is included in the exchange between infant and adult. From then the infant is able to coordinate object and person. The child becomes able to look at an object from the perspective of the adult. Bertau argues that the capacity of joint attention functions as a developmental condition for the emergence of self-reflection:

> Just as the infant can learn about *external* situations from the point of view of the adult, in face-to-face interaction the infant can now learn about the adult's perception and intention *toward her*, the infant, when the adult's attention is on her.
>
> (Tomasello 1993: 176, emphasis by Bertau)

In other words, via joint attention the child learns about him- or herself from the perspective of the adult. This creates the condition for the emergence of self-reflection, including self-criticism, in which the evaluative stance of the adult toward the child is incorporated.

In their neuroscientific analysis in Chapter 3, Lewis and Todd discuss the case of Yvonne who thinks of her familiar I-position as the 'Anxious Child', while she names the sarcastic parental voice, vaguely responding in her imagination, the 'Critic'. While the voice of the anxious child is mediated by the orbitofrontal cortex, the critical voice of the parent is, in Lewis and Todd's view, more mediated by another part of the brain, the anterior cingulate cortex (ACC). If it is true, Lewis and Todd reason, that the articulation of the ACC-mediated parental voice moves the conversation forward, one important goal for therapy might entail tuning in to the voice of the Critic more closely. Over time, Yvonne might learn to actively inhabit this voice as a fully articulated, volitional persona. In this way, not only would Yvonne experience the Critic's righteous anger as her own, but also, by elaborating this position, the Critic would allow the Anxious Child to respond in a more constructive manner. By moving the dialogue forward, such enhanced aware-ness of dialogical voices might also allow the Anxious Child to become more volitional. Such increased volitional force could redress power imbalances between the two positions allowing the Anxious Child to become stronger in response to a more articulate Critic. In this way Yvonne might move the conversation out of the repetitive, stuck mode that perpetuates her feelings of defensive anxiety.

In Chapter 7 on process-experiential psychotherapy, Whelton and Greenberg are doing precisely what Lewis and Todd are suggesting. They focus in their contribution on self-criticism as an example of conflict between parts of the self and use two-chair therapy to address maladaptive forms of self-criticism. This technique invites the client to move back and forth between two chairs. In one chair the client dramatizes the voice of the self-critic and in the other the voice of the 'experiencing' self, the object of the criticism, the part of the self that experiences the hurt of being criticized. Two-chair dialogue involves clearly separating out the two voices in spatial ways and having them speak directly to each other. The self-critic begins with general attacks and criticisms, then more pointed and specific criticisms. In response the experiencing self will often complain and will counterattack but very superficially. In the course of psychotherapy, the two voices learn to address each other in more symmetrical dialogues in which they deal with each other in more productive ways.

In Chapter 4 in this volume, Cooper, building on Buber's (1923/1958) dialogical philosophy, distinguishes an I–I and an I–It mode of relating. In the I–I mode there is a fundamental confirmation of the alternate I-position: by contrast, in the I–It relational mode, the alternate I-position is not fully accepted as it is, and may be criticized, dismissed or derided. In that case, there is a failure to accept the other *as* an Other: it is a demand for totaliza-tion and homogeneity (Levinas 1969) rather than an openness to alterity and difference of the other voice. In the I–Me self-relational stance, a derivation from the I–It mode, the on-line I-position does not meet the alternate posi-tion as it actually is. By contrast, in the I–I self-relational stance, there is a breaking-through of a genuine otherness into the on-line I's world. Cooper calls this recognition of the otherness a 'self–otherness', an attitude that is open to something new and unexpected. In this respect, it is a meeting in the present. Instead of reducing the alternate position to a homogeneous object, the I–I mode brings the alternate voice to expression in all its particular aspects.

As the above selected passages show, four different contributions from different (sub)disciplines deal with the same phenomenon from quite differ-ent angles: developmental psychology, brain sciences, psychotherapy and philosophy. Not only do they show a clear commonality in subject matter, but also they complement each other in their understanding of the phenomenon in question. Shifting from one theoretical stance to the other may enrich not only our understanding of the psychotherapeutic process but also our self-understanding as scientists and professionals.

Composition of the book

The book has four parts. The first part includes chapters that deal with the general theoretical foundation of the dialogical self. The second part includes chapters from different psychotherapeutic orientations dealing with theoretical and practical issues in the treatment of clients. The third part focuses more specifically on the reconstruction of dialogical processes in severely affected clients. The fourth and final part includes some contributions that address methodological and empirical issues related to dialogical aspects of psychotherapy.

References

Angus, L. and McLeod, J. (eds) (2004). *Handbook of Narrative and Psychotherapy: Practice, Theory and Research*. Thousand Oaks, CA: Sage.

Bakhtin, M.M. (1973). *Problems of Dostoevsky's Poetics*, 2nd edn. Trans. R.W. Rotsel. Ann Arbor, MI: Ardis. First edn published in 1929 under the title *Problemy tvorchestva Dostoevskogo* [Problems of Dostoevsky's Art].

Bakhtin, M.M. (1981). *The Dialogic Imagination: Four Essays*. Austin, TX: University of Texas Press.

Baldwin, M.W. and Holmes, J.G. (1987). 'Salient private audiences and awareness of the self.' *Journal of Personality and Social Psychology*, *52*, 1087–1098.

Barresi, J. (1994). 'Morton Prince and B.C.A.: A historical footnote on the confrontation between dissociation theory and Freudian psychology in a case of multiple personality.' In R. Klein and B. Doane (eds) *Psychological Concepts and Dissociative Disorders* (pp. 85–129). Hillsdale, NJ: Lawrence Erlbaum Associates.

Bruner, J.S. (1986). *Actual Minds, Possible Worlds*. Cambridge, MA: Harvard University Press.

Buber, M. (1923/1958). *I and Thou*, 2nd edn. Trans. R.G. Smith. Edinburgh: T. and T. Clark.

Ellenberger, H.F. (1970). *The Discovery of the Unconscious*. New York: Basic Books.

Elliott, R. and Greenberg, L.S. (1997). 'Multiple voices in process-experiential therapy: Dialogues between aspects of the self.' *Journal of Psychotherapy Integration*, *7*, 225–239.

Fonagy, P. (1997). 'Multiple voices vs. meta-cognition: An attachment theory perspective.' *Journal of Psychotherapy Integration*, *7*, 181–194.

Hermans, H.J.M. (1997). 'Dissociation as disorganized self-narrative: Tension between splitting and integration.' *Journal of Psychotherapy Integration*, *7*, 213–223.

Hermans, H.J.M. and Kempen, H.J.G. (1993). *The Dialogical Self: Meaning as Movement*. San Diego, CA: Academic Press.

James, W. (1890). *The Principles of Psychology*, Vol. 1. London: Macmillan.

Levinas, E. (1969). *Totality and Infinity: An Essay on Exteriority*. Trans. A. Lingis. Pittsburgh, PA: Duquesne University Press.

Levine, D.N., Calvanio, R. and Popovics, A. (1982). 'Language in the absence of inner speech.' *Neuropsychologia*, *20*, 391–409.

Lewis, M.D. (2002). 'The dialogical brain: Contributions of emotional neurobiology to understanding the dialogical self.' *Theory and Psychology*, *12*, 175–190.

McGuire, P.K., Silbersweig, D.A., Murray, R.M., David, A.S., Frackowiak, R.S.J. and Frith, C.D. (1996a). 'Functional anatomy of inner speech and auditory verbal imagery.' *Psychological Medicine*, *26*, 29–38.

McGuire, P.K., Silbersweig, D.A. and Frith, C.D. (1996b). 'Functional neuroanatomy of verbal self-monitoring.' *Brain*, *119*, 907–917.

Putnam, F.W. (1989). *Diagnosis and Treatment of Multiple Personality Disorder*. New York: Guilford.

Rowan, J. and Cooper, M. (1999). *The Plural Self: Multiplicity in Everyday Life*. London: Sage.

Sarbin, T.R. (1986). 'The narrative as a root metaphor for psychology.' In T.R. Sarbin (ed.) *Narrative Psychology: The Storied Nature of Human Conduct* (pp. 3–21). New York: Praeger.

Schore, A.N. (1994). *Affect Regulation and the Origin of the Self: The Neurobiology of Emotional Development*. Hillsdale, NJ: Lawrence Erlbaum Associates.

Smith-Benjamin, L. (1997). 'Human imagination and psychopathology.' *Journal of Psychotherapy Integration*, *7*, 195–211.

Stiles, W.B. (1997). 'Multiple voices in psychotherapy clients.' *Journal of Psychotherapy Integration*, *7*, 177–180.

Tomasello, M. (1993). 'On the interpersonal origins of self-concept.' In U. Neisser (ed.) *The Perceived Self: Ecological and Interpersonal Sources of Self-Knowledge* (pp. 174–184). Cambridge: Cambridge University Press.

Wilson, A. and Weinstein, L. (1992). 'An investigation into some implications for psychoanalysis of Vygotsky's perspective on the origin of mind, Part 1.' *Journal of the American Psychoanalytic Association*, *40*, 524–576.

Part I

General theory

Chapter 1

The dialogical self
Between exchange and power

Hubert J.M. Hermans

The two concepts, self and dialogue, that are central in this chapter, have their own specific connotations, when considered separately. The self is easily associated with something that is located 'within the skin' or 'deep down inside'. Dialogue, on the other hand, evokes the image of two or more people, involved in some kind of communication, typically a communication in which people are on common terms and understand each other quite well. As far as individuals are communicating with themselves, the term 'monologue' comes easily to mind, as suggested by the well-known term 'monologue intérieur'. As these connotations suggest, the self is often considered a 'within' concept and dialogue a 'between' concept.

The notion of the 'dialogical self' deviates from those associations and considers the self as a multiplicity of parts (voices, characters, positions) that have the potential of entertaining dialogical relationships with each other. Differences are as central to the dialogical self as they are to different partners in dialogue. Moreover, the different parts of the self are not only involved in communicative interchange, but also subjected to relative dominance, with some parts being more powerful or speaking with a louder voice than other parts. In other words, the dialogical self, as a 'between' concept, is based on the assumption that the processes that are taking place between the different parts of the self are also taking place in the relationship between the individual and him- or herself. The self functions as a society, being at the same time part of the broader society in which the self participates.

This chapter discusses the nature of the dialogical self in the context of classic and recent literatures. It starts with elaborating on an aspect that is crucial to the understanding of the present theoretical framework: the dialogue of the mind with itself. This will be followed by the notion of dominance or power as an intrinsic feature of dialogical relationships. After bringing together the components of 'dialogue' and 'self', I will discuss the implications of the dialogical self for psychotherapy.

Dialogue: the coexistence of exchange and power

The dialogical self can be seen as a theoretical effort to extend the self from a self-contained entity to a process that is extended to the other person and to society at large of which the self is a part. This widening of the theoretical 'reach' of the concept of self requires a discussion of two phenomena that are central to any society in which people live together: exchange and social power.

Internal dialogue and the imperfection of the mind

When we communicate with ourselves, the question can be posed whether 'we' are identical with 'ourselves' or not. When one part of the self communicates with another part, and the two parts would be exactly the same, both providing the same perspective on the world, and giving the same information to each other, not much progress in thinking and feeling could be expected. The human mind has the capacity to examine or interrogate itself, with one part addressing another part. When I ask myself a question, I would never be able to give any meaningful answer, as long as the part of the mind who poses the question, would be the same part as the one who is supposed to answer. The argument is that the mind is able to entertain a meaningful internal communication, only if the answering part is to some extent *qualitatively different* from the asking part.

In a thorough discussion of the dialogical nature of the human mind, the philosopher Blachowicz (1999) proposes the metaphor of the cooperation between a police artist and a witness for understanding the relationship of the mind with itself. Only from different perspectives they arrive, stepwise, at a final picture that may resemble the suspect:

> I propose viewing the 'dialogue of the soul with itself' as a series of proposals and disposals similar in function to the exchange between the police artist and the witness in their collaboration. The two parties represent the independent interests of meaning [accessible to the witness] and articulation [the capacity of the police artist]. At one moment we may possess a meaning but fail to articulate it; at another moment we may possess just such an articulation, but find that its meaning fails to correspond with our intended one. We talk to ourselves when we think because only a dialogue where each side provides proposals and corrective disposals for the other can achieve a simultaneous satisfaction of these twin requirements.
>
> (Blachowicz 1999: 182)

Dialogical self theory can be seen as an effort to extend the self from a self-contained entity to a process that is extended to the other person and to society at large. Along these lines we may understand that a person, faced with alternative actions, may ask herself 'Do I want this?' or 'Does this fit with my interests?' It may take some time before the person, after a process of proposals and disposals, arrives at a final answer to such a question.

Bakhtin (1929/1973), a source of inspiration to any student of dialogue, considered not only question and answer but also agreement and disagreement as basic dialogical forms. He uses the following example (see also Vasil'eva 1988). Take two phrases that are completely identical, 'life is good' and again 'life is good'. When we consider these phrases from the perspective of Aristotelian logic, they are connected by a relationship of *identity*; they are, in fact, one and the same statement. From a dialogical perspective, however, they are different because they can be seen as two remarks coming from two spatially separated people in communication, who in this case entertain a relationship of *agreement*. Although two phrases are identical from a logical point of view, they are different as utterances: the first is a statement, the second a confirmation. The confirmation is not just a repetition of the first statement but it adds something that was not included in the initial statement. The initial utterance is not finalized in itself. Instead, it is dialogically expanded by the contribution of the interlocutor and, therefore, also its meaning has been widened.

Similarly, the statements 'life is good' and 'life is not good' can be discussed. In a logical sense, one is a *negation* of the other. However, when the two phrases are taken as utterances from two different speakers, a dialogical relation of *disagreement* exists. In Bakhtin's view, the relationships of agreement and disagreement are, like question and answer, basic dialogical forms. In other words, dialogue can be understood only in terms of voices, characters or positions that are spatially located in actual, remembered or imagined relationships.

Although this example is applied to two different people in communication, it can also be applied to different positions or voices in the self. In dialogical self theory, question and answer, like agreement and disagreement, can take place in one and the same person who communicates with him- or herself. Plato was well aware of this when he described thinking in terms of a dialogical relationship of the mind with itself:

> I have a notice that, when the mind is thinking, it is simply talking to itself, asking questions and answering them, and saying yes or no. When it reaches a decision – which may come slowly or in a sudden rush – when doubt is over and the two voices affirm the same thing, then we call that 'its judgment'.
>
> (Theaetetus 189e–190a; quoted by Blachowicz 1999: 184)

Apparently, the mind needs itself, that is, it requires contact with another part of the mind, in order to accomplish the act of thinking. This insight led philosopher Gadamer (1989) to speak of the 'imperfection of the human mind' referring to the impossibility of the mind to being completely present to itself:

> Because our understanding does not comprehend what it knows in one single inclusive glance, it must always draw what it thinks out of itself, and present it to itself as if in an inner dialogue with itself. In this sense, all thought is speaking to oneself.
>
> (Gadamer 1989: 422).

Power differences in the self

It would be a misunderstanding to conceive of dialogue as free from any social power. As Linell (1990) has argued, asymmetry exists in *each* individual act–response sequence. Speakers can communicate in meaningful ways only if they are able to take initiatives and display their views in turn. As part of a turn-taking process, the actors continually alternate the roles of 'power holder' and 'power subject' in the course of their conversation. For example, when one party talks, the other party remains silent, so that, during a particular turn, the speaking party is more influential in the conversation than the listening party. Or, one party may simply talk more than the other party, creating a relative dominance as a result of the amount of talk. Or, one of the parties introduces a new topic or a new perspective on a topic and has as such more influence on the direction that the conversation takes and on the resulting actions. As these examples suggest, power is an intrinsic feature of turn-taking instead of something that is in contradiction with dialogue or alien to its nature. Verbal and even non-verbal dialogue (Fogel 1993) need some organization so that the partners in conversation are able to take their turns.

Apart from differences in dominance that are intrinsic to turn-taking processes, there are, moreover, institutional and societal factors that contribute to power differences in dialogue. For example, in a study of paediatric consultations, Aronsson and Rundström (1988) observed that parents routinely step in as the spokespersons for their children, even when the doctor addresses the child directly. Mothers spontaneously grasped their children's turn, reinforcing what the children said and explaining what they meant, so that the children did not get the opportunity to express it properly themselves (Linell 1990: 162). A more extreme example of institutionalized asymmetry is the interrogation, in which one of the parties, the suspect, is forced in a yes-or-no answer frame and is hardly allowed to take initiatives. Certainly, there are situations in which power differences are strongly reduced, as we can see in an intimate conversation between friends. However, asymmetry or relative dominance never disappears entirely.

The influence of institutional and societal expectations and norms comprises not only dialogues between different individuals, but also dialogues within individuals. The desire to take a day off, may involve two parts of the self in negotiation or conflict, for example, the hard-working scientist and the enjoyer of life. In a society or institution in which hard working and competition is strongly encouraged, the enjoyer of life may be suppressed or 'silenced' by the ambitious part of the self. As this example suggests, disagreement between two parts of the self is not taking place in a 'free internal space'. Instead, societal and cultural norms are reflected in the internal dialogue and, by implication, in the relative dominance of the conflicting or alternative voices. Groups, institutions, and cultures are represented in the self as 'collective voices' (Bakthin 1929/1973) that directly influence its balance of power.

Self as a multiplicity of *I*-positions

So far, I have discussed the dialogical self elaborating on the concept of dialogue. In this section I shall deal with the second term of the concept: the notion of self. It is my purpose to show that the dialogical self not only is dialogical, but also assumes the existence of a multiplicity of self-positions.

James' view on the self translated into narrative terms

When people are involved in a process of interchange, they have stories to tell: stories they heard from others, stories they construct about their environment, and stories about their own experiences. Typically, people are motivated to tell stories that somewhere involve the self. Therefore, in my view, any narrative conception of the self should start with a treatment of James' classic work on the subject. In James' (1890) view, the *I*, the self-as-knower, is characterized by three features: continuity, distinctness and volition (see also Damon and Hart 1982). The continuity of the self-as-knower is reflected in a sense of personal identity and a sense of sameness across time. The feeling of distinctness from others, or the sense of individuality, also characterizes the subjective nature of the self-as-knower. A sense of personal volition is expressed by the continuous appropriation and rejection of thoughts by which the self-as-knower manifests itself as an active processor of experience.

In James' view, the *Me* is identified as the self-as-known and is composed of the empirical elements considered as belonging to oneself. Talking about the *Me*, James formulated an insight that will be crucial for the elaboration of the dialogical self: the self as extended to the environment (see also Becker 1973; Rosenberg 1979, who both emphasized the extension of the self as one of its central features). James was well aware that there is a gradual transition between *Me* and *Mine*, and concluded that the empirical self is composed of all elements in the environment that the person can call his or her own,

not only his body and his psychic powers, but his clothes and his house, his wife and children, his ancestors and friends, his reputation and works, his lands and horses, and yacht and bank-account.

(James 1890: 291)

Drawing on James' *I–Me* distinction, Sarbin (1986) supposed that people, in the process of self-reflection, order their experiences in a story-like fashion. The uttered pronoun, *I*, stands for the author, the *Me* for the actor or narrative figure. That is, the self as author, the *I*, can imaginatively construct a story in which the *Me* is the protagonist (and the *Mine* as antagonist). The self as author can imagine the future and reconstruct the past and describe himself or herself as an actor. Such a narrative construction, moreover, is a means for *organizing* episodes, actions, and the significance of the actions as a process in time and space (Bruner 1986; Sarbin 1986).

The narrative translation of James' distinction between *I* and *Me* and the extension of the self to the environment has a significant theoretical advantage: it allows describing the self not only in temporal terms (the self in past, present and future), but also in spatial terms (the self as being composed of a variety of spatial positions and as related to the positions of other selves). This insight offers also a road to escape from a basic Cartesian assumption, that space (*res extensa*) is *outside* the self (*res cogitans*) (Hermans and Kempen 1993). One of the theorists who was well aware of the spatial dimension of the self, Jaynes (1976), described it as a *mind-space*. The *I* constructs an analogue space and metaphorically observes the *Me* moving in this space. Other people and objects are part of the spatial extension of the self. Narration is always spatialized and this is an essential characteristic of all of our activities. Seated where I am, Jaynes explains, I am writing a book, and this activity is embedded in the story of my life, 'time being spatialized into a journey of my days and years' (Jaynes 1976: 63). The self is, in Jaynes' thinking, a spatial analogue of the world, and mental acts are analogues of bodily acts. (For an elaboration of the spatialized self in psychodrama, see Verhofstadt-Denève 2000.)

From Bakhtin's polyphonic novel to the dialogical self

The conception of *I* as author and *Me* as actor can be pursued further by returning to Bakhtin's dialogical approach. Bakhtin goes one step further than Sarbin. In his view, the self consists of *more* than one author or narrator.

In *Problems of Dostoevsky's Poetics* (1973), Bakhtin created a peculiar metaphor for expressing artistic thought, the polyphonic novel. He argued that in Dostoevsky's works there is not a single author at work – Dostoevsky himself – but *several* authors or thinkers – who coincide with his characters, such as Raskolnikov, Myshkin, Stavrogin, Ivan Karamazov and the Grand Inquisitor. These heroes are depicted as ideologically authoritative and independent and as using their own voice to ventilate their own view and philosophy. There is *not* a multitude of characters and fates within a *unified* objective world, organized by an omniscient author (Dostoevsky's), but a plurality of independent consciousnesses and worlds. In Bakhtin's (1973: 4) terms, 'The plurality of independent unmerged voices and consciousnesses and the genuine polyphony of full-valued voices are in fact characteristics of Dostoevsky's novels.' As in a polyphonic musical work, multiple voices accompany and oppose one another in dialogical ways.

For Bakhtin, personal meanings (e.g. ideas, thoughts, memories) can become dialogical only when they are embodied. They are embodied when there is an actual or imagined 'voice' that creates utterances that respond in comprehensible ways to the utterances of another voice. Only when an idea, thought or feeling is endowed with a voice and spatialized as emanating from a personal *position*, do dialogical relations emerge (Hermans et al. 1992; Vasil'eva 1988).

In summary, the metaphor of the polyphonic novel expands on the original narrative conception of the *I* as an author and the *Me* as an actor. In Sarbin's (1986) view, a single author is assumed to tell a story about himself or herself as an actor. The conception of the self as a polyphonic novel goes one step further: each individual lives in a multiplicity of worlds, with each world having its own author, who may tell a story relatively independently of the authors of the other worlds. It is assumed, thus, that the individual consists of multiple authors entering into dialogical relationships with each other and creating a complex organization of the self.

On the basis of the foregoing considerations, Hermans et al. (1992) conceptualized the self in terms of a dynamic multiplicity of relatively autonomous *I*-positions in the landscape of the mind. In this conception *I* has the possibility to move, as in a space, from one position to the other in accordance with changes in situation and time. The *I* fluctuates among different and even opposed positions. The voices function like interacting characters in a story. Once a character is set in motion in a story, the character takes on a life of its own and thus assumes a certain narrative necessity. Each character has a story to tell about experiences from its own stance. As different voices these characters exchange information about their respective *Me*(s) and their worlds, resulting in a complex, narratively structured self. Depending on the individual history and the collective stories of the groups, cultures and communities to which the individual belongs, some of the positions become more dominant than other positions (Hermans 1996a, 1996b, 2003).

The other as another I

For a proper understanding of the dialogical self, it is important to note that the theoretical term *I*-position is not exclusively used for the internal domain of the self (e.g. 'I as a father', 'I as a sports fanatic', 'I as a piano player').

External positions, as parts of an extended self (e.g. 'my father', 'my wife', 'my friend', 'my enemy'), are also conceived as *I*-positions, as the other person has the potential to function in the self as 'another I'. This theoretical expansion has the advantage of liberating the self from any self-contained individualism (Neimeyer 1998).

One of the advocates of a dialogical approach, Watkins (1999) is well aware of the potentials of dialogue to broaden a person's worldview:

> Unfortunately, it has become necessary to stress the relationship between intrapsychic dialogue and dialogue on these other levels [interpersonal, cultural, imaginal, ecological, and spiritual]. Often interior life has become used as part of a veil of privatism: a buffer against cultural, economic, and ecological realities and sufferings. In recent Western culture and its psychology we have lauded the development of the autonomous, highly rationalistic individual, bounded from others and nature, presumably responsible for his or her own fate. The threads of interrelationship between self and other, self and community, self and nature, self and spiritual reality have increasingly been neglected by the enactment of such a paradigm of selfhood. Correspondingly, the 'inner' world has been more and more looked to for meaning, relationship, ritual, and spirituality. It is imagined by some as though an untouched wilderness, a rich preserve to which one can turn for entertainment, mystery, and nurture.
>
> (Watkins 1999: 254)

By expanding the notion of dialogue to these broader realms or levels, it is possible to go beyond James' extended self. Certainly, James (1890) made a formidable step in overcoming the Cartesian split between self and body (James: my body belongs to the extended self) and between self and other (James: my children belong to the extended self) (for discussion of these splits, see Hermans and Kempen 1993). In this way, James contributed in innovative ways to the extension and spatialization of the self. However, it should be noted that James' extension of the self is anchored in the self as known (the *Me*). The elements of his extended self ('his wife and children, . . . his lands and horses, and yacht and bank account') suggest that persons are, from a theoretical point of view, extension pieces of the self rather than separate individuals with their own memories, intentions, desires and perspectives on life. That is, dialogical self theory makes a step of extending the self on the level of the self as knower or *I*.

The conception of the other person as another I is in accordance with a central thesis of Bakhtin: 'For the author the hero is not "he", and not "I" but a full-valued "thou", that is another full-fledged "I" ' (Bakhtin 1973: 51). This theoretical 'upgrading' of the other as another person in the self implies that the other is considered more than an extension of the *Me* on the object level but first of all an extension of *I* on the subject level. It allows the other, as part of the self, to develop an original perspective on the world, to tell a story about him- or herself, and to do so as a relatively autonomous position or voice with an own point of view.

The conception of the other as 'another I' in the self has a far-reaching consequence: the other person, or another 'object', are not simply known as objectified realities or internalized objects, but can be known only as far as they are allowed to speak from their own perspectives. The other as 'alter ego' has two implications: the other is like me (ego) and, at the same time another one (alter). By implication, self-knowledge is not only knowledge of myself (internal domain of the position repertoire), but also knowledge of the other as alter ego (external domain of the position repertoire). Along these lines, self-knowledge and knowledge of the other become intimately intertwined (Levinas 1969).

The theoretical argument for including the other in the self as 'alter ego' is to be understood as a possibility of the human mind more than as an empirical reality. In reality, the other person can be included in the self as a subject or as an object. This was reason for Cooper (2003) to pose the question of what kinds of intrapersonal relationship exist in the dialogical self. Drawing on Buber's (1923/1958) distinction between the I–Thou and I–It attitude, Cooper proposed that intrapersonal relationships can take one of two forms: an I–I form, in which one I-position encounters and confirms another I-position in its uniqueness and wholeness; and an I–Me form, in which one I-position experiences another I-position in a detached and objectifying way. In his view, a key role for the therapeutic process is to assist clients to become more able to experience moments of an I–I intrapersonal encounter, which requires the therapist to confirm the client both as a whole and in terms of his or her different voices.

Implications for psychotherapy

What are the implications of dialogical self theory for psychotherapy? In order to address this question, a distinction is made between (a) the content of the position repertoire, (b) its organization, and (c) the nature of the dialogical relations between the positions involved.

Content of a position repertoire: what has a character to tell?

When a psychotherapist listens carefully to the stories and experiences of clients, he or she is able to articulate them in terms of different positions or characters cropping up in the story. As part of the goal of therapy, the therapist may facilitate those positions that are productive for its outcome. For example, a client who is used to adopt a dependent position and has a strongly idealized view of other people, may learn during psychotherapy to get access to a more active and stronger position that is helpful to realize her life goals and to see others in a less idealized way (Dimaggio et al. 2003).

In the course of the therapeutic conversation, the therapist may focus on a particular position and invite the client to tell a story from the perspective of that particular position. Let's illustrate this with an example. In a case study, more extensively described in an earlier publication (Hermans 2001), a client, Nancy, started therapy in a period in which she suffered from extremely egocentric behaviour, trying to be the centre of the stage in almost all social situations. In the discussion with the therapist (Els Hermans-Jansen), Nancy labelled this position as 'the child in myself'. After some exploration of this position, the therapist decided to invite the 'child' to tell her own story about her past, present and future. The client then told, among others, about her siblings as permanent rivals, about the behaviour of her hot-tempered father, and about her pessimism to see any perspective in the future. After several months of therapy, a new character seemed to emerge, which was labelled as 'I as independent'. The client was then invited to give a *response* to the stories she had told from the child position in the beginning of the therapy. She explained that she now dealt with her problems in a different, more satisfying way. For example, she told how she learned to 'take some distance' as soon as the child in herself would come up and to oppose 'child' in terms of 'You just stay where I put you!' Essential in this case was that the child position was not deleted from the position repertoire or 'replaced' by the independent position. Rather, by becoming more independent, Nancy developed a 'counter-position' (Leiman 2002) that was able to give a meaningful answer to the child position that dominated her repertoire in the beginning of the therapy.

The procedure followed in Nancy's case is just one example of a more general therapeutic strategy which implies (a) to assess the positions that are involved in the client's story and accept their existence; (b) to articulate their differences; (c) to listen in an empathic way to the specific stories they have to tell; (d) to give special attention to the affective qualities of the stories and the intonations during the act of telling; (e) to facilitate the emergence of those positions that are expected to give a meaningful response to the positions that are dominating the repertoire of the client in dysfunctional ways; and (f) to stimulate dialogical relationships between the positions involved, with attention to their relative dominance (Cooper 1999; Dimaggio et al. 2003; Hermans and Hermans-Jansen 1995; Honos-Webb et al. 1999).

Organization of the position repertoire

For both diagnostic purposes and the process of psychotherapy, the organization of the position repertoire is crucial. The organization of the repertoire assumes the existence of a multiplicity in the self. Examining the organization of this multiplicity does not only reveal how the different positions are ordered as parts of a pattern, it also gives relevant information about their relative dominance.

A useful example is Lysaker and Lysaker's (2002) analysis of schizophrenia as a 'collapse of the dialogical self'. Building on this idea, they demonstrate that self-experience and personal narrative can devolve into three forms of organization. The 'empty' form is characterized by a radically limited number of inflexible self-positions, with only the barest dialogical opportunities available. Another form is the 'internal cacophony': the client seems to switch between a large number of disorganized self-positions that are lacking in hierarchy and coherent interconnections and that strongly reduce the accessibility of the repertoire and the stories involved. The third one is the 'rigid' form with a repertoire dominated by singular monological position (e.g. in paranoid delusions). Although the client's self-narrative may show some internal consistency, it is so rigid that it resists any narrative evolution. As these formulations suggest, distinction of different types of organization of the self may contribute to the linkages between dialogical self theory and forms of pathology.

More generally, for the study of the organization of the position repertoire, the following concepts are of particular significance: (a) the presence of a certain *hierarchy* of positions: in order to avoid an overly fragmented repertoire, positions can be examined on their common meanings and brought together under a superordinate position that serves their integration (for an example, see Josephs 2002); (b) the *accessibility* of positions: when particular positions are introduced in the repertoire as a result of psychotherapy, they should be accessible enough to be actualized in those situations in which they are needed to facilitate the client's adaptation (Hermans 2003); (c) the *flexibility* to move from one position to another: the client learns to shift from one position to another in close correspondence to a change of situation and time (Stiles 1999); and (d) the *affective variety* of the positions: when the repertoire consists of negative (unpleasant) positions only, the facilitation of positive (pleasant) positions is considered to be appropriate; when the repertoire is filled with positive positions only, the therapist may facilitate the exploration of positions with negative shadings (Angus et al. 1999).

Some researchers have argued that the development of a meta-position (or observing position) is of particular importance for facilitating the therapeutic reorganization of the self (e.g. Dimaggio et al. 2003; Georgaca 2001; Hermans 2003; Leiman 2002; Watkins 1999). A meta-position has some specific qualities: (a) it permits a certain distance toward the other positions, although it is attracted, both cognitively and emotionally, toward some positions more than others; (b) it provides some overarching view so that several positions can be seen simultaneously; (c) it leads to an evaluation of the several positions and their organization; (d) it enables to see the linkages between positions as part of their personal history (or the collective history of the group or culture to which the individual belongs); (e) the importance of one

or more positions for future development of the self becomes apparent; and
(f) it facilitates the creation of a dialogical space in which positions and
counterpositions entertain significant dialogical relationships (Hermans
2003; Leiman 2002).

A meta-position is not to be considered the 'centre' of the position repertoire or an agentic force that guarantees the unity and coherence of the self in
advance. It should be noted that a meta-position is always bound to one or
more internal and external positions (e.g. the psychotherapist) that are actualized at a particular moment and in a particular situation and that it is a
dialogical phenomenon. This implies that, depending on time and situation,
different meta-positions can emerge. Moreover, as each position has its horizon, also a meta-position, although it may permit meaningful linkages
between a variety of positions, has its limitations and is far from a 'God's eye
view'. These limitations follow from the assumption that multiplicity pre-
cedes any unity or synthesis of the self. Unity and coherence are considered a
goal rather than a given (Hermans and Kempen 1993).

The nature of dialogical relationships

It is far from certain that a position or voice is automatically connected with
other positions or voices in dialogical ways. A position may remain for a long
time at the background of the system or may emerge from the background
without any contact with the foreground positions (Hermans 2001). Moreover, an emergent voice may be warded off, on emotional grounds, in the
beginning of therapy and only later allowed to enter the larger community of
voices (Honos-Webb et al. 1999). As soon as an ongoing dialogical interchange with the other voices of the community is actually taking place, the
integration of the emergent voice can make a start.

The nature of dialogical relationships can be further explored by taking
into account two observations formulated by Lewis (2002). The first one is
that not all positions in the dialogical self are evenly accessible and that there
may be a limited number of ordinary positions that a person is used to
identify with. For example, familiar parent – child relationships may be taken
up in internal dialogues and an individual may automatically take the position of a scorning parent in situations in which they address to themselves
phrases like 'You are stupid' or 'Too bad!'. When particular voices from the
past are ruling the position repertoire and the person is automatically and
frequently returning to such emotionally tuned positions, the flexibility to
move to a larger variety of positions may be seriously reduced.

Lewis' (2002) second observation, closely connected with the first one, is
that many internal dialogues do not have the quality of a highly conscious
and well-ordered turn-taking process, but are rather sublingual and inchoate.
On the basis of this observation he introduces the notion of 'expecting dialogues': we are involved in a dialogical relation with an anticipated, almost

heard other that has the quality of a familiar and rather continuous I-position in the self. Along these lines Lewis presents a model that is based on neuroscientific evidence and, at the same time, compatible with dialogical self theory. This model is consistent with Schore's (1994) work on the orbitofrontal cortex which produces, in its linkage to the subcortical limbic system, an affectively charged, gist-like sense of an interpersonal respondent, which is based on stabilized expectancies from many past interactions. The advantage of Lewis' model is that it shows how relatively stable, sublingual voices put limits on the linguistic, dialogical processes. The advantage of sublingual dialogues is that they may facilitate our action readiness and behavioural efficiency. The disadvantage, however, is that our capacity to innovate the self, is reduced as the self tends to return automatically to a limited range of familiar positions (Bertau 2004).

Sublingual dialogues become problematic when (a) the voices involved are split off or warded off from contact with the larger position repertoire, (b) when their existence is poorly acknowledged; (c) when they are not accessible, (d) when their affective properties are mainly negative or (e) when the flexibility to move to other positions is severely reduced.

In such cases, the therapeutic relationship plays a crucial role in the reorganization of the client's self. The therapist functions as an 'alter ego' in the client's life. As an extension of the client's 'ego' the therapist is experienced in terms of old positions that are part of expecting dialogues. As 'alter' the therapist represents a new position in the life of the client that may provide a viable perspective for the innovation and reorganization of the self. The development of the client's meta-position may play a crucial role in this process of innovation.

In the psychotherapeutic relationship the two forms of dialogue discussed, the lingual, well-ordered dialogue and the sublingual, inchoate dialogue both play their part in a successful therapeutic relationship. The sublingual dialogue is innovated by its elaboration on the lingual level. In turn, meaningful changes and discoveries at the lingual level can be stabilized only if they leave their traces on the sublingual level.

One person is like two persons in dialogue

In this chapter I have explored the implications of two basic features of any dialogue: exchange and power. In the dialogical self these two features are brought together in such a way that interpersonal and intrapersonal dialogues can be studied as interconnected phenomena. The social relationships of the person with other persons are a model for the study of the social relationships of the person with him- or herself. As C.S. Lewis (1967) said:

> A person cannot help thinking of himself as, and even feeling himself to be (for certain purposes), two people, one of whom can act upon and

observe the other. Thus he pities, loves, admires, hates, despises, rebukes, comforts, examines, masters or is mastered by, 'himself'.

(Lewis 1967: 187)

It is the potential of psychotherapy to facilitate the mutual understanding and cooperation among these people, with acknowledgement of their differences.

References

Angus, L., Levitt, H. and Hardtke, K. (1999). 'The narrative processes coding system: Research applications and implications for psychotherapeutic practice.' *Journal of Clinical Psychology, 55*, 1255–1270.

Aronsson, K. and Rundström, B. (1988). 'Child discourse and parental control in pediatric consultations.' *Text, 8*, 159–189.

Bakhtin, M. (1973). *Problems of Dostoevsky's Poetics*, 2nd edn. Trans. R.W. Rotsel. Ann Arbor, MI: Ardis. First edn published in 1929 under the title *Problemy tvorchestva Dostoevskogo* [Problems of Dostoevsky's Art].

Becker, E. (1973). *The Denial of Death*. New York: Free Press.

Bertau, M.-C. (2004). 'Introduction: The theory of the dialogical self.' In M.-C. Bertau (ed.) *Aspects of the Dialogical Self: Extended Proceedings of a Symposium on the Second International Conference on the Dialogical Self* (Ghent, October 2002).

Blachowicz, J. (1999). 'The dialogue of the soul with itself.' In S. Gallagher and J. Shear (eds) *Models of the Self* (pp. 177–200). Thorverton, Devon: Imprint Academic.

Bruner, J.S. (1986). *Actual Minds, Possible Worlds*. Cambridge, MA: Harvard University Press.

Buber, M. (1923/1958). *I and Thou*, 2nd edn. Trans. R.G. Smith. Edinburgh: T. and T. Clark.

Cooper, M. (1999). 'If you can't be Jekyll be Hyde: An existential-phenomenological exploration of lived-plurality.' In J. Rowan and M. Cooper (eds) *The Plural Self: Multiplicity in Everyday Life* (pp. 51–70). London: Sage.

Cooper, M. (2003). ' "I–I" and "I–Me": Transposing Buber's interpersonal attitudes to the intrapersonal plane.' *Journal of Constructivist Psychology*, special issue on the dialogical self, *16*, 131–153.

Damon, W. and Hart, D. (1982). 'The development of self-understanding from infancy through adolescence.' *Child Development, 4*, 841–864.

Dimaggio, G., Salvatore, G., Azzara, C. and Catania, D. (2003). 'Rewriting self-narratives: The therapeutic process.' *Journal of Constructivist Psychology*, special issue on the dialogical self, *16*, 155–181.

Fogel, A. (1993). *Developing through Relationships: Origins of Communication, Self, and Culture*. Hemel Hempstead: Harvester Wheatsheaf.

Gadamer, H.G. (1989). *Truth and Method*, 2nd edn. Translation revised by J. Weinsheimer and D.G. Marshall. New York: Continuum.

Georgaca, E. (2001). 'Voices of the self in psychotherapy: A qualitative analysis.' *British Journal of Medical Psychology, 74*, 223–236.

Hermans, H.J.M. (1996a). 'Voicing the self: From information processing to dialogical interchange.' *Psychological Bulletin, 119*, 31–50.

Hermans, H.J.M. (1996b). 'Opposites in a dialogical self: Constructs as characters.' *Journal of Constructivist Psychology, 9*, 1–26.

Hermans, H.J.M. (2001). 'The construction of a personal position repertoire: Method and practice.' *Culture and Psychology*, special issue on culture and the dialogical self: theory, method and practice, *7*, 323–365.

Hermans, H.J.M. (2003). 'The construction and reconstruction of a dialogical self.' *Journal of Constructivist Psychology*, special issue on the dialogical self, *16*, 89–130.

Hermans, H.J.M. and Hermans-Jansen, E. (1995). *Self-Narratives: The Construction of Meaning in Psychotherapy*. New York: Guilford.

Hermans, H.J.M. and Kempen, H.J.G. (1993). *The Dialogical Self: Meaning as Movement*. San Diego, CA: Academic Press.

Hermans, H.J.M., Kempen, H.J.G. and Van Loon, R.J.P. (1992). 'The dialogical self: Beyond individualism and rationalism.' *American Psychologist, 47*, 23–33.

Honos-Web, L., Surko, M., Stiles, W.B. and Greenberg, L. (1999). 'Assimilation of voices in psychotherapy: The case of Jan.' *Journal of Counseling Psychology, 46*, 448–460.

James, W. (1890). *The Principles of Psychology*, Vol. 1. London: Macmillan.

Jaynes, J. (1976). *The Origin of Consciousness in the Breakdown of the Bicameral Mind*. Boston, MA: Houghton Mifflin.

Josephs, I.E. (2002). ' "The hopi in me": The construction of a voice in the dialogical self from a cultural psychological perspective.' *Theory and Psychology*, special issue on the dialogical self, *12*, 161–173.

Leiman, M. (2002). 'Toward semiotic dialogism: The role of sign-mediation in the dialogical self.' *Theory and Psychology*, special issue on the dialogical self, *12*, 221–235.

Levinas, E. (1969). *Het menselijk gelaat: Essays*. Gekozen en ingeleid door A. Peperzak. [The human face: Essays. Chosen and introduced by A. Peperzak]. Utrecht: Ambo.

Lewis, C.S. (1967). *Studies in Words*, 2nd edn. Cambridge: Cambridge University Press.

Lewis, M.D. (2002). 'The dialogical brain: Contributions of emotional neurobiology to understanding the dialogical self.' *Theory and Psychology*, special issue on the dialogical self, *12*, 175–190.

Linell, P. (1990). 'The power of dialogue dynamics.' In I. Markovà and K. Foppa (eds) *The Dynamics of Dialogue* (pp. 147–177). New York: Harvester Wheatsheaf.

Lysaker, P.H. and Lysaker, J.T. (2002). 'Narrative structure in psychosis: Schizophrenia and disruptions in the dialogical self.' *Theory and Psychology*, special issue on the dialogical self, *12*, 207–220.

Neimeyer, R.A. (1998). 'Social constructionism in the counselling context.' *Counselling Psychology Quarterly, 11*, 135–149.

Rosenberg, M. (1979). *Conceiving the Self*. New York: Basic Books.

Sarbin, T.R. (1986). 'The narrative as a root metaphor for psychology.' In T.R. Sarbin (ed.) *Narrative Psychology: The Storied Nature of Human Conduct* (pp. 3–21). New York: Praeger.

Schore, A.N. (1994). *Affect Regulation and the Origin of the Self: The Neurobiology of Emotional Development*. Hillsdale, NJ: Lawrence Erlbaum Associates.

Stiles, W.B. (1999). 'Signs and voices in psychotherapy.' *Psychotherapy Research*, *9*, 1–21.

Vasil'eva, I.I. (1988). 'The importance of M.M. Bakhtin's idea of dialogue and dialogic relations for the psychology of communication.' *Soviet Psychology*, *26*, 17–31.

Verhofstadt-Denève, L. (2000). *Developmental Therapy from an Existential-Dialectical Viewpoint: A Theoretical and Practical Guide to Action- and Drama-Techniques.* London: Jessica Kingsley Publishers.

Watkins, M. (1999). 'Pathways between the multiplicities of the psyche and culture: The development of dialogical capacities.' In J. Rowan and M. Cooper (eds) *The Plural Self: Multiplicity in Everyday Life* (pp. 254–268). London: Sage.

Chapter 2

Developmental origins of the dialogical self

Some significant moments

Marie-Cécile Bertau

Starting points

The following considerations have been developed on the background of a concept of dialogicity, which is thought of as fundamental to humans from the moment they come into life, forming their condition in development as well as in outer and inner activities. This line of thought not only is attached to dialogical philosophy (Buber 1997), but also is found in the works of thinkers interested in language, such as Humboldt (1994) and Bakhtin (1986), and in contemporary dialogical psychology (Hermans and Kempen 1993).[1]

Relatedness is the core structure from where different kinds of being-related-to (others, self, world) develop, and these relations are to be conceived as structure of talk and reply. Because language is embedded in this dialogic-ity it is always speech, always an act and an event between at least two persons, and only understandable from there.

The self, in turn, is dialogical in so far as it is conceivable solely within this structure. Thus it is a genuine entity: it is not the case that the self – after the initial moment of coming into life – sometimes enters into dialogues and sometimes does not. Human beings cannot choose to be related and to be dialogical or not. But one may ask how this condition of relatedness and dialogicity shows itself within a given socio-historical, cultural present, how it manifests itself in concrete situations, e.g. in game-playing situations between mother and child, or in problem-solving situations involving two persons or only one person acting.

Positing the dialogical self as a genuine entity also applies to its develop-ment: there may be a predialogical and a preverbal stage in the ontogenesis of human beings but no extra-dialogical and no extra-verbal stage, no outside. From the very beginning humans are enveloped in dialogicity and speech. Transferring these abstract notions into concreteness means to acknowledge the presence of others, present as certain physical bodies defined by their socio-cultural life context, displaying themselves in certain physical and verbal activities.

So, one of the starting points is the idea of the relatedness and dialogicity of human beings; the second one is complementary to the first: it is the idea of detachment. Humans are relational as well as detached beings, relational in their social and communicational life, including developmental aspects (e.g. the development of joint attention); but also detached, in so far as one needs to be decentred to be able to carry out a dialogue sensitive to the listener, therefore to be social, turned toward. Detachment seems to be even more marked in cognitive, instrumental thinking: this is (always to a certain degree) decentred, objectifying, symbolizing, in a distance, up to the possibility of meta levels in metacognitions.

Thus, one aspect conditions the other, relatedness conditions detachment and vice versa. It seems to me that the role of others lies there: in making possible, moreover in calling for relation as well as for detachment; both are conditions of communication. We have to be related to one another, mutually turned to, and at the same time we have to be detached from the other, we have to discern him or her from ourselves in order to build up any communication.

Considering the development of the dialogical self will then entail developing relationship as well as detachment, through others and within a dialogical world.

This will be done first by a look at the ontogenesis of the infant from the perspective of some core notions such as rhythms, joint attention and perspective taking. In the light of the role of the other for the developing dialogical self as outlined above, the distribution of activities between caregiver and infant will be of special interest. The line of argument will be supported by my own study with adult problem solvers obviously speaking with an internalized other while performing their task. This finally leads to the notion of phonicity which gives a central role to the perceived voice of a certain person.

Looking for the beginning: ontogenesis

According to the assumptions I started with, infants are, from the very beginning, enveloped in dialogicity and in the speech of others, they come into a dialogical world shaped by structures of addressivity. Thus, before becoming a dialogical self, an infant is a being in dialogues. These are socioculturally shaped, enacted and conveyed by others and their voices.

But the dialogical structure does not only occur in the environment of infants. Infants themselves display behaviour which is interpretable as addressed to (early helplessness as appeal, smiling and gazing from 2 months on), so the powerful principle of imputing sense and intention in every behaviour of the infant may function. This can be described as an invitation to dialogue. Infants seem to offer themselves as partners. Once taken up and enacted by competent dialogue partners, the infant's behaviour becomes actually dialogic. After this base is build up, exchange starts and refines itself in means (from rhythms to speech) as well as in quality (intersubjectivity, perspective taking etc., see e.g. Bruner 1975; Ninio and Bruner 1978).

At an early stage rhythms shape the encounters of infant and caregivers; rhythms like sleeping and being awake are, from the first moment of life, involved in a social construction of how they should be, becoming thus modes of exchange, manifest in certain activities toward the infant and coordinated by the culturally competent; these rhythms are from the first moment not just mechanical sequences but reflect and convey individual as well as socio-cultural defined meaning which the infant is driven into. This leads to the first rhythmified routines (Bruner 1997), forms of relatedness at an emotional level, and forms of order at a cognitive level, both giving orientation.

Rhythm becomes mutual as soon as the novice shows some kind of responsiveness beyond mere physical satisfaction/dissatisfaction; then, mutuality begins to arise, first in a rather diffuse way in directedness and order, later in a more directed and sequenced way. A first beginning seems to be when the infant starts to smile in response to social stimulation – as Rochat et al. (1999) put it, 'there is an apparent change in the way they relate to the world'. Smiling emerges as a sign of mutuality by 2 months of age and is at first an affective attunement to the other. This new attitude leads in turn to a new attitude in the caretakers who will show different, enriched ways of interacting with the infant.

Another important step emerges by 9 months of age when infants start to 'understand others as intentional and monitor their attention toward objects in the environement' (Rochat et al. 1999: 956). Not only is the other understood as intentional and the infant is not only directed to people in its environment. Also things come into view *in relation to the other*. These developmental steps involved in object relation and the other's perspective are well described by the terms of joint attention and primary/secondary intersubjectivity.

Tomasello (1993) stresses the development starting with 9 months of age, calling it 'the 9-month miracle'. Starting from the fact that human infants are social creatures from the beginning, Tomasello arrives at the notion of 'cultural learning', which entails perspectivity:

> In cultural learning, learners do not just direct their attention to an individual and its behavior, they actually attempt to see the world as the other individual sees it – from inside the other's perspective, as it were. It is learning in which the learner is attempting to learn not *from* another but *through* another.
>
> (Tomasello 1993: 175, emphasis in the original)

Learning through the other is precisely possible because of the ability to take the role or the perspective of the other, to participate in the other intersubjectively, to engage with the other in joint attention. Prior to 9 months, the infant is able to engage only with an object *or* with a person, where the object is not a part of their interaction; after 9 months, a radical change happens, when the object is included in the exchange between infant and adult. From then the infant is able to coordinate object and person. As part of this process, gaze plays an important role: 'Joint attention is not just shared visual gaze but a true perspective taking' (Tomasello 1993: 176).

As a quite interesting point in the context of the dialogical self, Tomasello (1993) connects the inclusion of objects and the taking of perspective to the emergence of a self-reflexive attention:

> Just as the infant can learn about *external* situations from the point of view of the adult, in face-to-face interaction the infant can now learn about the adult's perception and intention *toward her*, the infant, when the adult's attention is on her.
>
> (Tomasello 1993: 176, emphasis added)

Sharing a common perspective on objects also means to be aware of one another's attention to that object, leading in turn to notice the other's attention on self *as object*. This process amounts to the 'forming of a true self-concept' (Tomasello 1993: 177). And the apex of development is to imagine oneself as an object without the actual attention of the other, in his absence: 'I may act *as if* I were another person looking at my behavior' (Tomasello 1993: 182, emphasis in the original).

Continued perspective taking can thus be understood as an internalization process: the self internalizes the attention of others on objects, one of them being the self. Thus, there is also an objectification process permitting a distance, and a first step in detachment. The self then emerges from a commonality of attention (relating both persons), as well as from a discernment of the source of that attention (distinguishing both persons): the infant is aware of the other's attention as *belonging to that other* and takes up this view on the common object.

Primary and secondary intersubjectivity come into play. Primary intersubjectivity is related to the affective attunement of infants to their caregivers before the age of 4 months, displayed through contingent smiling, gazing, and other socially elicited gestures. Here, the infant seems to be related in an undifferentiated, mainly affective way to the other (Rochat et al. 1999); it is a stage of diffuse social acts, nevertheless understood by the caregivers as if they were meant in a certain, personal way. According to Tomasello (1993: 174), this primary form does not lead to a self-concept, although it involves 'a kind of self-perception or awareness'. Secondary intersubjectivity starts with the manifested mutual engagement as displayed in joint attention, leading to the true self-concept named above: by the age of 9 months, infants begin to behave in several ways demonstrating their growing awareness 'of how other persons work as psychological beings' (Tomasello 1993: 174). Thus, in contrast to primary intersubjectivity secondary intersubjectivity displays directedness to the other and therefore introduces a distinction between the infant (self) and the other.

Development leads from diffuse social acts and rhythmified routines to clear mutual exchanges where the partners understand each other as an intentional self. Moreover, they understand themselves as objectifiable selves, selves that can be addressed, meant, talked to, and all this in a certain position in relation to the other and to the world. Dialogical talk is to be seen as a support of this development. This especially applies to the voices speaking and leading through different zones of awareness of self, giving structure to the exchanges of the emerging self. One can observe a certain distribution of activities between mother and infant changing with development.

The mother will first take up all the roles and all the non-verbal as well as verbal actions, in this way establishing a model of exchange and dialogicity, speaking with more than one voice. It is precisely through this that the infant is able to learn where and when to take up his role by adequate means. This role may first be bound to structure, like a scaffold to move onto, and may later become a genuine role in terms of a position experienced as related to a certain perspective. It is in this way that I call dialogue and voice a supporting structure: first a perceived, voiced and outer structure with which the infant can concretely align, then a felt and experienced, more inner structure becoming increasingly meaningful for the self as well as for the other and for their mutual exchange.[2] The double-voicedness of the mother is an offer to the infant to take up one of the voices as a conversational role, but at the same time it demonstrates that one person can speak and act with more than one voice.

A beautiful example of the mother's voice as supporting structure for the child's 'voicing in' and for the demonstration of the possibility of not only two but multiple voices, can be found in Fogel et al. (2002). Mother and child have played the lion game with a lion puppet many times with clear roles, the mother always being the lion. Then a change comes in as the child puts the puppet on her own hand and acts with the voice of the lion, as she previously experienced the mother doing it. The child aligns with the voice of the mother which is in turn an imagined one, nevertheless belonging to the mother and to her perspective (on lions, on her child, on playfulness etc.). So, the mother's voice leads the child into a new position and at the same time conveys the perspective and meaning of that position. Fogel et al. (2002) stress the importance of the voice of the mother, too:

> The presence and the voice of the mother constitute a fundamental pole of the dialogue. In the absence of the mother and of her voice, Susan may not have been able to go through this process of self-exploration.
>
> (Fogel et al. 2002: 201)

This example illustrates the voicing of an imagined position; but the alignment to the voice of the mother functions in everyday dialogues as well (and mainly there), where the child has to come in with his or her own voice, own role in turn-taking and own position as speaking self.

The everyday exchange of voices, first completely done by the mother, is described well in Jochens (1979). Jochens depicts the behaviour of mothers with their 12 months to 23 months old children as an introduction to reciprocity, to dialogue. They do this not only for the sake of the child but for their own sake as well. According to Jochens, mothers seek for the dialogue with their children in order to encounter the social situation with the child in a routinized way. The central element of mothers' interaction is therefore what Jochens calls a conversational training, where a high number of questions are typical; these questions are first of all communicative appeals to the child and a supply of turn-taking. This will soon lead to a dialogue where the child takes a role and gives it his or her own voice.

A step further is to be seen in the examples Holzman (1972) gives of a frequent dialogical frame between mother and child (question play). These examples are to be read as a developmental series where the child not only has taken up his or her role in conversation – regarding especially the adjacency pair of question and answer – but also has understood the role of the other. Acting out both roles the child displays a self-dialogue as an aloud form of internalized speech:

1   Mother (M) starts, initiates child:

   M: What's the baby's name? (Sarah's doll)

2   Child (C) starts, mother is pseudo-starter; child initiates mother for initiating herself:

   C: What's that?
   M: What is that?
   C: Shoe lace.

3   Child is self-starter and initiates himself:

   C: What dat?
          A trailer.
          Dat's a cow.
          Dat a barn.
          Dat's a street.[3]

What the child is acting out playfully here becomes quite important as a self-questioning technique for several problem-solving activities (see e.g. Baker and Brown 1984). That is, early mother–child dialogues lead to the internalization of the exchange structure supported by the voices of the interactants.

The voice of the mother is of primary importance as she is the one mainly heard at the beginning, shaping the dialogical patterns, therefore first shaping the position and perspective of her dialogical partner, later the internal dialogues of that partner.

In listening to problem-solving adults who are speaking aloud what they are thinking, one can hear passages spoken as if two voices are talking, arguing, discussing; in a word, one can hear dialogues between the adult and an internalized position. The next section briefly reports a study where internal dialogues of adults were actually observed.

Listening to adults in problem-solving situations

Following Vygotsky (1978, 1987) human cognition is fundamentally social, the outer, shared and verbally mediated activity is internalized in the course of ontogenetic development. In this course, the function of language shifts from a communicative to a cognitive one. Within this movement Vygotsky observes that the child is talking to himself in a certain way:

> In our view, something similar happens when *the child begins to converse with himself as he previously conversed with others*, when, speaking to himself, he begins to talk aloud in situations that require it.
>
> (Vygotsky 1987: 75, emphasis added)

It is important to notice the shift to speech which is used cognitively but at the same time to bear in mind from where this shift comes and remains bound to: sociality, interacting and speaking with others. Rubinstein (1977) has put the social aspect of thinking succinctly:

> In inner speech, language renunciates its original function. However, inner speech, like any language, possesses social character. . . . the transformed structure, too, shows clear traces of its social descent. . . . Inner speech is social also in regard to its content. The affirmation that it is a monologue is not really precise. . . . Any man's word expressed in thinking has its audience in whose atmosphere his considerations take place.
>
> (Own translation of Rubinstein 1977: 521)

The question then arises if it is possible to find traces of the social, communicative and dialogical speech in the cognitively oriented speech of adults as observable in thinking-aloud protocols of problem-solving situations. In terms of the dialogical self: if a (thinking, problem-solving) self is observable that manifests its inner dialogicity. This would not only confirm Vygotsky's and Rubinstein's approach to internalization and thinking and make it concrete in the manifested voice(s), but also support the view presented here on the development of a dialogical self on the basis of the voice of the mother.

In Bertau (1999) I have analysed the thinking-aloud protocols of six adult subjects solving the Raven Test.[4] The utterances of the subjects were investigated with regard to an assumed so-called primeval dialogue between mother and child belonging to a primeval dyad. The relationship between the interactants changes in the course of the child's development in a significative way; three general stages are discernible.[5]

First, there is an early stage in which the mother monitors and directs the activities of the child; second, in a complex transitory stage, activities and therefore also responsibility for these activities are more and more shared between the two participants. With its (verbal, cognitive, manual) activities the child comes more and more to the foreground while the mother goes to the background at the same time. Third, in the resulting stage the child has taken over the mother's role completely, the mother is now a benevolent public, no more active but listening to and gazing at the child: a mere presence but still quite important to the child acting within the mother's atmosphere – to use Rubinstein's words. The apex of this development is a situation where the child is alone and has internalized not only the activities of the mother but also her presence and her atmosphere. The internal dialogues as focused on by the study are supposed to happen then.

In all subjects, the analysis reveals an increasing verbalization with increasing task difficulty; moreover, this verbalization takes a more and more dialogical form, also in relation to increasing task difficulty. Thus, internal dialogues actually happen, and with marked specificities: in terms of personal tendencies, some subjects being verbose and dialogical from the beginning, others being quite laconic and showing short dialogical passages only in highly difficult tasks; in terms of the quality of the dialogues, the internalized mother being in some subjects supporting and confirming, in others more sceptic and admonishing; finally in terms of the internalized position being not so much a mother than a peer. The following example illustrates an unfolded dialogue with the internalized mother-position:

(1) C8/ [task number]
(2) aha/
(3) . . ./
(4) this must be hatched obliquely/
(5) aha/
(6) obliquely to the left or obliquely to the right?/ [M turn]
(7) therefore/ [C tries to answer]
(8) completely hatched/ [C answers]
(9) where's this?/ [M turn]
(10) . ./ [C is looking for the answer]
(11) that is/ [C begins to answer with an objection]
(12) that's not/ [like (11)]
(13) not so logical/ [C finishing objection]

(14) nevertheless/ [M counters objection]
(15) now I see the figure/ [C understands and answers (9)]
(16) this is number one C8.[6]

Thus, a difficult problem-solving situation leads to verbalizations, and these have, to a certain degree, a dialogical character; inner speech, rather contracted in adults, can be unfolded to dialogues, that is: the developmental step leading from communication to cognition can be reversed when needed. In terms of development of the dialogical self: the internalized other position (be it the mother or a peer) can be heard again, its voice can serve to structure the activities and thoughts of the self. This means that the internal position is not necessarily always speaking with the self, although it is to be thought as present. The three developmental stages in the relationship between mother and child sketched above are, in adults, to be read as possibilities in the explicitness of voices, in different degrees of inner dialogicity: from fragmental dialogues entailing only some dispersed dialogical turns to completely unfolded dialogues with connected dialogical turns.

The unfolded dialogues display a certain quality not only in what is said by the interactants and first of all by the position the acting self is addressed to, but also by how this position listens. This more or less silent aspect in the dialogical self is, in my view, an important one (Rubinstein's atmosphere), leading to questions of internal audiences and publics (see e.g. Baldwin and Holmes 1987; Bertau 2004). And it points to the fact that, in speaking, there is not only turn-taking where the listener becomes the following speaker, but the listener as such also has a powerful role, shaping what the speaker says and does, and how he or she evaluates and experiences both.

Phonicity

As seen, the voice plays a significant role in the development of the dialogical self. It is the voice of the mother which supports and leads the development from diffuse social acts to clear mutual exchanges; and this voice always speaks for two, according to the necessities of turn-taking in conversations and according to the necessity of talk and reply grounded in fundamental dialogicity.

Thus, the mother speaks alone at first, inviting her child through diverse strategies – one of the most powerful ones is asking questions – to come into the exchange, to take his or her place and role, that is: to speak with his or her own voice. The child does this by aligning first with the voice of the mother, precisely: with one of the roles she acts out. This role is a conversational one, obeying the structures of dialogical exchange; but it is also bound to a certain perspective, e.g. the one who asks and the one who answers. Thus, forming an own voice within the mother–child conversation also means for the child to come to a perspective and to a speaking self. The distribution of voices between mother and child is in this way a matter of speech acquisition *and* of self-development, precisely through the forming of the own voice.

So, the term 'voice' refers first to a vocal event coming from a certain person, a clear auditory perception, recognizable as the voice of this person, although the person may speak for more than one party. The view on development presented here uses the term in this way. This vocal event leads to the notion of phonicity (Greek *phonè*, voice, sound), stressing the fact that dialogicity is always bound to a concrete auditory voice experience, no matter how abstractly it may develop.

Once the child has begun to form his or her own voice, there are two persons speaking, two voices can be heard, manifesting two different bodies, positions in space and time, two perspectives, two selves. Soon, these two concrete voices can realize different positions, also fictitious ones as in the lion puppet example. With the internalization of these voices, with their shift into an inner world, the notion of the term 'voice' changes too: no more an actual and audible vocal event but an imagined one. This change is grasped in a second notion of 'voice', as found for example in Bakhtin (1986), Hermans and Kempen (1993) and Wertsch (1993). Voice is here more than the vocal act, it is a 'speaking subject's perspective, conceptual horizon, intention, and world view' (Wertsch 1993: 51); for Hermans and Kempen (1993) the I-positions of the imaginery inner landscape can be endowed with voices, can then become characters of a story, each voice telling her own story, leading thus to a multiplicity of inner voices (mother, father, friends, teacher etc.).

From the point of view of development the dialogical self speaks and listens to voices that refer to actual speakers with audible voices, although these voices may be altered by processes as condensation and displacement, by imagination and generalization (this may be the case in Mead's generalized other). Because of this rooting – as has already been stressed – the term of phonicity is used to describe several states in dialogicity. These states correspond to the diversification of voices and start, which is worth noting, from the assumption that monologue does not exist. In line with a consistent dialogical position, monologue is to be seen as a sublimated dialogue, or as a dialogue where the roles of speaking and listening are asymmetrically distributed, at least over time. Thus, phonicity will always refer to dialogicity.

In the first stage there is only the voice of the mother, speaking for both the infant and herself, which is understood as *monophonic dialogicity*. As soon as the child takes up his or her role in the dialogical exchange, beginning with attention giving and gazing, vocalizations at the right time and place, and becoming more and more speech-like, there are two voices. Thus, *diphonic dialogicity* has emerged, enriching and intensifying the exchanges between mother and child or caregiver because now there are really two persons talking. The described distribution of activities and roles takes place along with this development of phonicity. As it develops and refines, this stage leads to mature dialogues between interactants able to attune themselves to the other, to his or her perspective, and to his or her knowledge and communicative possibilities.

This attunement is reached through imagining the other, imagining the other's position and view on the world, so talking dialogically presupposes an imagined dialogicity. In my view, it is because we start with a diffuse, dense relation to the other which is differentiated in a me and a you only in the course of development, that we become able to imagine this other and his or her perspective. In this imagination one has to give imitation an important role. Imitating the other is a device to slip into the other, highly refined in role play and disguise games where the act of slipping is systematically and joyfully displayed and showed outside. Thus, diphonic dialogicity leads to a *polyphonic dialogicity*: the possibility of enacting and imagining a multiplicity of voices and positions, even fictitious ones (see again the lion puppet).

In the beginning, imagining the other resides in undifferentiated relatedness to him or her, and is at the same time the product of a detachment process from this other, resulting in objectifying tendencies due to the emerging distance between me and you. With the help of the other, the development then goes ahead to reach a me and you. This unfolding process corresponds to an increasing gain of voices, increasing possibilities of phonicity going along with I-positions (Hermans and Kempen 1993), thus building up the dialogical self in a more and more refined and complex way. Adding finally new means as reading and writing, and opening up the voices to different (national) languages, a wide and rather complex horizon appears. But it has started with one voice speaking for both participants.

Conclusion

The foregoing considerations posit a basic movement going via another to a discernible you and me; these two positions can then be internalized as I-positions. This movement corresponds to an unfolding process where diffuseness is built up to discernment, where mere presence is structured and sequenced, and where discernment leads to objectification of other and self. Here, imagination plays a significant role, in so far as it accompanies, maybe even leads to objectification and discernibility of the other (and in the end of self, too). It is worth noting that imagination as characteristic of detachment is rooted in the diffuse and dense relatedness to the other from the beginning, and is even possible only because of this root. Imagining the other may therefore be seen as a kind of mature regression: going back to diffusity which permits nearness and at the same time holding this nearness at a certain distance to be able to see its substance.

The unfolding, objectifying process leads to a gain of voices as positions in the self. But before voices come to be I-positions, there is the concrete, perceivable voice of the other that has first supplied the emerging self with meaningful structure. This voice envelopes the developing self in dialogicity because of its boundness to a talk-and-reply structure and to another person. This in turn means that human life never is extra-dialogical or extra-verbal. Preverbality and predialogicity exist only in the environment of verbality and dialogicity; preverbal and predialogical events are instantly interpreted, understood, replied, questioned by somebody else within this environment.

In holding this position with its emphasis on another person and her voice I consequently view dialogues as involving another person, two parties communicating from different bodies and with different positions, coordinated and oriented toward each other. (See Linell 1998: 4 for this definition of dialogue.) And it is from there that emerging dialogues and a developing dialogical self is conceived: there is somebody who is competent and via whom the developing self is driven into dialogicity. Self is not able to extricate itself from itself, it needs and seeks for the other, displaying a certain kind of signal which the other, in turn, is looking for; this holds even stronger for the dialogical self.[7]

A look at the beginning of the dialogical self shows first a being deeply involved in dialogicity and coming to be a self through this very involvement which supplies a certain (socio-culturally determined) structure in encountering the other, itself and the environment. Becoming self occurs through dialogues on different complexity levels, with the voice of the other as a competent *and expectant* dialogue partner. This voice is offering a meaningful structure in so far as it always addresses, as it is always turned toward somebody. Precisely by virtue of this, the dialogical self emerges as a certain self with certain dialogical experiences which he or she can then internalize, thus becoming a self with a plurality of external and internal dialogical positions.

Finally, it is worth noting that the notions talked about are all saturated by a socio-cultural and historical context, and here again there is no outside but there are different ways of distinguishing, of constructing meaning, of talk and reply, of voicing, and of internalizing voices.

Notes

1   These considerations mainly rely on thoughts which are outlined in more detail in my contributions to Bertau (2004), especially regarding the model of phonicity, as well as philosophical, linguistical and developmental foundations of dialogicity and addressivity.
2   A similar idea is expressed in Bruner (1975), who speaks of a 'prosodic envelope' as a place-holding pattern for lexical development.
3   See Holzman (1972: 318, 331). Children are about 2–3 years old.
4   This small sample belongs to the pilot study of Werani (in press).
5   These stages are formulated with references to several scholars and their experiments, first of all Wood and Middleton (1975), Wood et al. (1976) and Wertsch (1978).
6   Example translated from Bertau (1999: 9f.).
7   This is the reason why I am a little sceptical about the very interesting approach of

Fogel et al. (2002), relating the self-awareness of the first days of life with dialogical relationship (pp. 193f.).

References

Baker, L. and Brown, A.L. (1984). 'Cognitive monitoring in reading.' In J. Flood (ed.) *Understanding Reading Comprehension* (pp. 21–44). Newark, NJ: International Reading Association.

Bakhtin, M.M. (1986). *Speech Genres and Other Late Essays*. Edited by C. Emerson and M. Holquist. Trans. V.W. McGee. Austin, TX: University of Texas Press.

Baldwin, M.W. and Holmes, J.G. (1987). 'Salient private audiences and awareness of the self.' *Journal of Personality and Social Psychology*, 52(6), 1087–1098.

Bertau, M-C. (1999). 'Spuren des Gesprächs in innerer Sprache. Versuch einer Analyse der dialogischen Anteile des lauten Denkens' [Traces of conversation in inner speech. Attempt of an analysis of dialogical features in thinking aloud]. *Sprache und Kognition, 18*(1–2), 4–19.

Bertau, M-C. (ed.) (2004). *Aspects of the Dialogical Self: Extended Proceedings of a Symposium at the Second International Conference on the Dialogical Self* (Ghent, October 2000), including psycholinguistical, conversational and educational contributions.

Bruner, J.S. (1975). 'The ontogenesis of speech acts.' *Journal of Child Language*, 2, 1–19.

Bruner, J.S. (1997). *Wie das Kind sprechen lernt*. Bern: Hans Huber. (Trans. from Bruner 1983: *Child's Talk: Learning to Use Language*. New York and London: Norton).

Buber, M. (1997). *Das dialogische Prinzip: Ich und Du. Zwiesprache. Die Frage an den Einzelneu Elemente des Zwischenmenschlichen* [The dialogical principle: I and Thou. Dual talk. The question of the singular elements of intersubjectivity]. Gerlingen: Lambert Schneider.

Fogel, A., de Koeyer, I., Bellagamba, F. and Bell, H. (2002). 'The dialogical self in the first two years of life.' *Theory and Psychology*, 12(2), 191–205.

Hermans, H.J.M. and Kempen, H.J.G. (1993). *The Dialogical Self: Meaning as Movement*. San Diego, CA: Academic Press.

Holzman, M. (1972). 'The use of interrogative forms in the verbal interaction of three mothers and their children.' *Journal of Psycholinguistic Research*, 1(4), 311–336.

Humboldt, W. von (1994). *Über die Sprache: Reden vor der Akademie. 1827: Über den Dualis*. Edited by J. Trabant. Tübingen and Basel: Francke.

Jochens, B. (1979). ' "Fragen" im Mutter–Kind-Dialog: Zur Strategie der Gesprächsorganisation von Müttern' ['Questions' in mother–child dialogue: About a strategy of conversational organization by mothers]. In K. Martens (ed.) *Kindliche Kommunikation. Theoretische Pespektiven, empirische Analysen, methodische Grundlagen* (pp. 110–132). Frankfurt am Main: Suhrkamp.

Linell, P. (1998). *Approaching Dialogue: Talk, Interaction and Contexts in Dialogical Perspectives*. Amsterdam and Philadelphia, PA: John Benjamins.

Ninio, A. and Bruner, J.S. (1978). 'The achievement and antecedents of labeling.' *Journal of Child Language*, 5, 1–15.

Rochat, P., Querido, J.G. and Striano, T. (1999). 'Emerging sensitivity to the timing and structure of protoconversation in early infancy.' *Developmental Psychology*, 35(4), 950–957.

Rubinstein, S.L. (1977). *Grundlagen der allgemeinen Psychologie* [Foundations of a general psychology]. Trans. H. Hartmann. Berlin: Volk und Wissen.

Tomasello, M. (1993). 'On the interpersonal origins of self-concept.' In U. Neisser (ed.) *The Perceived Self: Ecological and Interpersonal Sources of Self-Knowledge* (pp. 174–184). Cambridge: Cambridge University Press.

Vygotsky, L.S. (1978). *Mind in Society: The Development of Higher Psychological Processes.* Edited by M. Cole, V. John-Steiner, S. Scribner and E. Souberman. Cambridge, MA and London: Harvard University Press.

Vygotsky, L.S. (1987). *Thinking and Speech.* Edited by R.W. Rieber and A.S. Carton. Trans. N. Minick. New York and London: Plenum Press.

Werani, A. (in press). *Funktion und Struktur selbstregulierender Sprache beim Lösen sogenannter nonverbaler Probleme* [Function and structure of self-regulating talk in solving so-called non-verbal problems].

Wertsch, J.V. (1978). 'Adult–child interaction and the roots of metacognition.' *Quarterly Newsletter of the Institute for Comparative Human Development, 1,* 15–18.

Wertsch, J.V. (1993). *Voices of the Mind: A Sociocultural Approach to Mediated Action.* Cambridge, MA: Harvard University Press.

Wood, D. and Middleton, D. (1975). 'A study of assisted problem-solving.' *British Journal of Psychology, 66*(2), 181–191.

Wood, D., Bruner, J.S. and Ross, G. (1976). 'The role of tutoring in problem-solving.' *Journal of Child Psychology and Psychiatry, 17,* 89–100.

Chapter 3

Toward a neuropsychological model of internal dialogue

Implications for theory and clinical practice

Marc D. Lewis and Rebecca Todd

Yvonne has arrived at work early. She is giving a presentation today, the fruit of months of work. Alone in her office, she checks her slides one last time, making sure there are no errors. As she runs through the presentation she feels a combination of nervous anticipation and pleasure. She has checked all her facts, she is wearing her favourite skirt, and she feels prepared to answer all questions. Then, as she rummages in her bag for a backup disk, she discovers her son's completed homework assignment. She has forgotten to give it to him when she dropped him off at school. She notices a sudden change in her mood, a rush of anxiety and guilt. Now his grade will be marked down because it is late, he will be upset, and his teacher will disapprove. As she dials the phone to try to reach the teacher, she decides to stop and 'look inward', as her new therapist suggests. She notices that there are phrases in her mind: 'I can't help it. I can't do everything on my own. It's not my fault.' And she notices that these phrases are directed at someone, but she isn't sure who it is. It seems a bit like her mother, who disapproves of her absorption in her work, or her boss, who thinks her family obligations are excessive, or perhaps her son. But the person she is addressing is apparently much closer, because that person now responds sarcastically, 'Oh, and whose fault is it?'

How can the self be one yet many? This question has preoccupied philosophers and writers for centuries. It is a question that bridges worlds as different as Buddhist meditation, psychoanalysis and cognitive science (Varela et al. 1991), and it guides theories of psychotherapy that try to make sense of self-induced suffering. Recently, social and personality psychologists have attempted to address the multiplicity of the self by replacing terms such as ego and superego with the more contemporary language of self schemas and narrative structure. However, these conceptualizations essentially exchange one set of metaphors for another, and they propose static mechanisms for explaining what appears to be a very active process (Hermans 1996). To move beyond this impasse, Hermans models the multiplicity of the self in terms of voiced positions engaged in dialogue. This formulation is clearly action based, and it captures some of the phenomenology revealed by clinical reports. But is it correct? Does it point toward tangible psychological mechanisms and useful therapeutic strategies, or does it simply provide another set of metaphors?

Psychologists are increasingly looking toward the brain in order to ground their modelling in biological reality, and the discipline of cognitive neuroscience has compiled a great deal of data to assist them. Using these data, we suggest a neuroscientific instantiation of Hermans' model of the dialogical self, in order to evaluate its core tenets, increase its precision, and consider its therapeutic applications. Following Hermans, we see the embodied, agentic notion of voicing as an important refinement, and we use it as a bridge to the brain. We discuss the brain's premotor systems (systems that mediate the planning of motor sequences) and the attentional states that guide them, and we show how these and related systems are rooted in emotion. We speculate on how these systems might be engaged in producing internalized voices and responding to those voices as if they came from someone else. We then address the claim that different voices or positions coexist, occupying the same mental space at the same time. This portrayal of multiplicity creates problems for neurobiology just as it does for psychology, yet they are creative problems that point toward a fundamentally new perspective in psychological research. Finally, we consider the therapeutic implications of such a brain-based model of dialogicity.

Voicing in the dialogical self: embodiment, agency and position

In order to move beyond modern metaphors of information-processing and narrative, Hermans (1996) highlights the active voice in the multiple self. The 'agentlike qualities of the I' (p. 42) give each of the self's various positions a vital, active part to play in the internal dialogue. In fact, *positioning* assumes the status of a verb to convey this activity, and this allows Hermans to break away from the more passive constructs of schema, script and storyline. Hermans frames the dialogical self as an interaction between various voices. These I-positions take turns in an internal dialogue, like interacting characters in a story. They agree or disagree and tell stories from their own perspectives. Moreover, they have the capacity to change or evolve by taking into consideration the perspective of the other. This means that they must hear as well as speak, and indeed the concept of voice is meaningless unless it is related to the perception of other voices. For Hermans (1996: 44), 'voice assumes an embodied actor located in space together with other actors'.

Hermans' focus on embodiment places him in league with contemporary cognitive scientists for whom information-processing is the most recent in a line of inadequate metaphors. Rather than information-processing, theorists now propose cognitive processes that are fundamentally embodied. First, these processes are viewed as emergent, self-organizing, global gestalts that arise from reciprocal interactions among processing units, not linear sequences (Clark 1996; Varela et al. 1991). Second, they are necessarily affect-ive or motivated, linking biological requirements to the formation and manipulation of societal meanings (Fogel 1993; Freeman 1995; Lewis 1995). Indeed, Hermans and Kempen (1993) provide a central place for emotion in their model, and Hermans and Hermans-Jansen (2003) propose that changes in voiced positions can be explained as phase transitions in nonlinear dynamic systems. Thus, their account of the multiple self fits with an emerging Zeitgeist in cognitive science.

In cognitive science at large, the move toward embodiment includes a commitment to understand the brain as the basis of cognition. The richly distributed, reciprocally interactive, and self-organizing character of neural activity provides a radical alternative to the linear sequences of symbol-processing machines (e.g. Thelen and Smith 1994). It follows that Hermans' move toward embodiment should be compatible with neural realism. More-over, Hermans' emphasis on voice provides a useful entry point to test this compatibility. Voicing, construed as action, points toward the brain regions and subsystems directly involved in planning and generating voluntary speech. Voicing, construed as listening, points toward the attentional systems that anticipate others' speech and prepare for one's own. Thus, a good place to look for dialogicity in the brain is in systems where attention and action are integrated. These are generally acknowledged to be the frontal and pre-frontal cortical systems, and they are held responsible for a focused sense of the self acting in the world. By studying the character of these systems, their dependence on emotion, and their contribution to learning and memory, we can speculate on how a dialogical self might actually be housed in a dialogical brain (Lewis 2002).

One of the most difficult and intriguing questions for the dialogical self is how one can be both subject and object in the same dialogue, as was the case with Yvonne. To address this question, this article is restricted to discussion of *internal* dialogues, that is, dialogues between one's various I-positions (Hermans and Hermans-Jansen 2003). This exploration is guided by a con-tention of Hermans that is particularly challenging from a neural perspective. Hermans (1996) emphasizes that the positions in the dialogical self are dis-tributed in an imaginal space. This leads him to propose the 'simultaneous existence' (p. 46) of internalized voices. However, as we shall see, attention, action and motivation appear to synchronize the brain, such that numerous subsystems become highly coordinated in real time. It is difficult to imagine how semi-autonomous positions could coexist at the same moment in such a unitary brain, and this problem indeed recapitulates the classic difficulty of seeing the self as both unitary and multiple. Thus, what is problematic for a neural explanation is problematic for the study of the self more broadly: the reconciliation of unity and multiplicity. We now look to the brain to see how this challenge can be addressed.

Neuropsychological mechanisms of attention, action and emotion

The first step to modelling the dialogical brain should be to refine the psychological reality of multivoicedness. What is the actual subjective experience of internal dialogue? Most people do not actually hear internal voices most of the time. Yet, people often notice that a word or phrase was about to be spoken, and they may even notice their lips move or speak audibly to themselves at times. Less often, people report hearing phrases that sound like they come from somebody else. After meditation, Gestalt therapy, or some other form of introspective learning, one may begin to notice that one is actually the author of these phrases, speaking to an objectified self from a different perspective. But if one attends closely, most of the phrases one hears are one's own. They emerge from a familiar I-position and there is no clear respondent to whom they are directed.

At first glance, this portrayal seems to contradict Hermans' (1996) notion of multivoicedness. However, one does not have to be actively speaking or actively listening to be in a dialogical relationship. If Yvonne normally proceeds in a familiar I-position, but then hears a self-directed comment, she may not be surprised. The experience of dialogicity may often be the experience of *expecting* dialogue, that is, the experience of acting *as if* someone might be listening to us, evaluating us, and ready to react verbally. Even in the familiar I-position, there may be a kind of listening going on that presupposes the presence of an other. Such assumptions of course need to be supported by research. But if they are close to being correct, they potentially clarify what self-reports and questionnaires miss: that internal dialogues are real, but they are usually sublingual and inchoate, and the voice of the other is a rare event, but it is not unexpected. In fact, the expectation of hearing that voice may be kept alive in implicit memory, just below the surface of consciousness.

Based on these assumptions, a neural model of the dialogical self that is precise and comprehensive must be able to do at least three things. First, it must be able to determine what position, either a familiar I-position or some other position, is doing the talking and the listening. In other words, who is the subject and who is the object at each point in the dialogue? Second, it should be able to specify the degree of articulation at which dialogical events are taking place, on a spectrum from vague, gist-like sensations to articulated words or phrases. Third, it should be able to specify whether a dialogical act is happening in the moment or else expected in the near future.

To think about the first issue, the subjectivity of self or other, it is helpful to utilize a canonical example of self-talk. Following McAdams (1985), we can identify many versions of a familiar parent–child relationship being voiced in the internal dialogue. The self can switch from the child, who is subjectively hearing the parent's criticism or who subjectively argues back, to the parent who criticizes or scorns the child (subjectively speaking from another position). A more user-friendly version comes from developmentalists such as Dore (1989) and Kegan (1982), who observe children enacting highly familiar exchanges with a pretend parent, often switching between the child's and parent's role. A 2½-year-old girl audiotaped by Dore repeated to herself, 'Big girls don't cry', after her father had left her to fall asleep by herself. According to Smith Benjamin (1997) similar processes continue throughout the lifetime. Even in adulthood we continue to internalize other voices (e.g. supervisors, therapists, spouses) to guide our actions. Sometimes we use these voices subjectively, imagining ourselves to be the supervisor. But perhaps more often they seem to come at us from elsewhere, as if we played no part in their development. As suggested by the psychoanalytic notion of transference, these later-acquired voices may differentiate out from the seminal voices of childhood, becoming new variants on well-established themes.

In order to think about the second issue, articulation, it is useful to conceive of actions and perceptions as evolving from a gist-like sense of the world to fully elaborated behaviours and percepts. Much cognitive processing remains at the level of gist, where a supramodal image of an object, action or situation lacks sensory details yet has emotional significance (Brainerd and Reyna 1990). Actions begin with global, gist-like intentions that can be rapidly refined into specific motor plans and finally into a sequence of muscle movements (including speech). Perceptions begin with a global sense of the world; they can remain gist-like for some time but then shift to a rapid extraction of the specific features of a situation (e.g. the actual words in the case of dialogue). In fact, for both action and perception, most attentional activity (and neural activity) is engaged below the level of articulated words or sounds. Thus, voices may be actively *intended* in speaking, or actively *attended to* in hearing, without any specification of words or phrases.

Finally, with regard to expectancy, a key principle of cognitive psychology can be applied to internal dialogues. Action is always guided by anticipation and anticipation always takes place in the context of perception (Neisser 1978). To complete the cycle, actions change or reinforce aspects of the perceived world, setting the occasion for further anticipation and action. From a neural perspective, the link between perception and action-planning takes place at an executive level of *anticipatory attention and control* subserved by the prefrontal cortices (Fuster 1996). Here higher-order processes of volitional attention arise from a gist-like integration across perceptual modalities, providing the foundation for emerging behavioural plans and actions. It has long been established that perception is guided by anticipation of action as well. Freeman (1995) describes how *preafference* (or, so to speak, pre-reception) travels from incipient motor plans to the sensory cortices, focusing them on particular aspects of the world in anticipation of intended behaviour. Putting these ideas together, we can see the brain as generating actions and perceiving events that fit an anticipated future, a model of the world just ahead of us in time. The brain is concerned with what is about to happen, not what is happening now. In terms of dialogue, attention (hearing) would be guided by the expectation of what 'I' am about to say, and action (speaking) would be guided by the expectation of what 'you' are about to say.

As mentioned earlier, cognition in an embodied system cannot be independent of emotion, and the importance of emotion is central to the dialogical self. But how might the interplay between cognition and emotion guide neural modelling? Psychologists have become increasingly aware that negative emotions (e.g. anxiety, anger, sadness) narrow the focus of attention and anchor it to particular aspects of the world (Derryberry and Tucker 1994). In fact, the biological purpose of emotion is to motivate action, that is, to move attention toward aspects of situations that are highly important, and to urge the production of actions to deal with them. However, the control of attention by emotion is reciprocally related to the control of emotion by attention (Lewis 1995, submitted). Attentional states amplify, and then regulate, emotions by appraising their causes and generating plans to resolve them. These plans, though they may not be executed immediately, relieve immediate concerns by taking control of whatever needs to be done to face challenges and alleviate dangers.

How is this reciprocal relation between attention and emotion played out in the brain? Executive attention, and cognition more generally, are usually ascribed to the cerebral cortex, the outer sheath of the brain, and particularly to the prefrontal cortex which synchronizes all sensory and motor regions according to a particular plan or goal (Fuster 1996). Emotion, on the other hand, is often associated with the limbic system, an assortment of structures including the amygdala and hippocampus, that are enfolded within the cortical layers, as well as more primitive brainstem systems. These subcortical systems are considered directly responsible for affective feeling, emotional conditioning, and action tendencies related to emotion (Buck 1999; LeDoux 1996; MacLean 1993). Communication among these cortical and subcortical systems allows for the interplay between attentional and emotional states. Bundles of fibres carry signals in both directions between the prefrontal cortex and subcortical regions, such that they activate each other simultaneously and reciprocally. Cortical attention regulates emotion through downstream paths, while emotional arousal feeds up from limbic and lower structures to activate and constrain attentional focus. However, once these systems recruit each other in an emotional process, they become entrained or coupled, producing a unitary and coherent attentional focus. This global state synchronizes activation throughout the brain and controls physiological changes in all parts of the body as well (Tucker et al. 2000). Most important for the present discussion, this global state, because it is fuelled by emotion and directed toward action, commands all of one's attention. Thus, any I-position that is autonomous, intentional and 'voiced' synchronizes the entire brain; apparently, only one such voice could be activated at a time.

Modelling the dialogical brain

We can roughly locate the epicentre of internal dialogues in the network of circuits between frontocortical and limbic regions. These reciprocal connections are where global attentional states emerge in conjunction with emotion and anticipated action. We have characterized these global states as unitary Gestalts. But this poses a problem: how can multiple, coexistent voices or positions be supported by a single, unitary attentional stance? Hermans' description of the 'simultaneous existence' of internalized voices appears contradictory in a brain that can do only one emotional-attentive thing at a time, and this fundamental paradox needs to be resolved in a plausible model of internal dialogue. One solution would be to model internal dialogues as turn-taking, such that one global attentional state, belonging to one voice, alternates frequently with another. Yet, the phenomenology of internal dialogues may not support this idea. To recapitulate, internal dialogues are normally sublingual, and one spends much more time in the familiar I-position than in any other state. Thus, one subjectively speaks one's own voice more readily than one subjectively speaks another's, and most of the time the (objective) voice of the other is expected rather than heard. Given these considerations, switching one's global, subjective stance back and forth in a turn-taking sequence is not very likely. What is more likely is that one remains in a continuous dialogical relation with an *anticipated, almost-heard* other.

Let us begin to model Yvonne's experience using this framework. When she realizes that she still has her son's homework, anxiety flickers quickly in the limbic system and brainstem, and begins to recruit attentional circuits in the prefrontal cortex. A global attentional state coheres, and anxiety is now directed toward an imagined reaction to the missing assignment (her son's distress or the teacher's disapproval). Now a gist-like sense of being 'in trouble' prevails as a corticolimbic gestalt, and plans for self-defence begin to arise in the premotor circuits extending upward (dorsally) through the frontal cortex. What is happening is that a subjective I-position is emerging spontaneously and generating behavioural strategies (i.e. verbal intentions) about what to say to the critical other. However, these speech-like plans need not be articulated in words. They may resonate in the premotor circuits without actually arriving at the motor cortex. Yvonne may have a general sense of being wronged, feeling grumpy and arguing or defending, without any words appearing on the screen of the mind. This anticipatory, inchoate, dialogical stance may last for a while. Then, perhaps spontaneously or perhaps because she stopped to examine it, this stance gives way to more articulated motor plans, resolving to actual words and phrases (e.g. 'It's not my fault') as the motor cortex is activated. These may not seem like an internal dialogue, because Yvonne hears only her own voice in passing, through feedback from motor circuits to the auditory cortex. Of particular importance, this *monological* state could go on almost indefinitely, and certainly without much awareness. It is not until Yvonne notices a second internal voice that a sense of dialogue emerges.

The internal monologue just described is surprisingly self-sustaining, and one way it sustains itself is by anticipating the other's response. Whether inchoate or articulated, the motor plans generated by anticipation of criticism are *in relation to* the imagined other. The construct of preafference suggests that these plans maintain the anticipation of the criticism, the reality of the critic, as an ongoing, but abstract, perceptual gestalt. According to Fogel (1993), relationality is responsible for the emergence and stabilization of psychological states throughout the lifespan. Fogel (1993) proposes 'consensual frames', stable patterns of interpersonal interaction, as the unit of analysis for all psychological processes. These frames are stable because they lock together anticipation and response between two interacting partners. But the stability of interpersonal states also relies on emotion (Lewis 1995). Emotion keeps both partners committed to the exchange and prevents it from dissipating. We can think of internal monologues as the enactment of internalized consensual frames, and the relational and emotional aspects of these internal duets may serve the same stabilizing function. One imagines the critical stance of the other, but without resolution or detail, and this stance has a particular emotional significance. This emotional significance rivets attention and continues to propagate anticipatory action plans. Moreover, the stance of the imagined other is not static. Rather, it continues to adjust itself to Yvonne's evolving action plans. Thus, Yvonne's monologue is self-perpetuating, not through static anticipation, but through a progression of updated action plans and anticipated responses. For example, Yvonne's monologue of argumentative self-defence is likely to elicit opposition from the imagined other, and the anticipation of that opposition continues to fuel her anxiety and motivate adjustments to her defensive posture. Here we can observe a full-fledged dialogical process, continuous and self-perpetuating, without ever leaving the familiar I-position.

But to model this internal monologue with precision, we need to go back to the brain for more detail. So far the prefrontal cortex has been portrayed as a single, undifferentiated, attentional system. However, as shown in Figure 3.1, the prefrontal cortex can be subdivided into several attentional systems. Two of these, each with access to its own premotor network and each with different limbic connections, will be sufficient to set out our argument. The hub of one attentional system that is of particular relevance to emotion is the *orbitofrontal cortex* (OFC). This region is at the very base of the frontal lobe, and it is tuned to rewards and punishments in the immediate environment, probably because of its dense connections with the amygdala (the limbic structure that mediates fear, anxiety and some kinds of anger). It is also closely connected to the temporal lobes, where perceptual (visual and auditory) input is processed and integrated, and to Broca's area, which controls speech

Motor cortex

Supplementary
motor area

Parietal lobe

ACC

OFC

Arcuate
premotor
area

Amygdala

Hippocampus

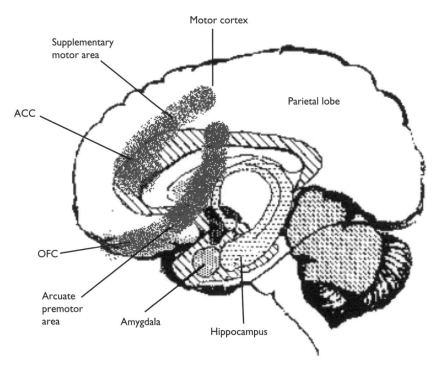

Figure 3.1 Drawing of a medial slice of the brain including amygdala and hippocampus. Two frontal attentional systems, the orbitofrontal cortex (OFC) and the anterior cingulate cortex (ACC), are shown along with their associated premotor areas, and their independent paths to the motor cortex are highlighted with 'spray paint'.

production and reception. Finally, it is closely related to a premotor system called the arcuate premotor area. Together, these linked systems have a particular style of functioning, characterized as controlled, responsive and input-driven (Goldberg 1985). A second attentional system has its hub in the *anterior cingulate cortex* (ACC), which is closer to the top and centre of the head (more dorsomedial). This system broadly integrates information across spatial and temporal perceptual elements. It is associated with a second premotor system, the supplementary motor area, where spontaneous volitional acts are generated. The outputs of these linked systems are characterized as coherent or packaged motor plans, projectional rather than responsive in style (Goldberg 1985; Luu et al. 1998). The ACC is also connected to the limbic system, but less closely to the amygdala and more closely to the hippocampus. Its motivational base is concerned with moving through familiar situations efficiently rather than carefully confronting challenges and threats. In summary, the OFC system attends to potential rewards and threats, and it drives behavioural plans, including speech, via careful monitoring of perceptual feedback. The ACC system integrates more diverse information into familiar Gestalts, is less 'hot' emotionally, and drives behaviour plans that are spontaneous, global and intact. It should be noted that both the ACC and the OFC are densely connected to the lateral prefrontal cortices, which mediate working memory, reflective thought, and other aspects of conscious attention.

The internal monologues described so far involved as much listening as speaking and, in Yvonne's case, they were fuelled by anxiety about anticipated rewards and punishments. These features suggest mediation by the OFC. However, there was no actual perceptual input from another person; thus, the OFC would have to create a gist-like imaginal figure while formulating its own voice. This should not be problematic for emotionally compelling monologues. According to Luu et al. (1998), the attentional system in this region has a short-term memory capacity sustained by the motivational significance of the recalled evaluations. It may also combine these evaluations into a categorical rather than specific sense of another person, explaining why Yvonne could not quite discern who was criticizing her.

Schore (1994, 1997) emphasizes the role of the right OFC in the 'valence tagging' of perceptions along a pleasure–unpleasure axis. He also sees the right OFC as key to implicit learning and memory from the time of early infancy. According to Schore, the right OFC produces an affectively charged, gist-like sense of an interpersonal respondent, based on expectancies from many past interactions. As a result, this gist-like image is the fundamental arbitrator of emotion regulation, and it sets the rest of the brain in a mode of readiness based on preconscious expectations. An image of a warm, soothing parent permits rapid emotional equilibration, whereas the expectation of rejection or criticism promotes defence or withdrawal. From Schore's perspective, these attachment-based appraisals would be the basis of individual differences in dialogical styles, consistent with case histories presented by Hermans and Hermans-Jansen (2003). Thus, internal monologues mediated by the OFC would be attuned to a highly predictable response from an imagined person or type of person, and this attunement would resonate with a particular emotional state, maintaining a particular style of other-directed speech.

The internal monologue described so far does indeed have a dialogical character, based on the creation of an expectable other in relation to whom one voices one's own position. It also addresses the problem of coexisting positions in a unitary attentional frame – at least partly – because subjectivity and agency reside in a single, coherent I-position. Such an I-position continuously awaits the other's response: no bifurcation of attention is necessary. However, these monologues do not have the vitality of Hermans' polyphonic self. They repeat familiar stances, are devoid of novelty, and miss any true exchange or confrontation between *autonomous* voiced positions. Regarding such monological rigidity, Morin (1995) wonders why some people seem to engage in constant self-talk without ever acquiring self-knowledge. He con-cludes that it is because they talk to themselves without taking the other's perspective.

Let us move on, then, to the final scene of Yvonne's internal dialogue. After her grumbling monologue, she seemed to hear another voice with an entirely different tone, saying 'Oh, and whose fault is it?' This implies a direct accusation coming at Yvonne from another. We know that the voice actually came from her. But does this imply a different I-position, as Hermans proposes? How would such a shift be modelled? We present the following speculative proposition.

The position of the 'other' may bubble up from a gist-like expectancy to an actual memory of a distinct word or phrase. If this is the case, Yvonne might hear the other's words yet retain her familiar I-position. But this possibility is not very interesting, because it maintains the same positioning as the mono-logue already described. It would be much more congenial with Hermans' polyphonic self if Yvonne's subjectivity switched from the familiar I-position to an alternative, autonomous I-position. Like the child who switches roles from the helpless little girl to the powerful parent, perhaps scolding and even punishing her favourite doll, adults also notice occasions when they take themselves as an object and speak subjectively as someone else.

How can this switch of subjectivity be modelled? One possibility is that internal monologues progress through many shades of emotional content as well as gradations of emotional intensity, along with the shifting images of the anticipated other. These changes would be expected to alter the frame and focus of attention, as discussed earlier (e.g. Niedenthal and Kitayama 1994). When anxiety gives way to sadness, for example, the narrow beam of atten-tion broadens, and when it gives way to anger, that beam switches to an object that can be construed as an obstacle. Such changes in emotion and attention may perturb the coherence of an attentional stance, changing the sweep of perception and anticipation, and this may be the point at which subjectivity switches. In previous work, we have suggested that fluctuating negative emo-tional states can shift the focus of an appraisal radically without changing its content (Lewis and Junyk 1997). For example, a blend of anxiety and rage felt toward a parent can shift to rage directed at the self, with only a small piece of the appraisal (i.e. its object) being replaced. Here we want to highlight the neurobiological fault line that subserves such changes, and one candidate is the distinction between the two attentional systems described earlier, the orbitofrontal and anterior cingulate systems. (Left and right-hemisphere dif-ferences may also play a critical role in the switching of subjectivities, but we save discussion of this topic for a future paper.)

Interestingly, the OFC is one of the only frontal regions whose activity can be independent of the ACC (Koski and Paus 2000). At times (and perhaps under suboptimal circumstances) these two systems may actually compete for the control of attention, depending on the type and intensity of emotion

(Bush et al. 2000). In the presence of negative emotion, and particularly anxiety, the orbitofrontal region may show heightened activation while the ACC becomes less activated; but in more cool or cognitive tasks, activation shifts to the ACC instead. While a scolding parental voice is not emotionally neutral, it is also not particularly anxious. In fact, it may be somewhat of a relief, emotionally, to become the perpetrator rather than the victim of rebuke. Thus, a shift away from anxiety, perhaps to anger or contempt, may be what triggers activation of the ACC, providing the occasion for a shift in subjectivity.

What is most intriguing about this hypothesis is that the rapid, spontaneous and projectional style of motor plans stemming from the ACC seem to match the phenomenology of the alternate I-position. For example, the critical rebuke launched by the 'internal parent' is preformed, of a piece, emerges without forethought, and is not attuned to perceptual feedback. In fact the child-self who bears the brunt of this rebuke is almost entirely ignored by the scolding parent, a point which is frequently made by therapists who encourage their patients to 'be nice to yourself'. The sudden parental tirade pays no attention to any environmental feedback, in sharp contrast to the anxious, preoccupied and attentive style of Yvonne's familiar I-position. Instead, it is well practised and smooth. In fact, we could suppose that the familiar and intact parental rebuke Yvonne hears is actually the performance of a voice she rehearsed when she practised her mother's role as a child.

If this hypothesis is eventually borne out by research, it will have remarkable implications for internal dialogues as well as for the therapeutic techniques that focus on such dialogues. The switching of activation between independent attentional systems provides the neural basis for semi-autonomous I-positions of the sort that Hermans postulates. Although the two systems cannot perform different tasks at the same time, the capacity to switch subjective positions rapidly and completely permits autonomous voices, engaged in something like a dialogical exchange. Furthermore, the switch from orbitofrontal to ACC activation allows a different premotor circuit to take control of motor output. The activity of this circuit is picked up perceptually (whether in the mind's ear or out loud). Now the brain finds itself confronted with new auditory information, and that information is bound to have an emotional impact. To actually hear an ACC-mediated parental rebuke regardless of its true author is likely to trigger an immediate emotional response in the OFC-mediated I-position, whether of fear, shame or anger. In turn, this emotional response should interrupt the present attentional frame, generate plans for new potential words or actions, and thus propel the internal dialogue forward, perhaps in a novel direction. Finally, under optimal circumstances, or when emotional intensity is reduced past some threshold, the ACC and the OFC systems can begin to operate synchronously, creating a voiced position that includes the ACC's rehearsed, volitional qualities as well as the OFC's immediate responsiveness. In this way, the vitality and creativity of internal dialogues can be squared with the constraints of biological realism, and we can begin to understand the power they have to colour the internal world. We can also begin to apply this understanding to the problems of clinical intervention, a topic we now introduce.

Clinical implications

In the vignette presented earlier, Yvonne's new therapist had asked her to look inward to identify her inner voices. Let us imagine that, at her next appointment, Yvonne is asked to name the voices she hears most often (Hermans and Hermans-Jansen 2003). She realizes that she thinks of her familiar I-position as the 'Anxious Child', while she names the sarcastic parental voice the 'Critic'.

At this point her therapeutic work might entail developing a heightened awareness of these voices. For example, if it is true that the articulation of the ACC-mediated parental voice moves the conversation forward, one important goal for therapy might entail tuning in to the voice of the Critic more closely. Increased awareness of the Critic would allow her to take on that perspective, consciously, for prolonged periods. Initially this voice might be experienced as both intrusive and elusive, bubbling up out of nowhere and then receding again. Over time, however, Yvonne might learn to actively inhabit this voice as a fully articulated, volitional persona. From that position, she might tell herself, 'The problem is, you're lazy! You know you should double-check your list before you leave the house. When you don't, you make stupid mistakes!' Not only can Yvonne enjoy the Critic's righteous anger as her own, but also, by elaborating this position, the Critic allows the Anxious Child to respond in a more constructive manner. Now, rather than wallowing in a generalized sense of failure, the Anxious Child can respond less defensively: 'It's true that I often neglect to take the extra step of double checking my list before I leave. Well . . . nobody's perfect.'

By moving the dialogue forward, such enhanced awareness of dialogical voices might allow the Anxious Child to become more volitional, while retaining her emotionally attuned listening stance. Such increased volitional force could redress power imbalances between the two positions (see Hermans 2003), allowing the Anxious Child to become stronger in response to a more articulate Critic. By allowing the initial, inchoate, partially heard voices to achieve full verbal articulation, Yvonne might move the conversation out of the repetitive, stuck mode that perpetuates her feelings of defensive anxiety.

As mentioned before, a fully articulated parental voice can generate a full-fledged emotional response. On the neural level, over the course of seconds, such a response can grow from an initial, barely conscious emotional reaction within the OFC into a full-blown, coherent, cognitive and emotional appraisal. This could entail an integration, or synchronization, of the ACC and OFC systems, which were previously functioning in a competitive, mutually inhibitory mode. Following a highly anxious condition, in which an aroused OFC operates in isolation, reduced anxiety may permit both systems to work together, creating a more balanced, volitional I-position (Goldberg 1985). Furthermore, synchrony between these systems may correspond with an extended, conscious appraisal, which in turn allows for deliberate evaluation of the developing conversation and the opportunity to choose among available I-positions.

According to Hermans and Hermans-Jansen (2003), however, the dialogical self contains more than two subject positions. The simple duality we have described does not fill out much of the imaginal landscape proposed by Hermans to include many interacting voices. Yet the tension and the interplay among the two neural systems we have described might provide the necessary force to carve out several unique dialogical frames. Different emotional constellations, triggered by self- and other-directed voicings, may recruit distinct cognitive appraisals, each laying down unique synaptic networks that consolidate over development. These distinct networks, reactivated on subsequent occasions, may provide the basis for a variety of stances or characters.

Once she has developed the dialogical exchange between the Anxious Child and the Critic, strengthening the Anxious Child's voice by integrating ACC and OFC activation on-line, Yvonne might begin to realize that she can identify other voices. Perhaps she discovers the faint voices of another dialogically linked pair of positions, drawn from another repertoire of internalized memories – voices that provide alternative stances to those of the Critic and the Anxious Child. She might begin to identify a second OFC-mediated child's voice (the Confident Child) saying, 'Well, I'm only human, and James' teacher will understand', in anticipation of a more soothing parental listener. Instead of a hostile ACC-mediated voice criticizing her as stupid, Yvonne might anticipate an encouraging parental voice assuring her, 'You've accomplished so much. Give yourself a break. After all, how many of your colleagues are raising three children?'

As Yvonne tunes into a new pair of linked voices, she may also begin to develop a meta-perspective, superordinate to any particular voiced position. According to Hermans (2003), a well-developed meta-position allows one to stand above the ongoing stream of perception. In other words, one takes the perspective of an author watching one's voiced positions functioning as actors in specific circumstances. As a result of increased self-awareness, one is able to strengthen the capacity for seeing relevant linkages. In our case, as she becomes aware of several linked pairs of voices, Yvonne begins to realize that she can choose among them. Rather than remain locked in the Anxious Child position, she discovers that she can inhabit the voice of another I-position, the Confident Child, whose expectations of an understanding interlocutor may indeed call up such an accepting parental voice.

But how might the idea of meta-perspective be modelled in neural terms? The ACC mediates the cognitive ability to choose among competing options, as well as such meta-processes as 'theory of mind' (Gallagher and Frith 2003). Drawing on such capacities, the ACC could supply a mechanism for deliberately recruiting networks underlying different positions. That is to say, beyond functioning as an actor, the ACC controller could also serve as Hermans' author. In addition to mediating such internalized parental positions as Yvonne's Critic, the ACC (which has dense connections with the lateral prefrontal cortices) could recruit the working memory circuits necessary for conscious choice among various positions. By first becoming aware of multiple positions, and then choosing the most constructive pair of voices for a particular context (in our situation, the Confident Child and the Soothing Parent), Yvonne would no longer be at the mercy of her anxiety. Rather, her cultivation of meta-awareness would permit her to author her own internal conversations with deliberation and increasing confidence.

Conclusion

In this account we have attempted to model an internal monologue, hypothesized to be the basis of the dialogical self, subserved by an attentional system in the orbitofrontal cortex and nearby affective and premotor systems. We have argued that this internal monologue implies the presence of another person, because it is directed toward an imaginal (but unspecific) sense of that person and it adjusts and updates itself through a changing anticipation of how that other person will respond. This model was extended to account for a switch to another, autonomous, voiced position, underpinned by the anterior cingulate cortex and its connections, as exemplified by a spontaneous rebuke directed by a parent-self toward the usual child-self. Finally, we discussed possible therapeutic applications of such a model. First, we suggested that increased awareness of voiced positions may allow for and be facilitated by longer durations of ACC activity and increased coherence between ACC and OFC systems, furthering the conscious, volitional nature of each voice. Second, we suggested that enhanced awareness of multiple dialogues may depend on ACC recruitment of working memory in the development of a meta-perspective, thus enabling more choice between voiced positions and their attendant affective values. We conclude that many characteristics of internal dialogue can be modelled with reference to the brain, and that insights from neuroscience can contribute to theoretical and practical formulations based on the dialogical self.

Acknowledgements

Portions of this chapter are reprinted by permission of Sage Publications Ltd from, Lewis, M. (2002) 'The dialogical brain: contributions of emotional neurobiology to understanding the dialogical self', *Theory and Psychology*, vol. 2, 2:175–190 © 2002 Sage Publications Ltd.

References

Brainerd, C.J. and Reyna, V.F. (1990). 'Gist is the grist: Fuzzy-trace theory and the new intuitionism.' *Developmental Review, 10*, 3–47.

Buck, R. (1999). 'The biological affects: A typology.' *Psychological Review, 106*, 301–336.

Bush, G., Luu, P. and Posner, M.I. (2000). 'Cognitive and emotional influences in anterior cingulate cortex.' *Trends in Cognitive Sciences, 4*, 215–222.

Clark, A. (1996). *Being there: Putting brain, body, and world together again.* Cambridge, MA: MIT Press.

Derryberry, D. and Tucker, D.M. (1994). 'Motivating the focus of attention.' In P.M. Niedenthal and S. Kitayama (eds) *The Heart's Eye: Emotional Influences in Perception and Attention* (pp. 167–196). San Diego, CA: Academic Press.

Dore, J. (1989). 'Monologue as reenvoicement of dialogue.' In K. Nelson (ed.) *Narratives from the Crib* (pp. 231–260). Cambridge, MA: Harvard University Press.

Fogel, A. (1993). *Developing through Relationships: Origins of Communication, Self, and Culture.* Chicago: University of Chicago Press.

Freeman, W.J. (1995). *Societies of Brains.* Hillsdale, NJ: Lawrence Erlbaum Associates.

Fuster, J.M. (1996). *The Prefrontal Cortex: Anatomy, Physiology and Neuropsychology of the Frontal Lobe*, 3rd edn. New York: Raven Press.

Gallagher, H. and Frith, C.D. (2003). 'Functional imaging of "theory of mind".' *Trends in Cognitive Sciences, 7*, 77–83.

Goldberg, G. (1985). 'Supplementary motor area structure and function: Review and hypotheses.' *Behavioral and Brain Sciences, 8*, 567–616.

Hermans, H.J.M. (1996). 'Voicing the self: From information processing to dialogical interchange.' *Psychological Bulletin, 119*, 31–50.

Hermans, H.J.M. (2003). 'The construction and reconstruction of a dialogical self.' *Journal of Constructivist Psychology, 16*, 89–130.

Hermans, H.J.M. and Hermans-Jansen, E. (2003). 'Dialogical processes and the development of the self.' In J. Valsiner and K.J. Connolly (eds) *Handbook of Developmental Psychology* (pp. 534–559). London: Sage.

Hermans, H.J.M. and Kempen, H.J.G. (1993). *The Dialogical Self: Meaning as Movement.* San Diego, CA: Academic Press.

Kegan, R. (1982). *The Evolving Self: Problem and Process in Human Development.* Cambridge, MA: Harvard University Press.

Koski, L. and Paus, T. (2000). 'Functional connectivity of the anterior cingulate cortex within the human frontal lobe: A brain-mapping meta-analysis.' *Experimental Brain Research, 133*, 55–65.

LeDoux, J. (1996). *The Emotional Brain: The Mysterious Underpinnings of Emotional Life.* New York: Simon and Shuster.

Lewis, M.D. (1995). 'Cognition-emotion feedback and the self-organization of developmental paths.' *Human Development, 38*, 71–102.

Lewis, M.D. (2002). 'The dialogical brain: Contributions of emotional neurobiology to understanding the dialogical self.' *Theory and Psychology*, *12*(2), 175–190.

Lewis, M.D. (in press). 'Bridging emotion theory and neurobiology through dynamic systems modeling.' (In press *Behavioral and Brain Sciences*.)

Lewis, M.D. and Junyk, N. (1997). 'The self-organization of psychological defenses.' In F. Masterpasqua and P. Perna (eds) *The Psychological Meaning of Chaos: Translating Theory into Practice* (pp. 41–73). Washington, DC: American Psychological Association.

Luu, P., Tucker, D.M. and Derryberry, D. (1998). 'Anxiety and the motivational basis of working memory.' *Cognitive Therapy and Research*, *22*, 577–594.

McAdams, D.P. (1985). *Power, Intimacy, and the Life Story: Personological Inquiries into Identity*. New York: Guilford.

MacLean, P.D. (1993). 'Perspectives on cingulate cortex in the limbic system.' In B.A. Vogt and M. Gabriel (eds) *Neurobiology of Cingulate Cortex and Limbic Thalamus: A Comprehensive Handbook* (pp. 1–15). Cambridge, MA: Birkhäuser Boston.

Morin, A. (1995). 'Characteristics of an effective internal dialogue in the acquisition of self-information.' *Imagination, Cognition and Personality*, *15*, 45–58.

Neisser, U. (1978). 'Anticipations, images, and introspection.' *Cognition*, *6*, 169–174.

Niedenthal, P.M. and Kitayama, S. (eds) (1994). *The Heart's Eye: Emotional Influences in Perception and Attention*. San Diego, CA: Academic Press.

Schore, A.N. (1994). *Affect Regulation and the Origin of the Self: The Neurobiology of Emotional Development*. Hillsdale, NJ: Lawrence Erlbaum Associates.

Schore, A.N. (1997). 'Early organization of the nonlinear right brain and development of a predisposition to psychiatric disorders.' *Development and Psychopathology*, *9*, 595–631.

Smith Benjamin, L.S. (1997). Contribution as a participant in a virtual discussion. In W.B. Stiles (moderator). 'Multiple voices: A virtual discussion.' *Journal of Psychotherapy Integration*, *7*(3), 241–262.

Thelen, E. and Smith, L.B. (1994). *A Dynamic Systems Approach to the Development of Cognition and Action*. Cambridge, MA: Bradford/MIT Press.

Tucker, D.M. Derryberry, D. and Luu, P. (2000). 'Anatomy and physiology of human emotion: Vertical integration of brain stem, limbic, and cortical systems'. In J.C. Borod (ed.) *The Neuropsychology of Emotion* (pp. 56–79). New York: Oxford University Press.

Varela, F.J., Thompson, E. and Rosch, E. (1991). *The Embodied Mind: Cognitive Science and Human Experience*. Cambridge, MA: MIT Press.

Chapter 4

Encountering self–otherness
'I–I' and 'I–Me' modes of self-relating

Mick Cooper

Stanley, 55, came to therapy to find a way of controlling his violence towards his partner.[1] 'I desperately want to stop,' he repeated again and again in our initial meetings, 'I just don't know why I do it.' In our third session, we explored one particular episode when he'd lashed out at his lover, Danny.

> He came home late [Stanley said] and he didn't say a word about where he'd been – no apology, no nothing – he just went straight into the kitchen and started cooking. I didn't want to start cross-examining him because I didn't want another row, but when I bit into the food and it was all raw inside . . . and just disgusting . . . I just started shouting at him and throwing plates. He told me that I was being childish and that completely did it for me. It was like some red sheet came down over me and I couldn't stop myself. I pushed him against the cooker and then . . . I think I smacked him in his face, and just shouted and ranted at him. It was completely weird, though, it was like it wasn't me doing it, like some monster or force had taken me over and I was just watching myself.

Sol was a computer technician in his mid-thirties. He had come to therapy to try and work out what he wanted to do in his life, and also to get over his feelings of depression and hopelessness. 'I just felt so lethargic this morning,' said Sol one session, as he had begun many before, 'I didn't have energy to do anything, didn't want to get out of bed. I just listened to the radio and went back to sleep and got to work over an hour late.'

'Do you have any sense of what the lethargy was about?' I asked.

> I dunno, it's just stupid. I hate being that tired and lethargic, but I don't seem able to stop myself. I just get to that place of feeling that everything's pointless – but it's crazy. I've got a decent job, a decent girlfriend, a decent house. What's going on?

Lynda, a client described by Cooper and Cruthers (1999), said that she felt like she was living in a war zone. 'Part of me wants to just lie down and cry and cry but then this voice says, "Don't stop you've got to keep on going . . . don't stop, don't stop, don't stop" ' (p. 198). During her therapy, Lynda came to label this first part of herself as 'Little Lynda' and the second part as 'Busy Coper'. Through therapy, she also began to notice that, whenever Little Lynda was about to express her tears and hurt, she would often shift into her Busy Coper mode as a way of pushing these feelings away. Later on in the therapy, when Lynda enacted a dialogue between these two parts of herself using sandtray figures (a monkey to symbolize Little Lynda and an owl to symbolize her Busy Coper), it became even clearer that her coping side was not willing to tolerate her vulnerability:

Monkey: Please let me out I need to play and have fun and I'm hurt and I need a cuddle and I hate it here behind this wall.

Owl: No – there's no room for you in my life, you muck everything up, I don't have time. I don't like you, I don't want you . . . shut up and go away.

Monkey: I'm going to scream and shout and make lots of noise and hammer on the wall and I'm not going to go away.

Owl: Well I'm not going to listen to you, you're trouble.

(Cooper and Cruthers 1999: 208)

Introduction

At the level of detail, each of these vignettes tells quite a different story. From a dialogic perspective, however, there is a shared theme that runs through each of them: in all three cases, one of the clients' I-positions is being disowned, or rejected, from an alternate I-position.

Within the self-pluralistic literature, much has been written about the tendency for some voices to become disowned (Stone and Winkelman 1989), 'cut off', or 'suppressed' (Hermans and Kempen 1993). There is also a substantial body of literature on the dissociation of certain parts of the self: dating back to Janet's (1889) late-nineteenth-century work on 'subconscious fixed ideas'. In recent years, Stiles and his colleagues' research into problematic experiences and their assimilation (e.g. Stiles et al. 1990) has also done much to advance our understanding of the disownment of certain voices: breaking the duality of owned/disowned into a much finer series of distinctions.

In this chapter, however, I want to propose a somewhat more expanded and holistic conceptualization of intrapersonal disownment. Certainly, in each of the three examples presented above, a central dynamic would seem to be the disownment of one voice from the position of another voice; but, in each of these cases, this would seem to be only one part of a more complex mode of intrapersonal relating. For a start, the disowned voice is not only pushed away, but also dehumanized in some kind of way: conceptualized as an impersonal drive or force rather than as a manifestation of human desires.

Along similar lines, there is a tendency to relate to only one aspect of the disowned voice, and there is also a tendency to avoid entering into dialogue with it.

Based on clinical examples such as these, it has been proposed that we might usefully talk of 'I–Me' modes of self-relating, which can be distinguished from 'I–I' self-relational forms (Cooper 2003b). This distinction is based on Buber's (1958) contrast between I–It and I–Thou interpersonal attitudes, respectively, and suggests that, just as we can relate to others as either it-like objects or whole human beings, so we can relate to our own I-positions in these two different ways.

'I–I' and 'I–Me'

Extrapolating from the distinction between I–Thou and I–It modes of interpersonal relating (see Cooper 2003b; Heard 1995; Woods 1969) to the intrapersonal plane, the distinction between an I–I and I–Me mode of self-relating can be characterized as follows.

Disowning versus owning

One of the primary dimensions along which these modes of self-relating vary is the degree to which one voice identifies with, or 'owns', the alternate voice. Indeed, this is a primary reason why the terms 'I–I' and 'I–Me' have been used: because, in the former case, the 'on-line' I-position (i.e. the I-position that is dominant at one particular point in time) acknowledges that an alternate I-position is part of the same greater I; while, in the latter form of self-relating, the on-line I-position distances itself from the alternate I-position, seeing it as something qualitatively distinct. This is not to suggest that it sees it as part of an entirely different person. Rather, it is that the alternate I's feelings, thoughts and behaviours are experienced as emanating from a different source as the on-line I's, and as if its way of being is not fully under the on-line I's control.

With this distancing also comes a fundamentally different mode of relating. In the I–I mode, the on-line I-position stands alongside its alternate, it moves in flow and dialogue with it without necessarily being aware of it as a discrete, separate I-position. By contrast, in the I–Me mode of self-relating, the alternate I becomes an *object* of experiencing: it is surveyed, studied or observed from a distance; it is talked *about* rather than directly engaged in.

Objectification versus subjectification

Buber's philosophy is rooted in an existential/humanistic/phenomenological paradigm, and from this standpoint, lived-experience is not a fixed, static, substance-like object, but a 'flux' (Merleau-Ponty 1962) or a 'psychic stream'

(Buber 1988: 70). In other words, at the time when Stanley is experiencing intense rage towards his partner, what he is experiencing is an ongoing flow of feelings, desires and thoughts. And yet, when he reflects on this mode of being from a dominant I-position, his rage is experienced as a more thing-like entity – a monster or a force – devoid of internally experienced temporal flow.

Dis-acknowledging agency versus acknowledging agency

From this standpoint, subjectively lived-experience is also characterized by a sense of agency and intentionality. We experience-towards-our-world in meaningful and purposeful ways: we choose towards goals and end-points and outcomes (Frankl 1986). In the I–I relationship, then, the on-line I-position not only enters into the temporal flow of the alternate I-position's world, but also comes to enter into its active, agentic, being-towards-meanings; to experience the subjectively lived choices infusing the alternate I-position's thoughts and behaviours. By contrast, in the I–Me self-relational stance, the purposefulness, meaningfulness and volition behind the alternate I-position's being-towards-the-world tend not to be acknowledged. Lynda's Busy Coper, then, can experience Little Lynda's neediness, but it is experienced as a threat or as an obstacle, rather than as a legitimate and intelligible desire.

In many instances, clients may dis-acknowledge the agentic aspect of alternate I-positions by construing them as causally determined reactions to external circumstances or their own past experiences. As Stanley, for instance, would sometimes claim, 'He wound me up so much I *had* to hit him'; or as Sol sometimes mused, 'I wonder if my lethargy has been caused by my parents splitting up when I was young.'

Fragmenting versus embracing

In the I–Me self-relational stance, the on-line I does not encounter to the totality of its alternate. While it may, for instance, respond to its behaviours, it ignores the feelings and desires within which that behaviour is contextualized. A four-dimensional lived-experience, then, becomes reduced down just to one or two of its facets.

Non-confirming versus confirming

In the I–I mode, there is a fundamental *confirmation* of the alternate I-position: 'an act of love through which one acknowledges the other as one who exists in his own peculiar form and has the right to do so' (Friedman 1985: 134). By contrast, in the I–Me relational mode, the alternate I-position is not fully accepted as it is, and may be criticized, dismissed or derided – as in the vignettes presented earlier. Here, then, there is a failure to accept the other *as* an Other: it is a demand for totalization and homogeny (Levinas 1969) rather than an openness to alterity and difference.

Present-based encounter versus past-based expectations or future-based needs

In the I–Me self-relational stance, the on-line I-position does not meet the alternate I-position as it actually is. Rather, what it meets is either its own, past-based assumptions about what that *kind* of voice is like; or else its 'aims', 'anticipations' or 'lusts' (Buber 1958) upon that voice. Here, then, the on-line I-position is doing little more than experiencing a mirror of its own schemata and interests (Woods 1969). In other words, when Stanley reflects on his rage, he is not actually encountering the rage-as-experienced, but either some pre-schematized monster, or else his desperate desire to rid himself of that rage. By contrast, in the I–I self-relational stance, there is a breaking-through of a genuine otherness into the on-line I's world – or what we might call a 'self-otherness'. Here, the on-line I-position encounters something new and unexpected. In this respect, it is a meeting in the present: a bringing into dialogue of an alternate voice, and an openness to the alterity that emanates through that voice.

Generalizing versus individuating

'Every real relationship in the world is exclusive', writes Buber (1958: 128), and in the I–I relationship, the on-line I-position experiences its alternate in all its uniqueness, distinctiveness and in-exchangeability. It is an encounter with *a* particular voice at *a* particular now which can not be replicated or repeated. By contrast, in the I–Me mode of self-relating, the alternate voice is experienced as just one representative of a more general class. Stanley's anger, then, becomes a faceless, generic monster; just as Sol's tiredness becomes a generic lethargy; and Lynda's Little Lynda becomes just one more irritating infant who must be silenced.

Fragmentary relating versus holistic relating

As with Buber's (1958) I–Thou attitude, the I–I attitude is characterized by not only the way in which the Other is experienced, but also the stance through which that experiencing takes place. In particular, in the I–I attitude, the on-line I-position encounters the alternate I-position with the totality of its being. It is not, as in the case of Sol's reflections on his tiredness, a cognitive appraisal of an earlier state of affairs. Rather, emotion, intuition and vulnerability, alongside cognition and reflection, are brought forward into the dialogue with otherness.

Defensiveness versus openness

Through bringing the totality of itself forward, the on-line I position also takes the risk of being changed in the encounter in ways that it can not control or predict. For, as with the I–Thou encounter (Buber 1958), a willing-ness to engage with an otherness in an immediate and spontaneous way – in a way that is open to the other's freedom and uniqueness – is 'perilous' and 'unreliable', in which 'the well-tried context' may be 'loosened' and one's 'security shattered'. By contrast, in the I–Me relationships, with its prefigured schemata and fragmentary relating, there is little possibility of the on-line I-position being transformed and changed in the meeting.

Monologue versus dialogue

Along the lines of Buber (1947, 1958), a useful way of drawing these distinc-tions together is to equate the I–I self-relational stance with a dialogic mode of self-encounter, and the I–Me self-relational stance with a monologic one. In contrast to Hermans' (2001) generic use of the term 'self-dialogue', then, or Shotter's (1999) conceptualization of human existence in terms of 'utter-ances' – dialogically formed once-occurrent events of being – the suggestion here is that much self-relating is neither dialogic nor temporally unique. Rather, in many instances, the individual relates to him or herself monologi-cally: through self-'speechifying' or manipulative talk in which the on-line I-position has no intention of being modified through encounter with its alternate (Linell and Markova 1993). From this standpoint, then, it is only when an I–I mode of self-relating is enacted that we can properly speak of 'self-dialogue' or 'self-utterances'. Only here is there a willingness to enmesh and engage with one's alterity, to thrust oneself into one's own otherness: an interpenetration in which both the on-line I and the alternate I may be changed in ways that they can not predict or entirely control.

A holistic understanding

Much overlap exists between each of the different qualities of the I–I and the I–Me self-relational stances outlined above. This is because they are not discrete qualities that can be added together, but integrated facets of a whole, which together describe and circumscribe two particular modes of intrapersonal relating.

This means that there are also many other qualities that could be attributed to these two forms of self-relating could be described. For instance, with the I–I relationship, one could also talk of a mode of self-relating that is characterized by mutuality: in which the relationship between the voices is symmetrical (Hermans and Kempen 1993), cooperative (Hermans and Kempen 1993; Shapiro 1976; Vargiu 1974) and reciprocal; as opposed to being asymmetric or disempowering (Hermans and Kempen 1993). One could also talk about the existence of open and fluid communication between the different I-positions (Cooper and Cruthers 1999; Greenberg and Elliott 1997; Hermans 2001; Shapiro 1976; Vargiu 1974; Watkins and Watkins 1979) and of intrapersonal relationships that are harmonious (Shapiro 1976; Vargiu 1974), respectful (Cooper and Cruthers 1999), compassionate (Schwartz 1999), accepting (Stone and Winkelman 1989; Vargiu 1974) and empathic (Greenberg and Elliott 1997; Vargiu 1974). In the I–I relationship, one could also talk, like Buber (1958), of the existence of independence-in-relation: that, while this mode of self-relating is characterized by openness to the Other, each of the I-positions also retains a certain degree of individuality, and does not become fused, or contaminated, by another I-position (e.g. Berne 1961; Shapiro 1976). There are also many parallels between the notion of I–I self-relating and the concept of 'internal narrative sequences' outlined by Angus and McLeod (Chapter 5 in this volume).

Connections with existential/humanistic thinking

This analysis of intrapersonal relationships forms a useful bridge between self-pluralistic models of human being and humanistic/existential approaches to psychology and psychotherapy. The I–Me form of self-relating, for instance, has many parallels with existential notions of 'inauthenticity' (Heidegger 1962) or 'bad faith': the taking up of oneself as a determined object. There are also many parallels between the notion of an I–Me mode of self-relating and the concept of a 'false self', as advocated by the existential psychiatrist R.D. Laing. Here, it is argued that schizoid-predisposed individuals withdraw their 'real selves' into an internal world for protection, leaving on the external, physical plane an empty, 'it'-like shell.

Similarly, at the intrapersonal level, the I–I self-relational stance has many parallels with the kind of *interpersonal* relationship that Rogers (1957) believed was necessary and sufficient for therapeutic personality growth. In the I–I self-relationship, there is a fundamental empathy towards an alternate I-position, a positive regarding of its particular way of being, and a congruence and honesty in relating to it.

A very similar form of self-relating is also proposed by feminist psychotherapists. Jordan (1991a), for instance, one of the key figures at the Stone Centre, Wellesley College, draws on psychodynamic and Kohutian notions of 'intrapsychic empathy' and 'retrospective self-empathy' to suggest that individuals, from the position of an observing ego, may be able to make empathic contact with another aspect of the self. In this relationship, she writes, 'the unacceptable is accepted and responded to in a caring, affectively present and re-connected manner' (Jordan 1991b: 286). Similarly, Surrey (1991) talks of the development of an attentive, listening, caring relationship to oneself, and refers to it as 'becoming one's own mother'.

Psychological well-being and intrapersonal relationships

Within the self-pluralistic literature, I–I-like forms of self-relating tend to be associated with psychological well-being, while I–Me-like forms of self-relating tend to be associated with psychological distress (e.g. Cooper 2003b; Greenberg and Elliott 1997; Jordan 1991a; Vargiu 1974). Theoretically, a number of good reasons exist why such associations should tend to be made.

First, from a humanistic perspective, the disowning of voices within the self is likely to mean that the individual will not be functioning at their full potential. Humanistic theorists like Rogers (1959), for instance, have argued that the sole motivating force within the individual is an actualizing tendency – the desire to maintain and enhance one's being – and this means that the basic need or striving for each I-position will be a legitimate one, however twisted or destructive its final form may appear (Vargiu 1974). Hence, if an individual it-ifies and attempts to deaden a particular I-position, he or she is also pushing away a valid need. So, for instance, when Stanley attempts to disown his rageful I-position, he also pushes away the anger and desire to be respected that might actually help him meet his needs and bring his violence to an end.

Moreover, because, from a humanistic standpoint, the fundamental needs of each of these I-positions are valid, they will not simply disappear when a more dominant voice commands them to do so. The organism-as-a-whole has these needs, and that means that, at certain times, these ways of being will become dominant (Hermans (2001) refers to this as 'dominance reversal'). Moreover, like a little child who is told to shut up and go away, the subjugated voices may temporarily disappear when related to in an I–Me way, but they are likely to return with even greater vigour once they find a way through. These voices *are* part of the person, they *are* what the person wants to say and feel (even if the dominant voices are not happy with this), and they are unlikely to allow themselves to be silenced unless that need or motivation can be heard and met in another manner.

This 'return of the repressed' has a number of implications. First, it means that the individual, in their more dominant, everyday mode, may be in a state of constant vigilance: fearing that, at any moment, their subjugated I-positions may return and take them over. Second, it means that the indi-vidual is likely to experience a great deal of inner conflict. Third, it means that the individual may be perturbed or concerned over their sense of inner duality. For instance, one of the most common metaphors that I have heard clients use in psychotherapy is that of feeling like 'Jekyll and Hyde' (Cooper 1999); many clients have also told me that they worry about being 'schizo-phrenic' – in the more popular usage of the term – or having a 'split personal-ity'. Fourth, in their more dominant mode of being, the individual may experience a great deal of hopelessness and frustration over this disowned, yet ineradicable, voice. Moreover, because this I-position has been stripped of its human intentionality, there is little sense of a possibility of dialoguing and negotiating with it: working with it towards some form of transformation. Rather, like a zombie in a horror film, the disowned voice is experienced as an impersonal, ever-threatening force that can only be remedied through annihilation; and if annihilation does not seem to work, then there would appear to be little hope.

Indeed, because the individual, from their more dominant I-positions, does not feel that it is possible to dialogue with this it-like force, then the possibility of finding more appropriate ways to express that subjugated position's most basic needs may be lost. Stanley's rage, for instance, is a raw, primal force, and it needs the cognitive abilities of Stanley's more adult I-position to help him find ways of appropriately expressing his anger. But if, from that adult I-position, he is simply attempting to push away his rage, then there is little opportunity for his cognitive, self-reflexive abilities to meet with – and permeate – his raging I-position. So he cannot ask himself, 'Why am *I* so rageful?' or, 'How could I get that need met in different ways?' In other words, just as the dominant I-position loses out from not having the input of the subjugated positions, so the subjugated positions lose out from not being permeated with the qualities of the more dominant ways of being.

This means that, when dominance reversal does take place, it is entirely untempered by the more dominant – and generally more 'adult' – voices. So when Stanley's 'red sheet' does come down, there are no strategies that he has developed for expressing his anger in ways other than violence. He has nothing to turn to, no thoughts in his head about how he could meet this situation differently. Indeed, as he feels the rage bubbling up in him, he has no way of standing outside of this position – no links or bridges to an alternate I-position from which he could assess or judge how to respond appropriately. Like an adolescent who is bullied in the school playground and now returns with an armful of semi-automatic weapons, the voice that has been it-ified now it-ifies its antagonists.

From a humanistic position, then, with its assumption about the inherent goodness of human beings' most fundamental needs and motivations, the move towards I–I modes of intrapersonal relating is a move towards greater psychological health. Indeed, it could be argued that one of the fundamental components of all the humanistic and existential therapists is a desire to help clients move towards a greater acceptance of the otherness within, as well as the otherness without. In Gendlin's (1996) focusing-oriented therapy, for instance, clients are encouraged to listen to, and empathically engage with, the voice of their bodily 'felt-senses'; while in transactional analysis (Berne 1961), clients are encouraged to establish respectful and dialogic relationships between their parent, adult and child ego states.

It is important to note, however, that not all forms of psychotherapy put such emphasis on the establishment of I–I intrapersonal relationships. Indeed, in the cognitive-behavioural therapies, there is often more of an emphasis on helping clients dispute and challenge those beliefs or voices that are deemed irrational (e.g. Trower et al. 1988). In the case of Sol, for instance, there may be more of an emphasis on challenging his totalized belief that *everything* in the morning feels completely pointless. Similarly, a key strategy within White and Epston's narrative therapy may be to help clients 'externalize' their problems (from McLeod 1997).

To some extent, one could argue that all self-pluralistic forms of psychotherapy – to the extent that they label and objectify certain voices within the self – could be seen as encouraging the development of I–Me, rather than I–I, intrapersonal relationships. Indeed, at an even broader level, it could be argued that the project of psychology as a whole – 'the scientific study of behaviour and cognitive processes' (Gross 1996: 19) – encourages people to relate to themselves in fundamentally it-ifying ways. Here, people are taught to view their thoughts and behaviours as determined reactions, devoid of freedom and volition; and to break their being down into constitutive elements. Many forms of psychotherapy, too, place great emphasis on helping clients to find the 'causes' for why they behave or feel in the way that they do: tracing current experiences back to past precursors and childhood events and conditions.

Such approaches, however, are not necessarily inconsistent with a more humanistic standpoint, and here it is useful to refer back to the work of Buber (1958) and his conceptualization of the relationship between the I–Thou and I–It attitudes. For Buber, these two interpersonal stances are by no means mutually exclusive (Woods 1969).

Rather, for Buber, there is a fundamental dialectic between them, such that an I–It attitude allows a human being to stand out of an initial, undifferentiated I–Thouness, and come to re-relate with an Other at a higher and more encompassing level. In this respect, then, the it-ification of certain voices within the self – whether through externalization, labelling, challenging or causal analysis – need not necessarily have a deleterious effect. Rather, it may be a way of lifting these voices out of an undifferentiated mass, identifying and understanding them, and then coming to relate to them in a more complex and sophisticated manner. From this standpoint, though, what would seem to be critical is that the it-ification of certain voices is not the last step of the therapeutic journey. In other words, if a voice is labelled, a belief questioned, or an explanation given, there also needs to be an attempt to empathize with, and re-engage with, the fundamental needs and motivations 'behind' these aspects of the I-position.

Implications for practice

How, then, can the development of I–I relationships between the different internal voices be achieved? In previous papers (Cooper 2003b; Cooper and Cruthers 1999), it has been suggested that chair-work and other creative-experiential techniques may be useful strategies for facilitating this process. However, it has also been argued that such techniques may serve to further re-ify and object-ify the different I-positions (Cooper 2003b).

An alternate approach may be for the therapist to model an I–Thou attitude towards the client, such that the client can begin to internalize this mode of relating towards him or herself (Cooper 2003b; Jordan 1991b). Here, however, it is not just a question of modelling an I–Thou relation to the I-position(s) that the client occupies when he or she is in therapy, but also to those subjugated or disowned I-positions that may be rarely externalized. Through relating to these voices in a confirming, empathic way, there is the possibility that the client may then, also, begin to acknowledge and accept these different voices. An example of this can be seen as Sol and I endeavour to develop a deeper understanding of his experiencing of lethargy:

Mick: So you're saying you hate that feeling of tiredness, but tell me more about what goes on for you when you feel it.

Sol: I just get this sense that everything is completely pointless. Like, why should I bother getting up, why should I go to work, what's the point of it all. It's just another pointless day: fixing printers, cleaning computer screens, reading the news on the internet. . . . It all seems totally futile. I may just as well stay in bed. And I just hate feeling like that, because it's so bloody stupid and it's such a bloody luxury to be able to say that . . . what about all those people with one arm or who have got Aids in Africa who are so much worse off than me. It's so self-indulgent.

Mick: I get a sense of your anger towards yourself, then, and feeling like you are really being self-indulgent, but the kinds of questions that you are asking yourself in the mornings don't seem to me that stupid, they seem like pretty intelligent questions.

Sol: I just don't feel like I've got any right to be feeling sorry for myself – it's so much worse for other people.

Mick: I know you're saying that you're feeling sorry for yourself and I can see that, but that's not how it sounds to me. It sounds to me like, at those times, you're wondering about your life and your job and what you're doing and whether it's something that is really satisfying for you.

Sol: I guess I've never seen it like that. I've just seen it as being self-indulgent.

The aim here, then, is to extend an attitude of confirmation and acceptance to the client's subjugated voices, while at the same time trying not to it-ify or antagonizing the more dominant selves (Mearns (2002) refers to this as 'multidirectional partiality'). In this case, Sol began to consider the possibility that his lethargy wasn't an entirely negative force; indeed, that it may have been telling him something important about how he felt towards his world.

As the work progressed, Sol came to increasingly acknowledge how frustrated and bored he *really* was at his computing job, and we moved away from focusing on his tiredness to look at the kinds of jobs that he might find fulfilling or satisfying.

In helping clients move towards a more thou-ifying mode of relating to themselves, a central element of the therapeutic work may involve encouraging them to 'unpack' (i.e. describe in increasing levels of detail) their actual, lived-experiences (Cooper 2003a). Through this process, behaviours or feelings that may have been seen as objects or as determined outcomes may increasingly come to be seen as parts of a volitional, intelligible flux of experiencing. An example from my work with Stanley illustrates this:

Mick: Can you tell me more about what was going on for you when you assaulted Danny?

Stanley: I just remember pushing him against the cooker. I was thinking, 'You can't bloody treat me like this. I'm not going to have it. You've got absolutely no respect for me.'

Mick: So, let me get this right. You thought, 'You can't treat me like this,' and then you pushed him against the cooker. And then what happened – how did you come to assault him?

Stanley: Yeah, I pushed him against the cooker, and he just glared at me, and I thought, 'I just can't get through to you, can I? You just ain't going to listen to me.' And I felt so frustrated and mad with him that I got to that point where I really wanted to hurt him – to let him know that he just couldn't treat me like that.

Having worked with Stanley to identify the intentionality behind his violence, it now became possible to explore appropriate ways of expressing these feelings and needs; indeed, Stanley did begin telling his partner more about his desire to be respected. He also reported that he was experiencing less rage towards his partner, and, throughout the therapy, no further violence was perpetrated.

Conclusion

In this chapter, I have outlined and illustrated one means of understanding the relationships between different intrapersonal voices. Buber's (1958) distinction between I–Thou and I–I attitudes to an Other has proved to be of great value on the interpersonal plane, and it is my suggestion here that such a distinction may also help us develop our understanding of relationships at the intrapersonal level. Just as we can treat an Other as a human being or as a thing, so, I am suggesting, we can relate to ourselves in one of these two ways. And, through such an analysis, not only may we form a bridge between dialogical models of the self and humanistic/existential modalities, but also between dialogical models of the self and our understanding of the goals and function of psychotherapy as a whole.

NOTE

1   To maintain confidentiality, details of all clients have been substantially altered. Dialogues have been reconstructed by the therapist.

References

Berne, E. (1961). *Transactional Analysis in Psychotherapy*. New York: Grove Press.

Buber, M. (1947). *Between Man and Man*. Trans. R.G. Smith. London: Fontana.

Buber, M. (1958). *I and Thou*, 2nd edn. Trans. R.G. Smith. Edinburgh: T. and T. Clark.

Buber, M. (1988). *The Knowledge of Man: Selected Essays*. Trans. M. Friedman and R.G. Smith. Atlantic Highlands, NJ: Humanities Press.

Cooper, M. (1999). 'If you can't be Jekyll be Hyde: An existential-phenomenological exploration on lived-plurality.' In J. Rowan and M. Cooper (eds) *The Plural Self: Multiplicity in Everyday Life* (pp. 51–70). London: Sage.

Cooper, M. (2003a). *Existential Therapies*. London: Sage.

Cooper, M. (2003b). ' "I–I" and "I–Me": Transposing Buber's interpersonal attitudes to the intrapersonal plane.' *Journal of Constructivist Psychology*, *16*(2), 131–153.

Cooper, M. and Cruthers, H. (1999). 'Facilitating the expression of subpersonalities: A review and analysis of techniques.' In J. Rowan and M. Cooper (eds) *The Plural Self: Multiplicity in Everyday Life* (pp. 198–212). London: Sage.

Frankl, V.E. (1986). *The Doctor and the Soul: From Psychotherapy to Logotherapy*, 3rd edn. Trans. R. Winston and C. Winston. New York: Vintage.

Friedman, M. (1985). *The Healing Dialogue in Psychotherapy*. New York: Jason Aronson.

Gendlin, E. (1996). *Focusing-Oriented Psychotherapy: A Manual of the Experiential Method*. New York: Guilford.

Greenberg, L.S. and Elliott, R. (1997). 'Varieties of empathic responding.' In A.C. Bohart and L.S. Greenberg (eds) *Empathy Reconsidered: New Directions in Psychotherapy* (pp. 167–186). Washington, DC: American Psychological Association.

Gross, R. (1996). *Psychology: The Science of Mind and Behaviour*, 3rd edn. London: Hodder and Stoughton.

Heard, W.G. (1995). 'The unconscious function of the I–It and I–Thou realms.' *The Humanistic Psychologist*, *23*(2), 239–258.

Heidegger, M. (1962). *Being and Time*. Trans. J. Macquarrie and E. Robinson. Oxford. Blackwell.

Hermans, H.J.M. (2001). 'The dialogical self: Towards a theory of personal and cultural positioning.' *Culture and Psychology*, *7*(3), 243–281.

Hermans, H.J.M. and Kempen, H.J.G. (1993). *The Dialogical Self: Meaning as Movement*. San Diego, CA: Academic Press.

Janet, P. (1889). *L'Automatisme psychologique*. Paris: Alcan.

Jordan, J.V. (1991a). 'Empathy and self-boundaries.' In J.V. Jordan, A.G. Kaplan, J.B.

Miller, I.P. Stiver and J.L. Surrey (eds) *Women's Growth in Connection: Writings from the Stone Center* (pp. 67–80). New York: Guilford.

Jordan, J.V. (1991b). 'Empathy, mutuality and therapeutic change: Clinical implications of a relational model.' In J.V. Jordan, A.G. Kaplan, J.B. Miller, I.P. Stiver and J.L. Surrey (eds) *Women's Growth in Connection: Writings from the Stone Center* (pp. 283–289). New York: Guilford.

Levinas, E. (1969). *Totality and Infinity: An Essay on Exteriority.* Trans. A. Lingis. Pittsburgh, PA: Duquesne University Press.

Linell, P. and Markova, I. (1993). 'Acts in discourse: From monological speech acts to dialogical inter-acts.' *Journal for the Theory of Social Behaviour, 23*(2), 173–195.

McLeod, J. (1997). *Narrative and Psychotherapy.* London: Sage.

Mearns, D. (2002). 'Further theoretical propositions in regard to self theory within person-centred therapy.' *Person-Centred and Experiential Psychotherapies, 1*(1–2), 14–27.

Merleau-Ponty, M. (1962). *The Phenomenology of Perception.* Trans. C. Smith. London: Routledge.

Rogers, C.R. (1957). 'The necessary and sufficient conditions of therapeutic personality change.' *Journal of Consulting Psychology, 21*(2), 95–103.

Rogers, C.R. (1959). 'A theory of therapy, personality and interpersonal relationships as developed in the client-centred framework.' In S. Koch (ed.) *Psychology: A Study of Science,* Vol. 3 (pp. 184–256). New York: McGraw-Hill.

Schwartz, R.E. (1999). 'The internal family systems model.' In J. Rowan and M. Cooper (eds) *The Plural Self: Multiplicity in Everyday Life* (pp. 238–253). London: Sage.

Shapiro, S.B. (1976). *The Selves Inside You.* Berkeley, CA: Explorations Institute.

Shotter, J. (1999). 'Life inside dialogically structured mentalities: Bakhtin's and Volshinov's account of our mental activities as out in the world between us.' In J. Rowan M. Cooper (eds) *The Plural Self: Multiplicity in Everyday Life* (pp. 71–92). London: Sage.

Stiles, W.B., Elliott, R., Firth-Cozens, J.A., Llewelyn, S.P., Margison, F.R., Shapiro, D.A., et al. (1990). 'Assimilation of problematic experiences by clients in psychotherapy.' *Psychotherapy, 27*(3), 411–420.

Stone, H. and Winkelman, S. (1989). *Embracing our Selves: The Voice Dialogue Manual.* Mill Valley, CA: Nataraj.

Surrey, J.L. (1991). 'The self-in-relation: A theory of women's development.' In J.V. Jordan, A.G. Kaplan, J.B. Miller, I.P. Stiver and J.L. Surrey (eds) *Women's Growth in Connection: Writings from the Stone Center* (pp. 51–66). New York: Guilford.

Trower, P., Casey, A. and Dryden, W. (1988). *Cognitive-Behavioural Counselling in Action.* London: Sage.

Vargiu, J.G. (1974). 'Psychosynthesis workbook: Subpersonalities.' *Synthesis, 1,* 52–90.

Watkins, J.G. and Watkins, H.H. (1979). 'Theory and practice of ego state therapy: A short-term therapeutic approach.' In H. Grayson (ed.) *Short Term Approaches to Psychotherapy* (pp. 176–220). London: Human Sciences Press.

Woods, R.E. (1969). *Martin Buber's Ontology: An Analysis of I and Thou.* Evanston, IL: Northwestern University Press.

Part II

Theory and clinical practice

Chapter 5

Self-multiplicity and narrative expression in psychotherapy

Lynne Angus and John McLeod

Introduction

For Jerome Bruner (2004), narrative expression is a self-making practice – narrative and self are inextricably interlinked. For Bruner, the sense of self originates in the embodied act of storying our experiences in the world in order to share those experiences with others as well as to facilitate self-understanding. In terms of self-understanding, he suggests that telling one-self about oneself is like making up a story about whom and what we are, what's happened and why we are doing what we are doing. The construction of selfhood, for Bruner, cannot proceed without a capacity to narrate. Once we are equipped with that capacity, we can produce a selfhood that joins us with others, that permits us to hark back selectively to our past while shaping ourselves for the possibilities of an imagined future.

Increasingly, the activity of storying personal experience takes place in a social world characterized by a high degree of narrative multiplicity (Gergen 1991; Van den Berg 1974). In contrast to those who lived in previous times, the pervasiveness of a global postmodern consumer culture has meant that most of us are faced with a confusing range of choices around lifestyle, occupation, religious and sexual orientation, and moral decision-making. Within contemporary culture, a major challenge for individuals is to achieve a sense of personal coherence and self-identity, while not denying the reality of the alternative standpoints that others may have adopted. Psychotherapy can be understood as a significant cultural arena in which a sense of personal coherence can be constructed and maintained (McLeod 1997, 2003, 2004).

The implications of social and cultural multiplicity for an understanding of the process of narrative, as a self-making practice, have been articulated by Hubert Hermans (2004). In particular his dialogical model of self-development, which highlights the social nature of identity construction. Hermans and Kempen (1993) view the self as akin to a polyphonic novel, that contains a multitude of internalized voices which 'speak' to each other, and relationally co-define each other, in dialogue. Hermans states that this conceptualization of the dialogical self emerges from a reformulation of the Jamesian I–me relationships in terms of Bakhtin's polyphonic novel. The spatial term 'position', and the dynamic terms 'positioning' and 'repositioning', are used to express the theoretical idea that the I is decentralized, not hovering above itself or the world. As parts of a polyphonic novel, the different I-positions are embodied as voices who entertain dialogical relationships, both internal and external, with other voices. On the basis of these considerations, the dialogical self can be described in terms of a dynamic multiplicity of relationally organized I–other (speaker–listener) positions. Conceptualized in a spatial structure, the I has the possibility to move position and take on the perspective of the other, in accordance with changes in situation and time. The I fluctuates among different and even opposed positions, and has the capacity to imaginatively endow each relational position with a voice so that dialogical relations between positions can be articulated. These voices function like interacting characters in a story. Each of them has a story to tell about their own experiences from their own relational stance. As different voices, these characters exchange information about the respective Me's that emerge from the observations of the relationally shifting I, resulting in a complex, narratively structured self (Hermans 2001; Hermans et al. 1992).

For Hermans (2004), internal and external voices are relationally intertwined and are constituted by a polyphony of consonant and dissonant voices. Accordingly, in a multivoiced self and a multivoiced society, there is an opportunity for intersubjective interchange. Second, both in society and in the self, dialogical relationships are shaped by dominance or social power. As some individuals or groups in a society have more social power and influence than other individuals and groups, the voices of some positions in the self are more easily heard and have, in a particular situation, more chance for expression and communication than others. For Hermans, dialogical interchange and dominance are intrinsic features of the dialogical self (Bhatia and Ram 2002; Gregg 1991; Hermans and Kempen 1993, 1998; Linell 1990; Taylor 1991).

In terms of psychotherapy specifically, Hermans (2004) suggests that the narrative construction of self is facilitated by I–me dialogical positioning in three primary ways. First, when clients disclose their stories in therapy sessions, they not only tell their story to their therapist, but also listen to the same story, through the voice of their therapists' empathic reflections. As such they not only tell their story to the therapist, but via the therapist's reflections, they are also able to rehear and make meaning of their story from a new perspective. For Hermans, it is precisely this special kind of listening which invites the possibility of a new retelling of the story.

Second, Hermans suggests that by telling their stories to their therapists, and to themselves, a 'dialogical space' is created that instigates the retelling of the story in such a way that new relational connections are established between existing story parts and/or new elements are introduced. This process facilitates the construction of a more comprehensive and coherent account of the client's self-story. This dialogical space functions as a field of tension in which a gradual transition is realized between the assessment of the story and the emergence of narrative change or innovation.

Third, and most importantly for this chapter, the construction of a dialogical space is facilitated when the two parties, the client and the psychotherapist, contribute to the process from their own specific expertise. Clients have an enormous autobiographical memory database from which they select events for the organization of a story. Moreover, they are knowledgeable about the inner experiences and meaning attached to these events as part of their life story. The therapist, on the other hand, has experience with a variety of clients and is, moreover, knowledgeable on theories, methods and specific interventions for the assessment and change of the client's narrative. Psychotherapy practitioners and researchers (Angus and McLeod 2004), representing a diverse array of therapy approaches, view client narrative expression as the essential starting point for the identification of client internal voice(s) and the construction of multi-perspectivity and meaning-making in psychotherapy.

The purpose of this chapter is to address the essential interrelationship between client self-multiplicity and narrative expression (Angus and McLeod 2004), in the context of effective therapist practices in psychotherapy. The Narrative Process model developed by Angus, Levitt and Hardtke (1999) will be used as an integrative framework through which the impact of therapist narrative practices and interventions can be understood, in relation to their effect on the client's sense of self-coherence. It is suggested that approaches to therapy that sensitize therapists to linguistic, narrative and discursive phenomena and processes are likely to highlight the client's sense of 'being many' (multiplicity). However, these therapies are unhelpful if they do not also enable clients to develop a capacity to reflect on their self-multiplicity, and through reflection develop a coherent macro-narrative or self-story. Some possibilities for future directions for theory, research and practice will conclude the chapter.

The Narrative Process model

The Narrative Process model (Angus et al. 1999) views narrative expression as arising out of a dialectical interplay of autobiographical memory, emotion and reflexive meaning-making processes. While personally significant narratives are marked by the expression and evocation of emotions, the significance of emotions can be understood only when organized within a narrative framework that identifies what is felt, about whom, in relation to what need or issue. The Narrative Process model is in agreement with a dialectical constructivist (Greenberg and Angus 2004) view of experiential therapeutic change. The core assumptions underlying this model reflect a sense of therapist's helping clients to access and differentiate emergent emotion schemes while clients shift to reflexive meaning-making processes in therapy sessions. The process of therapy is viewed as being co-constructed, arising from the interplay of client and therapist intentions. While we are in full agreement with the basic tenets of the dialectical-constructivist model (Greenberg and Pascual-Leone 1995, 1997, 2001) which views emotional processing and emergent meaning-making processes as central to the inception of change in psychotherapy, we also believe that narrative expression and the disclosure of salient personal memories is foundational to the inception of change experiences in experiential therapy.

According to the Narrative Process model of self-change, all forms of successful psychotherapy involve the articulation, elaboration and transformation of the client's life story (Angus and Hardtke 1994; Angus et al. 1999). Personal identity is construed as the coherent integration of emotionally salient personal narratives which either explicitly or implicitly represent core beliefs about self and others. The emotional tone of the narrative – anger, sadness, joy or fear – appears to be one of the primary ways in which personal memories and narratives are linked to one another. Accordingly, implicit emotion themes, and the personal memories they contain, become the lens through which we classify, story and make meaning of our new interpersonal experiences with others in the world.

External narrative sequences

In psychotherapy, it is crucial that clients remember and articulate real or imagined, past or recent events, in order to fill in the gaps in the narrative that may have been forgotten or never fully acknowledged and therefore not understood. This therapeutic process is represented by the *external* narrative mode of the Narrative Processes model, which addresses the question of 'What happened?' An external narrative sequence can be a personal story that is either autobiographical or non-autobiographical in content. Recent research findings (Angus et al. 2004) have established that 75 per cent of all external sequences, extracted from 180 experiential therapy sessions, contained an autobiographical memory.

Additionally, external sequences may entail a description of either a specific event, a general description of many repeated similar events or a composite of many specific events. The autobiographical form of external narrative processing provides the client with the chance to engage in storytelling, to create a visually rich picture for the therapist by means of verbally descriptive and specific details of life experiences and events. The client's description of 'what happened' might also entail non-autobiographical information or chronicles of factual information or events (McLeod 2002).

Internal narrative sequences

In the context of a secure therapeutic relationship, clients allow themselves to become more fully engaged in the experience of their own narratives told in the therapy hour. This type of storytelling activity brings to awareness feelings and emotions that had previously been silenced or tacitly processed but not symbolized in language (Greenberg and Angus 2004). Both therapist and client focus on the detailed unfolding and exploration of associated sensations and emotions which can emerge in the retelling of an autobiographical memory. This *internal* narrative process mode is associated with the description and elaboration of subjective feelings, reactions, and emotions connected with an event and addresses the question of 'What was felt?' during the event. Research supports the notion that emotional disclosure regarding traumatic events can result in positive immunological and psychological effects for survivors (Harber and Pennebaker 1992; Pennebaker and Seagal 1999).

Reflexive narrative sequences

The final goal of productive therapy involves the *reflexive* analysis of articulated experiences, which often leads to the construction of new meanings and perspectives on situations and can result in a reconstructed narrative. This reconstructed narrative may either support or challenge the implicit beliefs about self and others, which contribute to the construction of the client's life story. The reflexive narrative mode represents this therapeutic process and entails the articulation of new meanings emerging from the exploration of autobiographical memory narratives and subjective feelings.

The integration of modes of narrative processing within therapy events

Each of these three modes of narrative processing has a corresponding therapeutic goal. First, the *external* narrative mode allows clients to fill in the gaps of their self-story in terms of what has been forgotten or never fully acknowledged, and hence, understood. The external narrative mode enables the emergence of multiple, disjunctive narrative storylines which are inevitably in conflict with each other, heightening the client's sense of personal incoherence and fragmentation. With the assistance of the therapist, who functions as a sensitive audience to the emergence of the disparate storylines within the client's narrative, the client may become aware of a heightened sense of personal incoherence and fragmentation (McLeod and Balamoutsou 2001). Alternatively, the therapist may bring the sense of story incoherence to the attention of the client (Dimaggio and Semerari 2004).

Second, the *internal* narrative processing helps a client to relive an event that he or she has disclosed to the therapist, and to better sense its emotional significance, perhaps for the first time. The internal narrative mode can be viewed as a phase of holding or staying with conflicting narratives and developing dialogue; the therapeutic relationship allows a safe space for clients to experientially feel 'both' or 'many' sides to their story, without falling back into closing one side down.

Third, the *reflexive* narrative processing mode aids the client in forming new understandings about self and others, from a variety of relational perspectives. The reflexive mode also enables steps toward building a coherent macro-narrative: a creative process in which the person realizes that he or she is 'more than' (Todres 2003) each of his or her separate voices. Therapy is unhelpful if it does not enable clients to develop a capacity to reflect on their self-multiplicity, and through reflection develop a coherent macro-narrative or self-story. The role of the therapist can be seen, within the reflexive mode, as one of sensitively helping the client to connect the various storylines and co-create a sense of narrative coherence and personal meaning (Dimaggio and Semerari 2004).

Together, the three modes of narrative processing contribute to the development of more coherent, emotionally differentiated personal narratives, which provide individuals with a greater understanding of themselves and their interactions with others. In essence, the narrative process modes are viewed as essential components of a distinctive mode of human meaning-making which constructs, maintains and when needed, revises our sense of self in the world.

Jerome Bruner (1986, 1990, 1992, 2004) provides an alternative perspective on the integrative function of these different modes of narrative processing when he points out that narrative organizes and integrates actions, emotions and meanings within the context of an unfolding sequential time-line. He suggests that coherent personal narratives entail the articulation and integration of the dual landscapes of narrative action (e.g. describing the scene, setting and actions of the actors) and consciousness (e.g. articulating the emotions, beliefs, intentions, goals, purposes of self and others), from the situated perspective of the narrator.

From a Narrative Process model (Angus et al. 1999) perspective, accessing and articulating the client's world of emotions, beliefs, expectations, intentions and goals – what Bruner (1990) has termed the landscape of consciousness – is critical for the emergence of new ways of seeing and experiencing longstanding relationship problems and coming to terms with significant personal loss. In agreement with both Hermans (2004) and Bruner (2004), Angus and colleagues (1999) argue that it is the reflexive decentring from, and then re-engagement with distressing life experiences, from different relational vantage points, that facilitates the articulation of new understandings about the self in relation to others. It is the reflexive processing of emotions, beliefs, hopes, needs, motives, intentions and goals (landscape of consciousness) from different relational vantage points – and their inclusion in the events of the problem stories or narratives (landscape of action) – which enables the experience to be comprehensively represented and fully understood as part of the life story. In essence, it is the integration of the landscape of action – a description of the sequential, linear unfolding of an event which answers the question of what happened – with the landscape of consciousness – the internal responses of self and others addressing the question of what was felt and what does it mean – that enables the construction of a coherent and meaning-filled narrative account of our interpersonal experiences with others in the world. The metaphor of the 'landscape' used by Bruner provides a vivid image of what can happen in effective therapy: beginning with a set of reports of emotions and actions that are overwhelmingly salient and disconnected, the person gradually forms these elements into a territory which can be viewed and explored, and is in perspective.

To summarize: in the Narrative Process model, therapeutic change is viewed as entailing a process of dialectical shifts between narrative storytelling (external narrative mode), emotional differentiation (internal narrative mode) and reflexive meaning-making modes of inquiry. Influenced by the concept of a dialogical positioning of self and other voices in psychotherapy, we have begun to explore the interrelationship between narrative mode shifts and the emergence of what Hermans (2004) calls multivocal self-multiplicity in the therapy session hour. In the following section, we provide an example of the relationship between spontaneous, client-initiated internal and reflexive mode shifts, and the movement between self and other voices, in the context of an episode of a two-chair intervention in process experiential psychotherapy (Greenberg 2002). We hope to highlight specifically the ways in which two-chair and empty-chair interventions enable clients to shift between external, internal and reflexive narrative modes.

Facilitating dialogical shifts and narrative change in process experiential therapy

Process experiential psychotherapy (Greenberg 2002) is an emotion-focused, constructivist therapy approach rooted in an integration of both Gestalt and client-centred therapies. In the context of Gestalt psychotherapy, Fritz Perls suggested that a vulnerable internal voice – termed 'the underdog' – is often pitted against a more dominant voice – or 'top dog' – who bullies and harasses the underdog into silence. In order to facilitate a constructive dialogue between less dominant and more dominant internal voices or I-positions in psychotherapy, Perls encouraged his clients to identify, name and externalize their top dog and underdog voices in the context of empty-chair and two-chair interventions.

Greenberg (2002) points out that that process-directive experiential treatments encourage the emergence of different aspects of the self, so that these aspects can be brought into contact with one another. Chair dialogues are designed to facilitate clients' within session entry into an experiential/imaginal space such that internal or external voices of critic and self-experiencer can be externalized and engaged in a dialogical conversation.

Unfinished Business is a Gestalt therapy term that signifies the presence of longstanding, unresolved relationship concerns which are often accompanied by feelings of burden and resentment. Empty-chair work for Unfinished Business involves a client role playing a dialogue with a significant other who is viewed as sitting in the empty chair. In this imaginal dialogue, the client is encouraged to give expression to previously suppressed primary emotions – such as hurt and anger – and voice unmet needs experienced in relation to the significant other represented by the empty chair. Clients may also role play and voice the imagined perspective of the other in the context of an empty-chair dialogue, which may lead to the accessing of a new perspective on self and/or the significant other.

In the context of process experiential psychotherapy, two-chair and empty-chair role-play scenarios, play a particularly important role in the external-ization of internal voice and in the facilitation of client self-reflexive process-ing in relation to core emotional responses. The following excerpt, drawn from a good outcome process experiential therapy dyad (Greenberg and Angus 1995), illustrates the dialectical dance between reflexive and internal emotion-focused processing modes unfolding within the context of an empty-chair dialogue for Unfinished Business. In this case, the autobiographical memories narrated by the client in earlier sessions had allowed the therapist to identify two potentially conflicting, but relationally connected, role posi-tions in her marriage the voice of the critic or top dog (represented by her husband), and that of a hurt child (the client's experiencing self as wife in the marriage). The therapist (T) begins the empty-chair intervention by encouraging the client (C) to role play her husband in the empty chair and from that relational perspective, to reflect on how he makes his wife feel like a child, in the context of their marriage.

T: Be him . . . how do you make her feel bad, how do you make her feel like a child?

C: By laughing – just straight – not taking her seriously.

T: Ah. Tell her how you feel. You feel more powerful that way, right, like – sort of brush her off, how do you do that – how do you make her feel?

C: Um//(I say) 'you don't need that', or, you know, 'you can do without her', 'you've got to stay home' (*Client gives voice to the admonitions of the critical husband and gestures with her hands*) and

T: What's this? Like pushing her back? (*Therapist tentatively symbolizes the client's active gesturing in the session.*)

C: Um 'forget it, you don't need this', and – 'move out of my way so I can try to get dressed and go out' (*Client shift to external narrative mode and elaboration of gestured action in the context of an imagined scenario*) (laugh).

T: Mm-hm

C: 'You're not important' (*Client reflexive narrative mode shift to husband's core assessment of her importance to him, as a wife*) and you're just there for, because the kids are there, not because–
(sigh) (crying) (*Crying indicates shift to internal narrative mode and the active expression of bodily felt sadness and hurt in response to feeling unwanted as wife*) (p: 00:00:08),
I'm myself (client 306) again (*Client indicates to the therapist that she is now experiencing and voicing her own emotional responses – internal narrative mode – which is predicated on a shift in dialogical position to the experiencing self and she indicates that she is no longer able to role play husband*).

T: OK, come here (*Therapist acknowledges shift in dialogical position or voice and encourages the client to shift chairs in the session, further concretizing, differentiating and externalizing the representation of dialogical self positions*).
(*Client changes chairs and moves into the experiencing self position*).
What are you feeling? (*Therapist focuses on further differentiation of bodily felt sense/emotional response – internal narrative mode*).

C: (crying) As I was saying, that – that he just doesn't love me (*Client shift to reflexive meaning of feeling unloved in her marriage*).

T: So he sweeps you aside and you feel unloved. (*Therapist evocative reflection of client experience in which both feeling and narrative action is integrated*).

C: (sniff) Yeah.

T: Tell him about that feeling (*Therapist encourages the reflexive differentiation of the feeling of being unloved in the context of a dialogue with her husband*).

C: Um – it's like, I try so hard but you continue stepping on me, um, I feel like I'm there just for his slave, just, but not as your wife (*In the context of reflecting upon her feelings of being unloved by her husband and his hurtful actions towards her, a new subject position or voice emerges for the client which relationally captures a more differentiated sense of being treated unfairly in her marriage; of feeling more like a slave owned by her master rather than a child in relation to a parent or a wife loved by her husband*).

T: Uh-huh, what's it like to feel like a slave? (*Therapist encourages a further differentiation of complex feelings connected to the symbolized experience of being treated like a slave*).

C: Just, to do everything for, for you and the kids or everybody that, you know; but not to do anything together. (*Client shift to reflexive meaning-making mode*) it's like not having me there, you don't want me there.

T: Tell him what it's like to feel unwanted and unloved.

C: It's – it's very resentful, I resent you when (*Client shift to articulation of emotions and feelings experienced in response to being treated as a slave and unwanted as a wife*).

T: Uh-huh

C: When you push away, I resent you, I resent you . . .

T: I resent you, tell him (*Therapist encourages client to differentiate her feelings of resentment in the context of the imagined audience of her husband, in the empty chair*).

C: Yeah, why don't you want me to be there? (*Client shift to reflexive questioning of the intentions and motives for her husband's hurtful actions and her need to know why he neglects her as a partner in life, as a wife*) – for us to go out and have time to ourselves? Is there something about me, that you don't like me being there with you?

T: So you start to question yourself right?

C: Yeah . . .

In this therapeutic dialogue, both client and therapist focus on the differentiation of the client's emotional responses (internal narrative mode), and their symbolized meanings (reflexive narrative mode), in the context of an imagined dialogue with her husband. The client is encouraged to move into the dialogical position of her critical husband and to give expression to his dismissive actions that leave the client feeling like a child whose needs are brushed aside by an uncaring parent. Previously unvoiced emotions of sadness, hurt and resentment erupt in response to the role-played representation of her husband's uncaring and dismissive gestures. In conjunction with the emergence of this emotional reaction, the client spontaneously shifts to a new relational 'I' position and identifies that she now feels more like a slave in her marriage rather than a child relating to a parent. The therapist then encourages the client to further differentiate (internal narrative mode) and make meaning (reflexive narrative mode) of her previously unacknowledged – unvoiced – experiences of feeling unloved and being treated like a slave – not a partner, friend and/or wife – in her marriage. It is at this point that a new emotional landscape of hurt, justified anger and resentment emerges in the session. It is from this new subject position, and relational vantage point, that the client will begin to explore the intentions behind her husband's hurtful actions and the responsibility he must take for those actions in their marriage.

Additionally, it is clear that the process experiential therapist plays a pivotal role in the facilitation of the empty-chair dialogue by helping the client to shift from reflexive narrative processing with a focus on the meanings of actions and statements by her husband – 'you're not important (to me)' – to an internal narrative process mode and the active expression of emotional responses – crying and tears – evoked in the context of the imagined dialogue. The therapist also stays with the leading edge of the client's experiencing in the session and supports the client's articulation of emergent feelings of resentment and anger towards her husband.

The different dialogical shifts in client subject positions are both personal and unique to her, and at the same time typical of the discourses within which marriage and intimacy are constructed within contemporary society. The process of engaging in empty chair work, in the context of a strong therapeutic alliance, allows the client to tolerate the discomfort of experiencing and voicing the distressing emotions arising from the conflicting subject positions and relational perspectives. The expression of emotions emerging from a shift into a new subject position, or voice, allows the client to engage in a rehearing of the story of her marriage from a different relational vantage point. From this perspective, deep feelings of resentment, hurt and anger can now be acknowledged, expressed and meaningfully understood. Importantly, the articulation of this new way of seeing, experiencing and understanding her marital relationship enables a bridging between a confusing array of personal feelings, emotions, voices and subject positions. The articulation of a more differentiated relational landscape enabled the client to live with a greater sense of personal coherence, and self agency, in this area of her life.

Conclusion

It is our belief that the Narrative Process model offers a valuable framework for observing and understanding the moment-by-moment process of narrative meaning-making in experiential therapy. One of the unique insights generated by the Narrative Processes research programme (Angus et al. 2004) at York University has been the discovery that good outcome cases could be distinguished from poor outcome cases by a particular pattern of narrative processing. In these good cases, therapists focused clients inward when they were engaged in reflexive processing and clients once focused internally then reflected on their emotional experiences to create new meaning. Therapists shifted the clients' focus from reflexive to emotion processes and then clients shifted from internal emotional differentiation back to reflexive processing. In her intensive case analysis of three good outcome and three poor outcome process experiential therapy dyads from the York I Depression study, Lewin (Angus et al. 2004) found that in good outcome cases, almost a third (30 per cent) of the therapist's shifts in mode of processing were from reflexive modes to internal emotional differentiation. It appeared as if the therapist's specific focus on the differentiation of emotional meanings, in the context of the client's own self-reflections, helps the client to enter more fully into a sustained elaboration of his or her own internal world of felt emotions, as experienced in the therapy session. These findings suggest that there are consistent sequences of narrative processing associated with effective psychotherapeutic work.

Additionally, the intensive case analysis described in this chapter suggests that a critical component for the emergence of new emotions and self understanding may be the active engagement of the client in chairing interventions which facilitate the articulation of new subject positions and dialogical relationships (Hermans 2004) in the therapy hour. It is from the role-played vantage point of the significant other that new emotional schemas and perspectives seem to emerge. Further research is necessary to determine the extent to which productive sequences of internal and reflexive narrative processing modes are associated with the emergence of new subject positions in experiential psychotherapies and the extent to which they are present in other therapeutic orientations, with different client groups (Dimaggio and Semerari 2004; Hermans 2004).

The presence of facilitative narrative process patterns and the emergence of new dialogical subject positions (Hermans 2004) or voices (Osatuke et al., Chapter 15 in this volume) also has implications for training and supervision in psychotherapy. It may be valuable for psychotherapists to gain greater sensitivity to subtle shifts in the relational positioning of the client's experiencing self as a means of both identifying and bringing into life external, internal and reflexive moments within therapeutic conversations. It is of special interest to us that both Hermans and Bruner have drawn extensively from the field of literary criticism, and the concept of the decentred narrator (Lodge 2002), in formulating their theories of narrative and self-identity. Perhaps good therapeutic stories are those in which both multiplicity and coherence are present.

References

Angus, L. and Hardtke, H. (1994). 'Narrative processes in psychotherapy.' *Canadian Psychology*, *35*, 190–203.

Angus, L. and McLeod, J. (eds) (2004). *Handbook of Narrative and Psychotherapy: Practice, Theory and Research*. Thousand Oaks, CA: Sage.

Angus, L., Hardtke, K. and Levitt, H. (1996). *Narrative Processes Coding System Training Manual*. Department of Psychology, York University, North York, Ontario, Canada.

Angus, L., Levitt, H. and Hardtke, K. (1999). 'The narrative processing coding system: Research applications and implications for psychotherapy practice.' *Journal of Clinical Psychology*, *55*, 1255–1270.

Angus, L., Lewin, J., Bouffard, B. and Rotondi-Trevisan, D. (2004). 'What's the story? Working with narrative in experiential psychotherapy. In L. Angus and J. McLeod (eds) *Handbook of Narrative and Psychotherapy: Practice, Theory and Research* (pp. 87–102). Thousand Oaks, CA: Sage.

Bhatia, S. and Ram, A. (2002). 'Locating the dialogical self in the age of transnational migrations, border crossings and diasporas: Commentary.' *Culture and Psychology*, special issue on culture and the dialogical self: theory, method and practice, 7, 297–309.

Bruner, J. (1986). *Actual Minds, Possible Worlds*. Cambridge, MA: Harvard University Press.

Bruner, J. (1990). *Acts of Meaning*. Cambridge, MA: Harvard University Press.

Bruner, J. (1992). 'The narrative construction of reality.' In H. Beilin and P.B. Pufall (eds) *Piaget's Theory: Prospects and Possibilities* (pp. 229–248). Hillsdale, NJ: Lawrence Erlbaum Associates.

Bruner, J. (2004). 'The narrative creation of self.' In L. Angus and J. McLeod (eds) *Handbook of Narrative and Psychotherapy: Practice, Theory and Research* (pp. 3–14). Thousand Oaks, CA: Sage.

Dimaggio, G. and Semerari, A. (2004). 'Disorganized narratives: The psychological condition and its treatment.' In L. Angus and J. McLeod (eds) *Handbook of Narrative and Psychotherapy: Practice, Theory and Research* (pp. 263–282). Thousand Oaks, CA: Sage.

Gergen, K.J. (1991). *The Saturated Self: Dilemmas of Identity in Contemporary Life*. New York: Basic Books.

Greenberg, L.S. (2002). *Emotion-focused Therapy: Coaching Clients to Work through their Feelings*. Washington, DC: American Psychological Association.

Greenberg, L.S. and Angus, L. (1995). 'How does therapy work?' *Social Sciences and Humanities Research Council Standard Research Grant (1995–1998)*.

Greenberg, L.S. and Angus, L. (2004). 'The contributions of emotion processes to narrative change in psychotherapy'. In L. Angus and J. McLeod (eds) *Handbook of Narrative and Psychotherapy: Practice, Theory and Research* (pp. 331–351). Thousand Oaks, CA: Sage.

Greenberg, L.S. and Pascual-Leone, J. (1995). 'A dialectical constructivist approach to experiential change.' In R.A. Neimeyer and M.J. Mahoney (eds) *Constructivism in Psychotherapy*. Washington, DC: American Psychological Association.

Greenberg, L.S. and Pascual-Leone, J. (1997). 'Emotion in the creation of personal meaning.' In M.J. Power and C.R. Brewin (eds) *Transformation of Meaning in Psychological Therapies: Integrating Theory and Practice* (pp. 157–173). New York: Wiley.

Greenberg, L.S. and Pascual-Leone, J. (2001). 'A dialectical constructivist view of the creation of personal meaning.' *Journal of Constructivist Psychology*, *14*, 165–186.

Gregg, G.S. (1991). *Self-representation: Life Narrative Studies in Identity and Ideology*. New York: Greenwood Press.

Harber, K.D. and Pennebaker, J.W. (1992). 'Overcoming traumatic memories.' In S. Christianson (ed.) *The Handbook of Emotion and Memory: Research and Theory* (pp. 359–387). Hillsdale, NJ: Lawrence Erlbaum Associates.

Hermans, H.J.M. (2001). 'The dialogical self: Toward a theory of personal and cultural positioning.' *Culture and Psychology*, special issue on culture and the dialogical self: theory, method and practice, 7, 243–281.

Hermans, H.J.M. (2004). 'The innovation of self-narratives: A dialogical approach.' In L. Angus and J. McLeod (eds) *Handbook of Narrative and Psychotherapy: Practice, Theory and Research* (pp. 175–192). Thousand Oaks, CA: Sage.

Hermans, H.J.M. and Kempen, H.J.G. (1993). *The Dialogical Self: Meaning as Movement*. San Diego, CA: Academic Press.

Hermans, H.J.M. and Kempen, H.J.G. (1998). 'Moving cultures: The perilous problems of cultural dichotomies in a globalizing society.' *American Psychologist*, *53*, 1111–1120.

Hermans, H.J.M., Kempen, H.J.G. and Van Loon, R.J.P. (1992). 'The dialogical self: Beyond individualism and rationalism.' *American Psychologist*, *47*, 23–33.

Linell, P. (1990). 'The power of dialogue dynamics.' In I. Marková and K. Foppa (eds) *The Dynamics of Dialogue* (pp. 147–177). New York: Harvester Wheatsheaf.

Lodge, D. (2002). *Consciousness and the Novel*. London: Secker and Warburg.

McLeod, J. (1997). *Narrative and Psychotherapy*. London: Sage.

McLeod, J. (2002). 'Lists, stories and dreams: Strategic invitation to relationship in psychotherapy narrative.' In W. Patterson (ed.) *Strategic Narrative: New Perspectives on the Power of Personal and Cultural Stories* (pp. 89–106). Lanham, MD: Lexington.

McLeod, J. (2003). 'The significance of narrative and storytelling in post-psychological counselling and psychotherapy.' In R. Josselson, A. Lieblich and D. McAdams (eds) *Healing Stories*. Washington, DC: American Psychological Association.

McLeod, J. (2004). 'Social construction, narrative and psychotherapy.' In L. Angus and J. McLeod (eds) *Handbook of Narrative and Psychotherapy: Practice, Theory and Research* (pp. 351–366). Thousand Oaks, CA: Sage.

McLeod, J. and Balamoutsou, S. (2000). 'Narrative process in the assimilation of a problematic experience: Qualitative analysis of a single case.' *Zeitshcrift fur qualitative Bildungs – Beratungs – und Sozialforshung*, *2*, 283–302.

Pennebaker, J. and Seagal, J. (1999). 'Forming a story: The health benefits of narrative.' *Journal of Clinical Psychology*, *55*, 1243–1254.

Taylor, C. (1991). 'The dialogical self.' In D.R. Hiley, J.F. Bohman and R. Shusterman (eds.) *The Interpretative Turn* (pp. 304–314). Ithaca, NY: Cornell University Press.

Todres, L. (2003). 'Humanising forces: Phenomenology in science; psychotherapy in technological culture.' *Counselling and Psychotherapy Research*, 3, 196–203.

Van den Berg, J.H. (1974). *Divided Existence and Complex Society*. Pittsburgh, PA: Duquesne University Press.

Chapter 6

Encounters between internal voices generate emotion

An elaboration of the assimilation model

William B. Stiles, Katerine Osatuke, Meredith J. Glick and Hannah C. Mackay

Introduction

Psychological theorists from Allport (1946) to Zajonc (1980) and from Rogers (1959) to Skinner (1953) have agreed that affective reaction – assigning some degree of positive or negative valence to the events one encounters – is automatic, universal and adaptive. Rogers (1959) described this as an *organismic valuing process*, an evaluative or affective response to each experience that reflects its potential to enhance or damage the organism. The precise tuning of people's ability to discern each experience's value and react accordingly is a product of adaptive biological evolution.

The concept of automatic valuing becomes more complex when considered in the context of internal multiplicity. Each internal voice may value experiences differently; that is, a person may have different feelings about an experience depending on which voice is the current centre of experience. Further, one internal voice may encounter another, so a person may have evaluative or affective reactions towards parts of him- or herself. These latter reactions are the stuff of psychological problems and psychotherapy.

In this chapter, we explore how affective reactions can be understood within one theory of internal multiplicity, the assimilation model (Stiles 2002; Stiles et al. 1990). Our purpose is theory-building (elaboration of the assimilation model), and we do not attempt to review the many similar or related ideas advanced by other writers, such as the authors represented in this volume. We present some evidence bearing on our conjectures; however, we realize that they call for far more research.

First, we describe the assimilation model, including its account of internal voices. We explain the relation between affective reactions and the sequential stages of assimilation of problematic voices. We then suggest that the assimilation sequence can be understood as the development of a dialogue between internal voices. In particular, we explore a conjecture that the salient affective differences across assimilation stages reflect changes in how long contact with a problematic voice can be sustained.

The assimilation model

The assimilation model (Stiles 2002; Stiles et al. 1990) is an evolving description of how people change in successful psychotherapy. Its core strategy involves distinguishing themes or topics and tracking them across sessions, using recordings or transcripts of sessions. This strategy has shaped the model's concepts. First, the model understands people as made of psychological parts – constellations of traces of experiences that constitute a theme or topic and have a degree of independent agency. In concert with the other authors in this volume, we describe these constellations of traces as *internal voices, I-positions, characters, self states* or the *centre of experience*, among other terms (Hermans 2002; Honos-Webb and Stiles 1998; Stiles 1997, 1999). Second, the model takes a developmental perspective, which we call *assimilation of problematic experiences*. It seeks regularities in the process by which problematic voices are reconciled and integrated into the rest of the person.

Much of the research on the assimilation model has been intensive case studies, meant to elaborate the model so that it better represents clinical observations (Stiles 2003). We have drawn cases from a variety of client populations and therapeutic approaches, including psychoanalytic, interpersonal, client-centred, cognitive-behavioural and process-experiential (see Stiles 2002 for references).

Voices as traces of experiences

According to the model, experiences leave traces, which can be reactivated. An experience encompasses the full awareness and activity of the moment, incorporating intentions and actions as well as sensory images. Thus, when traces are reactivated, they are active agents. They are not inert information like books in a library or files in a computer, waiting to be acted upon by some central agency. Calling the traces *voices* emphasizes their ability to act and speak, but we sometimes use other terms (e.g. *centre of experience, self state, character, I-position*) to emphasize other properties.

Traces tend to be activated by (or, equivalently, voices tend to be addressed by and respond to) new events that are similar or related to the original events. When traces are active simultaneously, they leave further, joint traces and so tend to become assimilated to each other (Stiles 1999, 2002). Thus, traces of previous events tend to become linked to traces of newer experiences that are similar or related, forming coherent constellations of mutually linked traces. That is, voices grow over time, amassing more experiential material. Normally, the constellations of traces that form different voices tend to become interlinked too, forming a *community* of voices. The assimilative links bridge the traces, so they are smoothly accessible from each other and can serve as a repertoire of resources. Voices within the community emerge when they are needed, addressed by circumstances that recall their formation. For example, feeling hungry and being in the kitchen will trigger traces of experiences of finding food and cooking – typically, precisely the resources needed in such circumstances. Metaphorically, we can say that members of the community of voices emerge to deal with the current demands in relevant situations.

Some experiences are problematic, however, for example, traumatic experiences or destructive primary relationships. The voices (traces) of such problematic experiences may not be integrated into the community but instead are treated as unwelcome or foreign. Because they are not mutually interlinked, they are not available as resources. Their emergence (e.g. when triggered by external circumstances) is signalled by negative emotion, and they may be quickly suppressed or avoided. When and if they speak, transitions tend to be abrupt, unexpected, and painful, rather than smooth and appropriate. (In a somewhat similar way, when dangerous situations emerge suddenly, they tend to produce negative emotion, and they tend to be abruptly escaped or avoided.) In some clients, whole communities of voices may be problematic (e.g. a community formed around prolonged experience of early abuse and neglect: see Osatuke and Stiles, in preparation).

As reported elsewhere in this volume, a person's different internal voices often sound different. They can be empirically distinguished in session audiorecords by vocal, phonological characteristics as well as by content, that is, by how they sound as well as by what they say (Osatuke et al., Chapter 15 in this volume). Expressions by a problematic voice may sound as if the speaker angrily interrupted herself. This is illustrated in a previously reported passage from the case of Debbie (transcribed in Stiles 1999: 15; audio available on the Internet at http://www.psychotherapyresearch.org/journal/pr/pr9-1.html or at http://www.users.muohio.edu/stileswb/debbie-1a.htm).

We use the terms *voice* and *community* in flexible and overlapping ways. Even very delimited problematic voices involve some range or sequence of traces (even isolated traumas are not instantaneous), and hence may be considered as (small) communities. On the other hand, even large, diverse collections of experiences in a well-integrated personality can speak coherently, as if through a representative, and hence be considered as voices.

In therapy, problematic voices can be assimilated into the community. Based mainly on the case studies, we have inferred a sequence of stages or levels through which problematic experiences/voices may pass as they are assimilated. We call this sequence the Assimilation of Problematic Experiences Scale (APES). A version of the APES is shown in Table 6.1. It is written to describe the relation of a problematic voice to a dominant community at each stage, but it could be recast to describe relations between any two voices. Different problematic voices may pass through these stages at different rates or remain stuck at different stages. We use the APES as a way to summarize and accumulate ongoing observations drawn from the case studies and other research (Stiles 2003). Thus, the APES changes to accommodate new

Table 6.1   Assimilation of Problematic Experiences Scale (APES)

0 Warded off/dissociated. Client is unaware of the problem; the problematic voice is silent or dissociated. Affect may be minimal, reflecting successful avoidance. Alternatively, problem may appear as somatic symptoms, acting out, or state switches.

1 Unwanted thoughts/active avoidance. Client prefers not to think about the experience. Problematic voices emerge in response to therapist interventions or external circumstances and are suppressed or avoided. Affect is intensely negative but episodic and unfocused; the connection with the content may be unclear.

2 Vague awareness/emergence. Client is aware of a problematic experience but cannot formulate the problem clearly. Problematic voice emerges into sustained awareness. Affect includes acute psychological pain or panic associated with the problematic material.

3 Problem statement/clarification. Content includes a clear statement of a problem – something that can be worked on. Opposing voices are differentiated and can talk about each other. Affect is negative but manageable, not panicky.

4 Understanding/insight. The problematic experience is formulated and understood in some way. Voices reach an understanding with each other (a meaning bridge). Affect may be mixed, with some unpleasant recognition but also some pleasant surprise.

5 Application/working through. The understanding is used to work on a problem. Voices work together to address problems of living. Affective tone is positive, optimistic.

6 Resourcefulness/problem solution. The formerly problematic experience has become a resource, used for solving problems. Voices can be used flexibly. Affect is positive, satisfied.

7 Integration/mastery. Client automatically generalizes solutions; voices are fully integrated, serving as resources in new situations. Affect is positive or neutral (i.e. this is no longer something to get excited about).

Note: Assimilation is considered as a continuum, and intermediate stages are allowed, for example, 2.5 represents a stage of assimilation half way between vague awareness/emergence (2.0) and problem statement/clarification (3.0).

observations while it continues to summarize what had been observed previously.

Affect and feeling across assimilation stages

Theoretically, encounters with a new experience or the traces of previous experiences generate *affect*, particularly if the experiences are problematic. The affect is an automatic organismic response to the encounter, which, we suggest, happens very quickly. The affect is produced in a fraction of a second and can recede almost as quickly, though it may be repeated or prolonged if the voices remain in contact (that is, if both sets of traces remain activated). Recognition of the affect, which may be called the *feeling*, happens somewhat more slowly and lasts longer. The recognition may depend partly on the sensation of the affect's physiological concomitants, such as patterns of autonomic activation. We suggest that the process of recognition requires repeated or at least slightly prolonged (seconds, perhaps) contact between the voices.

Whereas an affect is an organismic process that is not assignable to any one voice, a feeling is located within the current centre of experience (the currently speaking voice). It is possible for an affect to go unrecognized. One may have an affect of fear, for example, while not consciously feeling frightened, or one may mislabel one's affect. Indeed, others may sometimes recognize a person's affective state when he or she does not. As a further subtlety, one may verbally express an emotion when one is not in the corresponding affective or feeling state, for example, truthfully stating that one is angry at one's boss or frightened of spiders even though one is not feeling angry or frightened (or in an angry or frightened affective state) at that moment. In distinguishing levels of emotional processing and using the common words *affect* and *feeling* for this purpose, we follow the example of Damasio (1994), though our distinctions are framed within assimilation theory and so differ from Damasio's in their specifics.

As indicated in Table 6.1, each APES stage is associated with a characteristic range of feeling. At low stages of assimilation, emergence of problematic voices tends to produce terror, rage, disgust, anguish or other sorts of intense emotional pain. At the most extreme, the negative affect leads to dissociation of the problematic experience from the rest of the community of voices (APES stage 0), as manifested, for example, in warding off, flashbacks or state switches (Varvin and Stiles 1999). Dissociation reflects an intensity of affect so great that one of the voices is automatically suppressed before it is recognized by the other. Voices do not remain in contact and do not become linked. For example, Karen, a psychotherapy client described by Osatuke et al. (2001), first presented with complaints of time management difficulties at work; only later in the course of therapy did she painfully realize how important her family issues were and how much distress they caused her.

In slightly less extreme conditions, the feeling of dysphoria is intense (the affect is recognized) but very brief, as the problematic voice is quickly avoided and not allowed to speak (APES stage 1). This may be manifested by forgetting to do things or forgetting events or by active refusal to consider or discuss problematic experiences. At somewhat higher assimilation stages the voices acknowledge each other, the problematic voice emerges, and strong negative feeling is manifested by crying or other intense expression (APES stage 2). As an illustration of forgetting and crying at APES stages 1 to 2, Karen invited her colleagues to her home to discuss a work issue that she felt nervous about. She had counted on her husband's support, but he said he would not be home at the time of the gathering. She expressed her disappointment to him 'not very nicely', and then forgot what exactly she had said. One of the main conflicts addressed in Karen's therapy was that she tended to feel bad when she failed to meet her perceived obligations towards others. Concordantly, she had forgotten her remark to her husband exactly because it was 'not very nice'. When the therapist's active questioning made her remember, she cried for about a minute out of guilt and remorse (Osatuke et al. 2001).

As the problem is formulated into a statement (APES stages 2 to 3), the raw negative affect is moderated and reduced. Just acknowledging the pain and confusion represents the beginning of a meaning bridge. For example, after heavy crying expressing her emotional pain, Karen made this statement of her main difficulty: 'I don't know how to make life fun, how to relax – I just don't know how to do it . . . I don't know how to do things other than work.'

Construction of a meaning bridge in the range of APES stages 3 (problem statement) to 4 (understanding) may produce mixed positive and negative feelings, manifested, sometimes, by laughing. For example, toward the end of her therapy, as she was gaining an understanding of her problem, Karen reproached herself for not spending enough time with her son, and used the word 'should', a word actively discouraged by her therapist during previous sessions. Prompted by the therapist, she corrected herself, but then immediately directed another reproach to herself, for having used the word 'should'! The therapist pointed this out, noting that Karen had worked on the maladaptive pattern of using 'should' and did not deserve the reproach. Karen agreed and laughed, presumably, because she noticed the pattern. Reproaching herself for reproaching herself was too many 'shoulds' indeed (Osatuke et al. 2001).

At still higher assimilation stages, when the understanding is being actively applied in daily living, encountering the formerly problematic content may yield feelings of satisfaction or pride in having overcome the problem (APES stages 5 and 6). For example, close to the end of therapy, Karen reported satisfaction in correcting a difficult office situation in a way that considered her own emotional needs. Her formerly opposing voices (one expressing her emotional needs, and one concerned with her obligations towards others) were working in collaboration.

The feelings curve

A schematic plot of clients' feelings across APES stages yields an S-shaped curve, as illustrated in Figure 6.1. Across the early stages, clients' feelings become more negative – feeling worse before feeling better. Feelings reach a low point at APES stage 2, emergence. Then, in the APES range of 3–5 feelings improve steadily, reaching a peak at stage 6. At the highest stages, the feeling level returns to neutral as the experiences are integrated.

The S-shaped feelings curve was used descriptively early in assimilation research (Stiles et al. 1991), but we realized only recently that it represents the mathematical product of the two simpler curves plotted as broken lines in

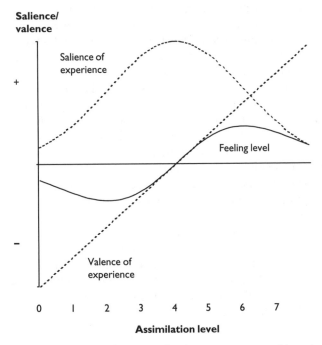

Figure 6.1 Theoretical relations of valence of and attention to a problematic experience with characteristic feeling level at each stage of the Assimilation of Problematic Experiences Scale (APES). APES stage: 0 = warded off; 1 = avoided; 2 = emerging; 3 = recognized; 4 = understood; 5 = applied; 6 = solved; 7 = mastered (see Table 6.1)

Figure 6.1. The mathematical relations point usefully to psychological ones. The ascending diagonal *valence* curve represents the degree to which the affect on encountering a particular experience is negative (at low assimilation levels) or positive (at high assimilation levels). The normal curve represents *salience*, that is, the amount of attention paid to the experience. This is low if the experience is warded off or avoided (APES = 0 or 1) or if it is integrated and therefore unremarkable (APES = 7), and highest in the middle (APES = 3 to 5) range when the problem is being clarified and understanding is being achieved and applied. With suitable scaling, the feeling level is equal to the affective valence level multiplied by the salience level at each point on the assimilation continuum. In other words, the characteristic feeling associated with each APES stage is the product of (a) the valence associated with the community's encountering the voice and (b) the probability or duration of such encounters. (We are not proposing units for measuring either valence or salience, though this may be possible. The basic shape of the feelings curve is the same regardless of scaling.)

Psychologically, considering feelings as the product of valence and salience of problematic experience suggests the following. When a problematic voice is unassimilated, the potential for dysphoria is great, but encounters are rare or fleeting, so the average feeling level (e.g. as observed in therapy sessions) is only mildly negative. As assimilation increases, the potential intensity decreases gradually, but the salience increases rapidly, so the feeling is more negative, reaching a low point at APES stage 2. This is typically the most intense phase of exploratory therapies, characterized by moments of emotionally painful breakthrough, in which previously-avoided problematic experiences are acknowledged and confronted. The improvement in feelings across APES stages 3–5 reflects the high salience of a voice whose valence is becoming more positive as the problem is recognized, discussed, and understood and the understanding is applied. The peak of positive feelings comes at APES stage 6, when the problem is resolved and the formerly problematic experiences are recognized as resources. The return to neutral at higher stages reflects a decline in attention to the formerly problematic experience.

We hasten to acknowledge that a few graphed lines cannot capture the range or subtlety of human emotional experience. The schematic representation in Figure 6.1 focuses on only two general dimensions of emotion, valence and salience. The specific flavours of emotion vary hugely (e.g. see Osatuke and Stiles 2003).

Emotion as a dialogical position

We suggest that a dialogical process, an encounter between voices, underlies the curves in Figure 6.1. In an important contribution, Leiman (Chapter 16 in this volume) pointed out that, in each utterance, its author expresses a position (an attitude, an evaluation) toward its addressees (the people or things to whom the utterance is directed) and/or toward its referents (the people or things that the utterance is about). Utterances are tangible (e.g. auditory or visual) events in the world and hence are open to observation by others, in particular, by researchers.

We extend Leiman's reasoning as follows: first, we suggest that the concept of emotional expression is an extension of the concept of position. That is, emotional expression a (strong) position the author takes toward the expression's addressee or its referent. Second, we note that both addressee and referent are known by the author, that is, they are traces of the author's experience (past experience or current experience). It follows that author, addressee and referent can be considered as internal voices as well as entities in the world. In this sense, each utterance can be considered as an encounter between voices – between the utterance's author and those whom the utterance is directed to and about. Conversely, then, any emotion expression signals some sort of contact between voices. Putting this together with foregoing sections suggests that clients' feeling states can serve as markers for APES stages (cf. Honos-Webb et al. 1999). That is, clinicians or researchers might infer the APES stage of a problem by noting the feeling associated with it.

Each utterance can be understood as expressing a position (an emotion) at a point in time, thus sampling the author's continuous stream of experience (Stiles 1992: 66–67). In what follows, we describe two studies where utterances were considered as internal voices' emotional position-taking with respect to each other and hence as tracking clients' feeling.

Encounters between voices lengthen with assimilation

In this section, we explore a conjecture that has emerged from our observations of therapy discourse: encounters between internal voices become more sustained as the voices become more assimilated to each other. The lengthening of encounters appears emotionally mediated. We examine this conjecture in terms of clients' response to problems at each APES stage, or, more technically, in terms of the emotional reaction by a representative of the dominant community to a problematic voice.

At APES stage 0 (see Table 6.1 and Figure 6.1), as noted earlier, even brief contact is so intensely negative that contact is broken before the dominant community can recognize the problem. Signs that address or trigger the problematic voice generate dysphoric affect, and the problematic voice is quickly dissociated. The problematic voice may be expressed in unrecognized (and hence affectively safe) ways, as through somatic symptoms or acting out.

At APES stage 1, the encounter is long enough for partial recognition, but the potential negative feeling is so intense that the client actively avoids the problematic experience. In effect, the presence of the problem is sensed or even acknowledged, but the problem is not engaged. For example, when a therapist inquires about a past trauma, triggering the traces may signal such intense emotional pain that the dominant community may abruptly change the topic, in effect, denying full awareness to the problematic material, and hence avoiding the pain that full awareness would entail.

At APES stage 2, the problem is engaged, in the sense that it is repeatedly addressed and repeatedly responds. We suggest that the encounters are intensely painful but not continuous. That is, the engagement consists of repeated brief encounters, each of which is affectively very negative. The problematic voice emerges long enough to say something (perhaps one utterance or part of an utterance), but not long enough to be understood, much less, resolved. As a result clients feel worse than at previous (or subsequent) stages, but they are often confused about why they're feeling so bad. In the next section, we illustrate the emotional processes of APES stage 2 drawing on a study in which the degree of positive or negative feeling was rated in each sentence of selected therapy sessions (Mackay et al. 2002).

At APES stages 3 to 4, the problematic voice expresses itself directly. At APES stage 3, it can respond and speak when it is addressed. Typically, however, it is quickly interrupted by the dominant voice. The feeling associated with these encounters is negative, but less intensely so than at lower APES stages. The problematic voice is recognized and named by the dominant community's representative (that is, the problem is explicitly described and addressed). Between APES stage 3 and APES stage 4, there appears to be a gradual lengthening of the time that the problematic voice can hold the floor, so the interruptions decrease and each voice speaks for longer periods. At the same time, the negative feeling becomes less intense and more mixed (with positive as well as negative moments), and the voices appear to converge on a mutual understanding, or *meaning bridge*. In a subsequent section we illustrate these dialogical processes in drawing on a case study of a client's progress through APES stages 3 to 4 (Glick et al., in preparation).

At higher APES levels, encountering the voice is no longer problematic. The formerly problematic voice can be considered as a member of the community. Contact is sustained and may even be a source of positive feelings (e.g. satisfaction as the former problems are overcome and used as resources).

Although emotion is important, according to the assimilation model, catharsis is not enough. Encounters with the problematic experience, with attendant affect, may be necessary for change, but change additionally requires building a meaning bridge. Understanding and application of understanding must follow the encounter (cf. Table 6.1).

Emotional volatility at APES stage 2

In a study directly addressing emotional expression in therapy (Mackay et al. 2002), three raters independently rated the degree of pleasure–displeasure expressed by each client sentence in sessions drawn from the Second Sheffield Psychotherapy Project (Shapiro et al. 1994). The raters responded to the question: 'How positive or negative is the client's emotion in this sentence?' on a nine-point rating scale with anchor points of -4 (very negative) and $+4$ (very positive). These ratings were meant to assess the feelings curve shown in Figure 6.1.

The rated sessions were all middle sessions (i.e. not one of the first three or last three sessions) of eighteen clients who each received sixteen sessions of either psychodynamic-interpersonal therapy or cognitive-behavioural therapy in the Sheffield project. The sessions were selected because they were rated by therapists as being particularly helpful, high-impact sessions (see Mackay et al. 2002 for details). Figure 6.2 shows the results for two sessions that appeared to represent the emergence of problematic voices. They could be considered as characteristic examples of APES stage 2 (see Table 6.1), corresponding to the low point on the feelings curve (see Figure 6.1). Sessions containing APES stage 2 emergence events, like those containing insight

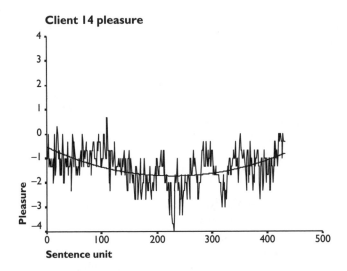

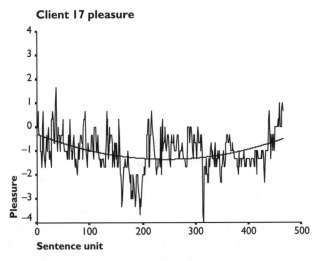

Figure 6.2 Means of ratings of feeling expressed in each client sentence by three independent raters. Raters responded to the question: 'How positive or negative is the client's emotion in this sentence?' on a nine-point rating scale with anchor points of −4 (very negative) and +4 (very positive). One session from each of two clients is shown.

events (APES stage 4), can be dramatic. Consequently, they may be particularly likely to be rated as helpful by therapists.

Both of the sessions shown in Figure 6.2 were psychodynamic-interpersonal therapy. In each session, the client focused on a difficult and emotionally charged issue. In each case, the therapist and client had evidently negotiated in a previous session that this issue would be discussed.

Early in her session, Client 14 said that, despite a joint decision to 'pin down' what had happened to her, she was frightened to talk about it, and that, at least partly for this reason, she had been too upset to attend the previous scheduled session (avoidance characteristic of APES stage 1). The therapist acknowledged the client's reluctance but supported her wish to proceed. The client then described the events of the rape in detail, and, with the therapist, explored her distressing feelings and the lack of support she experienced from friends and family. Later in the session, she linked this experience with her tendency to avoid emotional commitment, so as not to be let down again.

Client 17, somewhat similarly, started the session by saying she was intentionally late because she was scared about what they had planned to do. She described fearing that if she spoke the things she had been hiding, she would be so upset that she would hurt the therapist physically. However, she also felt determined to tell him. She went on to describe adolescent sexual experiences that she found embarrassing and difficult to discuss. The therapist and client explored these experiences in relation to power and guilt and to the client's tendency to see people either as her parents or as her victims (the latter was illustrated by her fear of hurting the therapist). Although she found this exploration painful, by the end of the session, she felt glad she had done it.

Note that the distress indicated in the graphs was not sustained dysphoria, but rather a series of intensely negative spikes. That is, sentences expressing great emotional pain were interspersed with those expressing much milder feelings. Only the smoothed curves in Figure 6.2 plausibly resemble the low segment of the feelings curve shown in Figure 6.1.

Our theoretical interpretation argues that the volatility in the measured feelings curves represented real volatility in the clients' feelings. The encounters between the dominant community representatives and the voices of the problematic experience were brief, intense, painful and, to a significant extent, uncomprehending. Brief moments of great emotional pain were interleaved with less painful moments in which the dominant community was out of contact with the problem. Nevertheless, the pain was not so great nor the contact so quick that the problematic material was completely suppressed or avoided, as it had been in these clients' previous sessions. There were repeated, rapid, irregular cycles in which contact was made and then withdrawn, each contact producing strong dysphoria.

On the other hand, the smoothed curves in Figure 6.2 can also be considered as accurate summaries of session process. That is, both of these sessions were indeed characterized by globally negative feeling, with an initial descent from a relatively defended (and hence slightly less negative) early period to a mid-session period of more intense dysphoria, followed by an easing of the pain associated with consolidation of the contact late in the session.

Cross-fire slows with progress toward mutual understanding

Progress between APES stages 3 (problem statement/clarification) and 4 (understanding/insight) was studied in an assimilation analysis of the case of Margaret, a 58-year-old woman treated for depression in seventeen sessions of client-centred therapy (Glick et al., in preparation). Margaret was a client in the York Depression Project (Greenberg and Watson 1998), chosen for study because she had one of the best outcomes in the project, as measured by standard symptom intensity inventories.

The assimilation analysis of verbatim session transcripts identified two prominent voices in Margaret's discourse: (a) The **caretaker** voice (in bold face in the following examples) represented the dominant community. This voice expressed pride in skilfully caring for husband, children, ageing parents and felt an obligation to attend to others' needs. (b) The *care for me* voice (in italics) was problematic. It seemed to represent suppressed experiences of neediness, entitlement, desire to be cared for, and resentment at being the caregiver. Margaret complained that she received little help or acknowledgement, particularly from her husband.

Margaret's transition from APES stage 3 (where the voices and problem became clear) to stage 4 (where shared understanding was reached) took roughly nine sessions, progressing through substages of changing relations between the two prominent voices:

(3.2)   Rapid cross-fire. Opposing voices fought for the floor, interrupting and contradicting each other.
(3.4)   Entitlement. The *care for me* voice became bolder, acted entitled to speak, spoke for longer periods, was more demanding and aggressive.
(3.6)   Mutual respect and attention. The *care for me* voice could speak without interruption as if expecting respect. The **caretaker** voice displayed greater empathy.
(3.8)   Active search for understanding. The voices seemed to listen intently to each other and offered tentative shared understandings.

Examples of substages 3.2 and 3.8, drawn from Margaret's sessions 3 and 11, respectively, illustrate the increasingly sustained contact between the voices. Even at APES 3.2, the problematic voice could make several utterances before being interrupted:

Margaret: **When you've been from my generation,**
Therapist: mm-hm.
Margaret: **you know that you've always got your husband's supper.**

              It's very difficult to change,
              like to say, like, *'get your own'* (slight laugh), you know.
              And, but I know that he doesn't expect it.
              because he has said if I [inaudible] that's my problem
              and if you're in the middle of something, because
              For a long time,
              if I was in the middle of something,
              I did resent it.
              I felt, well I had my dinner.
              He's-he's the one who's ruined the routine,
              not me.
              Why should I stop what I'm doing?
Therapist: Right.
Margaret: **But I still felt I should do it** (laughs)
              because this is my generation you know.
              and, um,
              But I resented doing it.
              So I kind of I'm sort of resolving that as I go along.

At APES 3.8, the exchanges were more prolonged, and there was a suggestion of agreement, rather than contradiction.

Margaret: *mm-hm. so this is how I, you know, I mean, as I say,*
              I'll admit like, it really was a bad time
              And, as I say, part of it was my fault too,
              I guess maybe I pushed [my husband] away in a lot of ways
              so that he got to the point he thought
              okay, that's the way she feels,
              she can, I'm not gonna, you know, try any more.
              even now he's very careful what he says about my family (laughs).
Therapist: So somehow that started this kind of thing
              where he was afraid to, maybe, say, or get involved?
Margaret: **mm-hm.**
Therapist: It was more like,
              he thought you wanted him to keep his distance?
Margaret: **Yeah, I think yeah.**
              and, and, I think,
              and then when something like that happens,
              it leads to other things too, you know, like quite unwittingly,
              I think people just say,
              okay fine, enough, if that's the way she wants it, or
Therapist: yeah maybe he, just kind of,
              I can imagine him maybe just getting confused
              about what you did want.

Margaret: **yeah.**
Therapist: just kind of feeling like,
maybe you need some space,
when it sounds like probably that was the last thing you really
wanted.
Margaret: yeah.
I just needed somebody.

This sequence illustrates mixed emotions, gradually becoming more positive. Shortly after the second passage, Margaret reached a new understanding that her insistence on acting as caretaker had blocked her husband's efforts at support, and this was accompanied by a sense of accomplishment and optimism. This insight (APES stage 4) pointed to ways she could change, and she subsequently applied it (APES stage 5). Later, she reported enjoying her daughter's wedding more by allowing others to take responsibility for some of the arrangements. In theoretical terms, she found meaning bridges that allowed the *care for me* voice to become a resource permitting satisfactions in life (APES stage 6), rather than a source of resentment and antagonism.

Conclusion

Theoretically, the smooth mutual accessibility of resources, illustrated by Margaret's meaning bridge from her dominant **caretaker** community to her *care for me* voice, represents the opposite pole from the automatic, dissociative warding off of affectively intolerable traces of problematic experiences. The process of assimilating problematic voices can be understood as progress along a continuum of dialogical engagement governed by the affective concomitants of contact between voices. As meaning bridges become stronger, progressing from partial awareness through recognition and naming to understanding and integration, the client's feeling gradually emerges and then changes from intensely negative to positive. In concert, encounters lengthen from instant dissociation through active avoidance, painful affective volatility, rapid cross-fire dialogue, and a search for mutual understanding, to coordinated joint activity.

Acknowledgements

We thank Michael A. Gray, Hani M. Henry, Mikael Leiman and Lisa M. Salvi for comments on drafts of this chapter.

References

Allport, G.W. (1946). 'Effect: A secondary principle of learning.' *Psychological Review*, *53*, 335–347.

Damasio, A.R. (1994). *Descartes' Error: Emotion, Reason, and the Human Brain*. New York: G.P. Putnam's Sons.

Glick, M.J., Salvi, L.M., Stiles, W.B. and Greenberg, L.S. (in preparation). 'Building meaning bridges: Therapeutic progress from problem formulation to understanding.'

Greenberg, L.S. and Watson, J. (1998). 'Experiential therapy of depression: Differential effects of client centered relationship conditions and active experiential interventions.' *Psychotherapy Research*, *8*, 210–224.

Hermans, H.J.M. (2002). 'The dialogical self as a society of mind.' *Theory and Psychology*, *12*, 147–160.

Honos-Webb, L. and Stiles, W.B. (1998). 'Reformulation of assimilation analysis in terms of voices.' *Psychotherapy*, *35*, 23–33.

Honos-Webb, L., Surko, M., Stiles, W.B. and Greenberg, L.S. (1999). 'Assimilation of voices in psychotherapy: The case of Jan.' *Journal of Counseling Psychology*, *46*, 448–460.

Mackay, H.C., Barkham, M., Stiles, W.B. and Goldfried, M.R. (2002). 'Patterns of client emotion in helpful sessions of cognitive-behavioral and psychodynamic-interpersonal therapy.' *Journal of Counseling Psychology*, *49*, 376–380.

Osatuke, K. and Stiles, W.B. (2003). 'Emotional flavour and historicity.' *Psychology and Psychotherapy: Theory, Research and Practice*, *76*, 47–50.

Osatuke, K. and Stiles, W.B. (in preparation). *On Different Kinds of Problematic Internal Voices: Elaboration of the Assimilation Model*.

Osatuke, K., Stiles, W.B., Shapiro, D.A. and Barkham, M. (2001). 'Laughing, crying, and forgetting: Signs of different degrees of separation between internal voices on the Assimilation of Problematic Experiences Scale.' In W.B. Stiles (moderator) *Applications of the Assimilation of Problematic Experiences Scale*. Panel presented at the meeting of the North American Society for Psychotherapy Research, Puerto Vallarta, Mexico, November.

Rogers, C.R. (1959). 'A theory of therapy, personality, and interpersonal relationships as developed by the client-centered framework.' In S. Koch (ed.) *Psychology: A Study of a Science, Vol. 3, Formulations of a Person and the Social Context* (pp. 184–256). New York: McGraw-Hill.

Shapiro, D.A., Barkham, M., Rees, A., Hardy, G.E., Reynolds, S. and Startup, M.J. (1994). 'Effects of treatment duration and severity of depression on the effectiveness of cognitive/behavioral and psychodynamic/interpersonal psychotherapy.' *Journal of Consulting and Clinical Psychology*, *62*, 522–534.

Skinner, B.F. (1953). *Science and Human Behaviour*. New York: Macmillan.

Stiles, W.B. (1992). *Describing Talk: A Taxonomy of Verbal Response Modes*. Newbury Park, CA: Sage.

Stiles, W.B. (1997). 'Signs and voices: Joining a conversation in progress.' *British Journal of Medical Psychology*, *70*, 169–176.

Stiles, W.B. (1999). 'Signs and voices in psychotherapy.' *Psychotherapy Research*, *9*, 1–21.

Stiles, W.B. (2002). 'Assimilation of problematic experiences.' In J.C. Norcross (ed.)

Psychotherapy Relationships that Work: Therapist Contributions and Responsiveness to Patients (pp. 357–365). New York: Oxford University Press.

Stiles, W.B. (2003). 'When is a case study scientific research?' *Psychotherapy Bulletin, 38*(1), 6–11.

Stiles, W.B., Elliott, R., Llewelyn, S.P., Firth-Cozens, J.A., Margison, F.R., Shapiro, D.A. and Hardy, G. (1990). 'Assimilation of problematic experiences by clients in psychotherapy.' *Psychotherapy, 27*, 411–420.

Stiles, W.B., Morrison, L.A., Haw, S.K., Harper, H., Shapiro, D.A. and Firth-Cozens, J. (1991). 'Longitudinal study of assimilation in exploratory psychotherapy.' *Psychotherapy, 28*, 195–206.

Varvin, S. and Stiles, W.B. (1999). 'Emergence of severe traumatic experiences: An assimilation analysis of psychoanalytic therapy with a political refugee.' *Psychotherapy Research, 9*, 381–404.

Zajonc, R.B. (1980). 'Feeling and thinking: Preferences need no inferences.' *American Psychologist, 35*, 151–175.

Chapter 7

From discord to dialogue

Internal voices and the reorganization of the self in process-experiential therapy

William J. Whelton and Leslie S. Greenberg

Rick, a composite of several clients we have known, is feeling angry, frightened and immobilized. He has been in therapy for four months with Dominique and is beginning to voice painful longings and deep, inchoate fears. Rick is a single, 32-year-old computer engineer whose hard work and discipline have won him great professional success but this has done nothing to assuage growing feelings of emptiness, loneliness and depression. A lonely man, he wants more connection with others and the joys of sex and romance but his sporadic attempts in this direction always end in an almost physiological paralysis.

Rick's internal world has the air of a crowded and claustrophobic space peopled with voices of both hope and fear. The taunts and badgering of parts of himself carry echoes of voices he has known now become his own, but they alternate with the enthusiasm of anger and desire and determination. It would be hard to find a dramatic action on the stage more poignant and conflictual than the one played out each day in Rick. Elements of Rick's story can be heard in the stories told by many clients in therapy. Individual clients bring 'a self' to therapy but the therapist soon discovers that the individual is a microcosm of disparate, sometimes conflicting, selves, often accompanied by the still tangible emotional presence and voices of important figures from the past.

The purpose of this chapter is to present the approach taken in process-experiential therapy (Greenberg 2002; Greenberg et al. 1993) to the dialogue between, and the reorganization of, the many self-aspects that comprise the relational microcosm of a client's internal world. Process-experiential therapy is an emotion-focused therapy that lies firmly within the tradition of humanistic, experiential and existential therapies. Within this view people are seen as multivocal (Elliott and Greenberg 1997). There are many voices and possibilities within each person. Some have been marginalized and silenced and others openly assent to and participate in the oppression. One goal of all humanistic therapies is to offer distance, perspective and the freedom to reject and dismiss those voices which appear alien and intrusive, which harass and poison the self creating fear, pain and discord. Likewise, there are other voices, often buried, usually living in fearful and oppressive silence, voices which bespeak potential and hope if given a chance to speak and be heard. Process-experiential therapy takes the view that 'multiple internal voicedness' is a valuable, even essential, therapeutic resource and it has elaborated structural paradigms of the most common internal conflicts between parts of the self and how these can typically be resolved. This chapter will elaborate these propositions and present basic cases using elements from Rick's struggles and other therapy cases to illustrate.

Process-experiential therapy

Process-experiential (PE) therapy is an emotion-focused approach to therapy in the humanistic and experiential traditions which was largely formed by amalgamating the Rogerian sensitivity to the basic conditions of a healing relationship and the Gestalt therapy focus on tasks that require completion within an affective science framework (Greenberg et al. 1993). This view posits that the self has many parts and many voices within a complex and variably organized framework. This multivocality is a basic element of our human heritage. A very frequent goal of therapy is to heal, strengthen or unify the self by a reorganization of these parts and voices.

One of the forerunners of PE therapy was the Gestalt therapy of Perls et al. (1951). This therapy was exquisitely attuned to the delicate balance between the self and other. The satisfaction of basic needs requires awareness and action in the social world but many social norms, processes and events as experienced by a given person can serve to deaden awareness and to dampen individual initiative and action.

Person-centred therapy (Rogers 1959) also emphasized the inherently relational nature of the self. This therapy has deeply influenced PE therapy because PE therapy views the person-centred conditions of empathy, congruence and unconditional positive regard as setting the essential framework for the therapist's attitude and presence to the client in therapy. The attuned and valuing 'other' allows the self to begin to relax the beliefs about self that constrain and diminish it, in order that it might itself become attuned and accepting of its tacit emotional experience. Rogers trusted that the experience of the self would prove to be a complex and diverse source of potentials and 'possible' selves that had remained unaccessed as a resource because they had been disallowed.

Theory of the self

In this theory, the self is viewed as constructed and as an ongoing, self-organizing process in which emotion acts as the central organizing process. There are two principal theoretical bases for this model of the self.

The first is the mathematical concept of dynamic systems that has been applied to complex systems in many domains, including geography, meteorology and developmental psychology (Mahoney 1991; Thelen and Smith 1994). The theory posits that given the dynamic interaction of countless variables across subsystems in an organizing system, stable patterns emerge out of apparent chaos and these patterns are called attractor states because they pull toward a certain stability and order. These are not fixed structures but are continually synthesized in the moment and a new emergent order can be created if a certain threshold of change in the underlying variables is attained. This theory is meant to be understood here in a metaphorical sense. The metaphor of dynamic systems applies very well to biological systems whose very survival depends on the constant subtle interaction and balance between shifting internal and external environments. The self is also a shifting organization of more basic elements that are synthesized from moment to moment in response to conditions in the internal and external environments. The self in this view is fluid and dynamic, is not directed by a central agency or homunculus, and is built up over time from a sense of ownership of the complex array of self states that have been organized into a narrative identity.

The second central theoretical framework for understanding the self is the theory of dialectical-constructivism (Greenberg and Pascual-Leone 2001; Pascual-Leone 1987). The self in this view is a multi-process, multilevelled organization built up at the highest level from the dialectical interaction between ongoing, moment-by-moment experience and higher-level conceptual processes of reflection, which attempt to interpret, order and explain these elementary experiential processes. In this model, basic experiential self-organizations are tacitly constructed from a dynamic synthesis of physiological processes and other basic elements. The next stage in the construction of the self entails the conscious and deliberate pole of the dialectic. This constructive process flows from attending to the feelings and sensations of the self state and symbolizing and interpreting it through one's acquired and constructed language, narratives and beliefs. Attention to both poles of the dialectic is vital. Both the wisdom that biological patterns display and the wisdom refracted through the prism of culture and thought are crucial to healthy survival and to try to live by the integration of both is to live most viably.

This model of the process construction of the self is the basis for the way in which PE therapy conceptualizes and works with dialogues between parts of the self. In the modular view of the self being proposed, the self contains many habitual self states which may function in unison, in competition, or in fierce opposition and contradiction with each other. Some of these, however habitual, have never been really noticed or explored in conscious awareness. Other possible self states have been poorly actualized or directly suppressed. And the network of bodily, sensorimotor and affective subsystems whose information is synthesized into self states can be organized in ways that have never been tried. Some self states are fundamentally maladaptive (though these states may have served an adaptive function at some earlier point in life). People who come for therapy are often organized into positions of anger, cynicism, defeat, passivity and shame. In many cases, deeper self-experiences of sadness and pain remain largely buried. Possible self-organizations of hope, pride and constructive anger may flicker by but seem out of reach. Each self-organization needs to be understood as an actual or potential process, not as a reified structure. Active self-organizations have and deserve a voice within the self and a crucial part of therapy is to allow them to speak and to be heard (Elliott and Greenberg 1997; Stiles 1999). In the dialectic that has been described, disjunctions often exist between what is experienced and the cognitive, representational self. Many self-organizations have never been attended to, symbolized in language or allowed to speak. Ironically, they may be central to bodily organization and behaviour without ever having been brought into conscious awareness. Allowing different aspects of the self to be brought into awareness and to speak is a core activity in PE therapy.

Emotion and cognition in PE therapy

As this book attests, a number of therapies currently posit views of the self in which self-modules, self states or the voices of aspects of the self interact or dialogue within the self. The issue of dialogue within the self has emerged in our time as central to both theory and practice in therapy (Hermans 1996; Stiles 1999). Recent approaches to multivocality in therapy tend to be overtly postmodern. They share many family resemblances while differing substantially in their emphases. Most of these approaches hold in common that narrative and the constructions of voice, story and metaphor are important to both the multivocality and the coherence of the self. What principally distinguishes the PE perspective is the degree of emphasis on the organizing role of emotion in the construction of the self and in the conduct of therapy (Greenberg and Van Balen 1998; Whelton and Greenberg 2001). In PE therapy the self is irreducibly situated in the body and bodily processes of sensation and emotion form the foundation for self states. In practice, PE therapy stands in agreement with Stiles (1999) about the therapeutic necessity of assimilating problematic experiences by allowing them into awareness and offering them a voice as an aspect of the self. But to offer them a voice is dialectical: it is the cognitive and narrative construction of a fundamentally emotional and bodily based experience. Experience both directs and limits possible constructions so our view would be most at odds with those multivocal views that are most radically socially constructionist and which neglect the biological and bodily basis of emotion.

Many perspectives focus on cognition and cognitive information-processing in human functioning and it is true that the importance of cognition for human life can hardly be overstated. Cognition, though, is a relatively recent evolutionary development and it is built on and interacts with a foundation of emotional processing which seems central to attachment, social bonding and status seeking and other relational processes which are fundamental in generating distress or well-being. Emotion has a more ancient evolutionary provenance (LeDoux 1996) and preverbal affective attunement with a caregiver seems to be at the root of the development of the self and emotional regulation (Siegel 1999). Research in the domains of social psychology (Zajonc 2000), problem-solving (Damasio 1994; Fredrickson 2001) and the neuropsychology of resilience (Davidson 2000) are all pointing to the fundamental role of emotion in facilitating and directing the adaptive function of cognition in embodied, real-world situations. Emotion is the fuel and rudder (and at other times the anchor) of the motivated self, directing cognition toward solving what matters to the self. The PE view is that emotion is integral to the processes by which self states are dynamically organized from moment to moment.

PE therapy contends that the self is an organizing process that builds from the synthesis of innumerable, integrated subsystems a relatively stable, unified sense of its own being and presence in the world. Stability is provided consciously by an organized net of familiar stories and beliefs that contribute to creating an enduring identity and tacitly by the familiarity of one's body and by the bodily sensations and emotional states that serve as habitual attractors. At its core the model is dialectical constructivist and the basic dialectic is between automatic sensorimotor, bodily, emotional processes and the attentional, perceptual and higher-order linguistic, cognitive processes that edit and interpret this experience. Various cognitive processes and various bodily, sensory and emotional processes are dialectically synthesized at several levels both in and out of awareness to construct the self (Greenberg and Pascual-Leone 2001). A core concept in this model is the emotion scheme. At the level of the emotion scheme many constituent elements are synthesized and the emotion scheme is a tacit, learned construct that serves as the framework for all self states that an individual has developed in interaction with the environment. The emotion scheme serves as a template that structures how new experience is processed but it differs from the cognitive concept of the schema in that it is understood to be dominated by affect with cognitive factors being secondary. Emotion schemes contain sensorimotor elements, bodily sensations, emotion, needs and wishes, action tendencies, as well as learned perceptual cues and the rudiments of beliefs. All of these are integrated to provide the bodily based tacit sense of an emotional state. Emotions such as sadness, anger or joy are innate and biological but emotion schemes are learned and can be adaptive or maladaptive (Greenberg 2002).

Rick, for example, is often suffused by a global sense of loneliness and rejection. If he were able to put his feeling into words he might say that he feels alone, cut off from others, as if impregnable walls of indifference existed between others and himself. But the fundamental elements of the emotions and sensations which wash over him are more basic if hard to symbolize in language: His body is heavy and tense, and there are gnawing sensations of anxiety and fear in his stomach and legs. Tears collect and burn behind his eyes and his throat is tight and choked. His body wants to curl up but it wants to do so in order to be caressed so it is already automatically resisting the action tendency out of a bodily based, tacit sense of futility. His chest is weighed down with hurt which bespeaks both a sad longing for connection and a feeling of abandonment. His face would be a mask of mixed sadness and anger if he weren't trying to hide it. This loneliness/rejection emotion scheme might be largely under the radar screen of awareness, or it might be crudely symbolized as 'I don't feel so good', but it is how his self is organized at an experiential level and if brought into awareness this is Rick's current self-experience.

Figure 7.1 represents the construction of the self. At its basis is the synthesis of emotion schemes into self-organizations which are themselves the basis of experience when brought into awareness. At the core of the process of constructing the self is a dialectic between experiencing and explaining, experiencing being an automatic process through which feeling and bodily sensations are apprehended as a global and immediate state and explaining being the deliberate cognitive process, mediated by language, through which experience is symbolized and interpreted.

A house divided: the nature and therapy of self-criticism

The rest of the chapter will focus on self-criticism as an example of conflict between parts of the self and two-chair therapy to address self-criticism as an example of structured dialogues within PE therapy. However, self-criticism is only one difficulty for which self-modules are used to structure healing dialogues in PE therapy. A different approach of equal clinical significance is unfinished business, in which representations of significant persons from one's past remain as powerful and toxic aspects of one's current self.

A puzzling fact about human reflexivity is the extent to which self-awareness is imbued with self-evaluation and, for many (perhaps most) people, self-attack and self-condemnation. An immense amount of pain is generated in people by themselves, by the ways in which they passionately berate themselves for perceived shortcomings and flaws. This is a central and basic instance of a division of the self into two parts. A very basic and still largely unresolved issue is to explain how this process is adaptive and fundamental to the self and how the benign and functional aspects of it differ from the ravages of self-imposed psychological abuse.

Humans, like wolves, horses and elephants, for example, are intensely and constitutively social animals and must learn the norms and prohibitions of the group early and well. Emotions are crucial to the regulation of all social

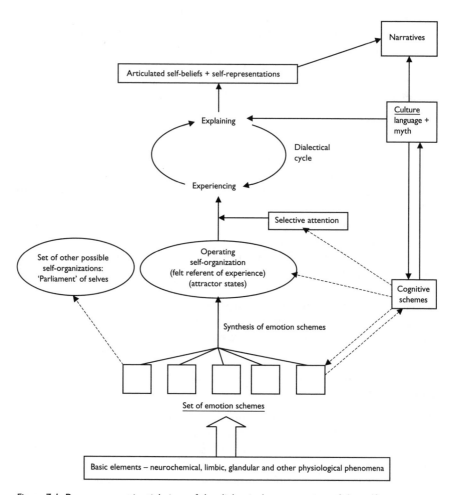

Figure 7.1 Process-experiential view of the dialectical construction of the self

interactions (Greenberg 2002). Some researchers (e.g. Robins et al. 1999) contend that the evolutionary development of a conscious self in humans largely served to organize and facilitate the interactions of their complex, multivalent social identities. Emotions continue to be a central regulator of these social selves. These processes are possible because being a self and being consciously aware of oneself are both integral aspects of selfhood, creating within the self a fundamental bifurcation (Hermans and Kempen 1993). This self-awareness helps to regulate one's connection to the group and one way in which this happens is through assessing and evaluating the self in the light of social standards. The self and the internal self-evaluator to some degree are themselves social constructs and external evaluations in early life are internalized and become aspects of the self. The internal voice of self-criticism is one of the most basic aspects of a decentralized self in most people and certainly one of the most salient to psychopathology and psychotherapy.

The self-critical aspect of the self (henceforth the 'self-critic') is not only a collection of beliefs and thoughts held about the self or directed at the self in the form of demands and admonishments. What has been internalized is more than the content of negative cognitions, it is also the emotional tone which accompanies these attitudes and the scorn and rejection which are the action tendencies of emotions like contempt and disgust. In a study of emotional processes in self-criticism, Whelton (2001) selected a sample of college students according to their level of self-critical vulnerability to depression on the Depressive Experiences Questionnaire (Blatt et al. 1976). These students were videotaped criticizing themselves and responding to the criticism after an imagination exercise in which they recalled an experience of failure. Observer codings showed that those with self-critical personalities displayed more contempt for themselves in the process of self-criticism than did those in the control group. Furthermore, in their response to the self-criticism the students with more self-critical personalities showed less resilience in the face of the criticism: they were less assertive, more submissive and more sad and ashamed than the students in the control group. Clearly, self-criticism is both a cognitive and affective process and one of the central emotions in the generation of depressive states appears to be contempt. What was also made apparent in this research was the latent sense of an inadequate and powerless self in the depressively vulnerable, their inability to organize around a resilient and resourceful core to fend off the attack. Their self-criticism was more potent not only because more contemptuous, but also because it tended to evoke an inner self-organization rendered fragile by shame and a sense of inevitable exposure and defeat.

Greenberg (1984) made the elaboration of effective techniques for healing the split between the self-critical aspects of the self and the self proper (the object of the criticism) a cornerstone of the development of PE therapy. The goal is a sense of harmony and peace developed through an emotional shift that allows a shift in perception and meaning on both sides.

The process of working with self-criticism in PE therapy is often called the two-chair dialogue (Greenberg et al. 1993). It involves having the client move back and forth between two chairs. In one chair the client dramatizes the voice of the self-critic and in the other the voice of the 'experiencing' self, the object of the criticism, the self-aspect who experiences the hurt of being criticized. The two-chair process is initiated when in the course of the therapy session a marker indicates that a struggle between two parts of the self is currently causing distress. This could be the client saying 'If I weren't such a damned idiot, this would never have happened', for example. Two-chair dialogue involves clearly separating out the two voices, the two self-aspects, and having them speak directly to each other, not the therapist. The therapist facilitates the process of the dialogue. The dramatic embodiment of the voices allows for all the physical and emotional dimensions of the self-organization to be expressed, not merely the thoughts or the point of view. The self-critic begins with general attacks and criticisms, then more pointed and specific criticisms. The expression of criticisms is often intense and it provokes in the self the pain that the critic is causing. In response the experiencing self will often complain and make excuses or will counterattack but very superficially. Eventually, however, the self experiences and expresses deep, authentic pain and sadness in response to the criticism. At this point, changes begin to happen in both chairs. In the experiencing chair the self begins to express its wants and needs in a stronger and more assertive way. It may for example reorganize around more positive and assertive emotions like anger and pride. The critic weakens a little and may begin to express the fear which underlines so many of the critical demands. Within this fear is a core of true standards and values which are genuinely held. In a full resolution the critical side softens into a compassionate embrace of the self with the continued assertive expression of the experiencing chair. Then something like a genuine dialogue can begin because both sides are expressing authentic values and needs of the self which must be negotiated and reconciled.

Example of two-chair work in therapy

In this brief example, which focuses on the early stages of two-chair work, the client (Valerie is her pseudonym) arrives at her therapy session after having passed a couple of difficult days during which she felt hurt, angry, worthless and vulnerable. Working with the chairs functions as a sort of therapeutic heuristic device whose function is precisely to help differentiate out the most salient aspects of the self in order to allow them to speak and to allow the dialogue to develop. It is evident in Valerie's discourse that numerous self-aspects are active in her self-process, that her sense of self waxes and wanes according to which is dominant, and that each, if allowed, can give voice to differing dimensions of her experience and perspective. In the early part of the session, she expresses her impatience at the degree of pain and vulnerability she is feeling and this helps to identify a principal critical voice, one that contributes to her sense of worthlessness:

C: I was very anxious coming today. Very anxious. I've been very angry the past couple of – I'm just sick of it. I'm sick of feeling angry because then I start analysing it and I know its because I'm hurt and I can't stand feeling hurt.

T: Mmhmm. And the anxiety?

C: Plus I'm very tired. Just been waking up and when I first get up just feeling really anxious.

T: I see.

C: These anxiety attacks – I can't breathe.

T: OK, it sounds like things are really percolating.

C: But –

T: You're saying angry but really hurt. And then not wanting to be hurt, right? And then anxious about coming here or just anxious about bringing all this stuff here.

C: Yeah.

T: Uh-huh.

C: Like bringing it all up and looking at it and talking about it. It's like I'm so sick.

T: Sick of it.

C: Sick of it (mmhmm). So sick of it.

T: Mmhmm. I just want it to all not be there.

C: Yeah.

T: That kind of thing.

C: Or just like there's part of me that says, 'Get over it, Valerie.' You know?

T: Mmhmm mmhmm.

C: Get over it. Get on with your life. What's the problem? Why do you have to spend so much time analysing it, figuring it out, understanding?

T: Mmhmm.

C: Working through.

T: Right right right right. And yet it's there.

C: It's there – and like we talked a couple of weeks ago and yet I'm so frustrated because I don't think I should be stuck (mmhmm). You know – I've got so much going on for me that I should be beyond this stuckness (mmhmm).

T: Right. So there's this whole conflict about I shouldn't be there and should be beyond it and we've sort of been around that before, but then there is the stuckness and the feeling that the stuckness also really means anger and hurt, right? So can you tell me a bit more about that – this is the stuff you don't want but is really there.

C: (sighs)

T: Mmhmm. It kind of wells up but then

C: I don't know where to start with it all – and I – and every time I think of something I always just dismiss it because it's like so stupid

T: mmhmm mmhmm mmhmm.

C: So dumb and I'm so overwhelmed by stupid piddling everyday life things. You know just

T: So again it's those two parts right (yeah). The one is so dismissive

C: but I know there's this part that wants to be validated and recognized so much (right right) but I just think I want to give up because it will never be validated. You know, I will never have enough affirmation for myself. I will never be able to feel good enough for myself (mmhmm mmhmm). And so I want to learn how to live with that discontentment. It will never feel good enough. It will never be enough.

T: Which part is saying: 'I'll never feel enough', do you know?
C: The part that just is never enough. Like I just can't –
T: The part that feels so empty or deprived or
C: yeah – I will never be a good enough parent. I will never be a good enough friend. Everyday I try to get up and attempt to do things and just – it just never measures up. I'm just always failing somewhere somehow. And I'm just always restlessly discontent and not feeling like.

At this point the therapist is able, in a collaborative fashion, to help identify the emergence of one of the central voices of the Critic and to have Valerie speak from one of the chairs as that critical voice. As we have seen, it is often the case in therapeutic practice that it takes time to sort out many voices to identify and differentiate those self-aspects that are crucial in generating painful dysfunction. Each person is unique and it is equally important to develop a therapeutic sense of how these voices are interacting in a given individual: what their demands, values, fears and tactics are. Jumping ahead a little in the transcript, the Critic is demanding perfection and berating the self for its inability to measure up:

C: You're not perfect. You have to be everything in every way for your children, for your friends. You just have to. You just have to – that is the standard. That is – that's the standard. And you will never measure – you will never measure up.
T: So tell her: You will never measure up.
C: You'll never measure up. Ever. So just deal with it.
T: What doesn't she do right? What doesn't –
C: She doesn't – she doesn't provide enough –
T: Tell her 'You –'
C: You you you don't provide enough um you don't provide enough um presents for your children because who you are is not enough. Being there. You have to provide more – more conversation, more humour, more insight, more knowledge. You you you do that but it's not enough. It will never be enough.
T: You will never be enough.
C: Never.
T: Say it again.
C: You'll never be enough.
T: Again.

C: (sighs)
T: You will just never be good enough.
C: (sigh) You'll never be good enough (very subdued voice).

When Valerie is moved from the Critic's chair to the chair of the Self (the object of the criticism) it becomes quickly evident that the burden of these demands and expectations is a torment for her to bear. This leads ultimately to the emergence of a previously ignored voice:

T: I'll never be enough according to that standard.
C: Yes. I feel worthless not being all those things.
T: Uh-huh. And this is really the heart of it, right? This painful awful feeling of worthlessness that makes you live up to somebody's expectation.
C: I just can't stand feeling it (sniffs).
T: What's 'it' feel like?
C: I just feel so despairing and like nothing. I'm just not even a person (uh-huh). I'm drowning.
T: Uh-huh. So just your whole self is drowning and just. Tell me more about it. I mean, you're saying, 'I just feel so –'
C: I just feel empty. Like I'm nothing. I'm empty. I'm nothing. I'm not worth even. I'm not even noticed – I'm not even there (uh-huh). I'm not even there. I'm not even recognized anywhere without being that.
T: uh-huh. So – unless I'm living up to some kind of expectation of perfection I'm nothing. I'm worthless. I don't even exist.
C: That's how I feel inside. And I just get panicky and anxious and afraid.

Valerie here starts to allow her vulnerability to pour out in the form of tears. She has reached a deeper voice of worthlessness, the voice at the core of her distress, and in doing so a tiny voice of resistance emerges from her affectively based tendency to survive and thrive:

C: (sobs)
T: Can you let some of those tears come? These are the tears you don't want to have but they're there.
C: It's too overwhelming (sniff)
T: Mm-hmm.
C: (sigh)
T: So it's just overwhelming to be so wiped out unless you're perfect.
C: Yeah. And I'm supposed to function normally (sniff) and take care of four kids on my own and
T: mm-hmm. It's just too much. I can't.

C: I hear myself telling myself that but I'm just resisting these days.
T: Yeah – resist her. What are you saying?
C: I just can't take it anymore.
T: Uh-huh. Tell her what you can't take. 'I can't carry on pushing –'
C: I just want to lay down and stop.
T: Uh-huh, mm.
C: I just can't take the pressure and the pushing and you have to do this in order to be loved and acceptable to your children, to your friends. I'm just so tired of it. I just cannot stand that voice anymore.
T: Uh-huh. Tell her. 'I'm just so tired. I can't –'
C: Yeah. So tired of it.
T: Uh-huh.
C: I just feel so depleted – it's hard to even stop you, to fight you. (begins to weep).
T: Uh-huh.
C: (cries)
T: Let it come. Breathe. Breathe.
C: (cries) Just can't take it anymore (cries).
T: I didn't hear.
C: I can't take her anymore.

Later in the session, as she enters more deeply into her pain and sadness, and buoyed a little by the internal resources that she has been able to muster against the Critic, Valerie gets increasingly in touch with her adaptive needs and goals. As she is able to articulate these, small gains in resilience are achieved because in the face of the perfectionistic Critic she becomes more than an object of abuse; she becomes a subject who can make plans and have needs and articulate goals. In a small way, we are already seeing a more empowered voice:

T: I just need something more (C sobs) comforting. More . . .?
C: Yes (tearfully) (sobs).
T: Caring.
C: (sobs) Oh god (quiets, breathing deeply).
T: I just need rest from that pounding.
C: Yeah (exhales).
T: Mm-hmm.
C: I'm so tired of always having it attacking me.
T: Uh-huh.
C: In such a harsh harsh way. I just always listen to it so readily and agree with it and lose a sense of myself when I hear it and I just can't take it today (uh-huh). I just don't want to hear it (mm-hmm, mm-hmm) (exhales deeply).

T: So what do you need? 'I just need –'
C: I want to be. I just want to be comforted . . .
. . . (a little later)
T: What do you need in your pain and your depletion and exhaustion?
C: (sniffs) I need to be understood (uh-huh) and listened to and comforted (OK) and yet encouraged and challenged (uh-huh) just to not give up (mm-hmm) (mm-hmm).
T: That sounds very real, right? Can you tell this to her? What you need? (client sighs) From her as well as from others but from her?
C: (sigh)
T: Tell her what you need her to understand.
C: (sigh) I need you to understand that I have needs and it's OK to have them.
T: Uh-huh. What needs?
C: Just needs to be. Just needs to be there (small laugh).
T: Uh-huh
C: Just to be OK in who I am (uh-huh). Just to be nurtured (uh-huh).
T: Somehow to be accepted for what I can and do do.

Change occurs by accessing her core maladaptive voice of worthlessness and making it accessible to new input from the healthier need-based voice. All this also takes place within a validating relationship that facilitates the emergence of the different voices and supports the emergence and strengthening of the adaptive voice.

Conclusion

The transcript conveys an example of one type of dialogue between parts of the self. A very different kind of dramatized intrapsychic dialogue emerges from therapeutic efforts to resolve hurts and injuries that linger from unresolved emotional experiences with important figures in one's past. The pain, resentment and shame that lingers from these experiences, especially when conceptualized as the result of unexpressed emotions and needs, is often referred to as 'unfinished business' (Greenberg et al. 1993; Perls et al. 1951). Dialogue is initiated by imagining the other and expressing with unconstrained emotion the resentment, hurt, grief and sadness that one has toward them. This can initiate a lasting reorganization of the self, a process through which the power invested in the other is reclaimed by the self, and the other not the self is now perceived as weak. In whichever form the dialogue takes, major therapeutic change can stem from dialogues between aspects of a multivocal self. In this process people contact and experience the emotions which organize each of the self-aspects while finding the voice to articulate their various fears, demands and desires.

This experiential self-theory emerged principally from reflections stemming from observations of techniques and processes that were effective in therapy. We do not pretend to a theoretical clarity about the self that is not even close to existing. The nature of the self and the ontological nature of self-modules is still highly elusive and problematic. Theory immensely exceeds what has been empirically demonstrated. Nevertheless, the process of therapy can also serve as a productive laboratory of sorts and watching the self change offers many insights into how the self might be constructed in the first instance. What is less disputable is that the type of dialogues described in this chapter have been shown to promote profound therapeutic self-reorganization.

References

Blatt, S.J., D'Affliti, P. and Quinlan, D.M. (1976). 'Experiences of depression in normal young adults.' *Journal of Abnormal Psychology*, *85*, 383–389.

Damasio, A.R. (1994). *Descartes' Error: Emotion, Reason, and the Human Brain.* New York: Quill.

Davidson, R.J. (2000). 'Affective style, psychopathology, and resilience: Brain mechanisms and plasticity.' *American Psychologist*, *55*, 1196–1214.

Elliott, R. and Greenberg, L.S. (1997). 'Multiple voices in PE Therapy: Dialogues between aspects of the self.' *Journal of Psychotherapy Integration*, *7*, 225–239.

Fredrickson, B.L. (2001). 'The role of positive emotions in positive psychology: The broaden-and-build theory of positive emotions.' *American Psychologist*, *56*, 218–226.

Greenberg, L.S. (1984). 'A task analysis of intrapersonal conflict resolution.' In L. Rice and L.S. Greenberg (eds) *Patterns of Change* (pp. 67–123). New York: Guilford.

Greenberg, L.S. (2002). *Emotion-focused Therapy: Coaching Clients to Work through their Feelings.* Washington, DC: American Psychological Association.

Greenberg, L.S. and Pascual-Leone, J. (2001). 'A dialectical constructivist view of the creation of personal meaning.' *Journal of Constructivist Psychology*, *14*, 165–186.

Greenberg, L.S. and Van Balen, R. (1998). 'A theory of experience-centered therapies.' In L.S Greenberg, J. Watson and G. Lietaer (eds) *Handbook of Experiential Therapy: Foundations and Differential Treatment* (pp. 28–57). New York: Guilford.

Greenberg, L.S., Rice, L.N. and Elliott, R. (1993). *Facilitating Emotional Change: The Moment by Moment Process.* New York: Guilford.

Hermans, H.J.M. (1996). 'Opposites in a dialogical self: Constructs as characters.' *Journal of Constructivist Psychology*, *9*, 1–26.

Hermans, H.J.M. and Kempen, H.J.G. (1993). *The Dialogical Self: Meaning as Movement.* New York: Academic Press.

LeDoux, J. (1996). *The Emotional Brain: The Mysterious Underpinnings of Emotional Life.* New York: Touchstone.

Mahoney, M. (1991). *Human Change Processes.* New York: Basic Books.

Pascual-Leone, J. (1987). 'Organismic processes for neo-Piagetian theories: A dialectical causal account of cognitive development.' *International Journal of Psychology*, *22*, 531–570.

Perls, F.S., Hefferline, R. and Goodman, P. (1951). *Gestalt Therapy*. New York: Dell.

Robins, R.W., Norem, J.K. and Cheek, J.M. (1999). 'Naturalizing the self.' In L.A. Pervin and O.P. John (eds) *Handbook of Personality: Theory and Research*, 2nd edn (pp. 443–477). New York: Guilford.

Rogers, C.R. (1959). 'A theory of therapy, personality, and interpersonal relationships as developed in the client-centered framework.' In S. Koch (ed.) *Psychology: The Study of a Science*, Vol. 3 (pp. 185–256). New York: McGraw-Hill.

Siegel, D.J. (1999). *The Developing Mind: Toward a Neurobiology of Interpersonal Experience*. New York: Guilford.

Stiles, W.B. (1999). 'Signs and voices in psychotherapy.' *Psychotherapy Research*, 9, 1–21.

Thelen, E. and Smith, L.B. (1994). *A Dynamic Systems Approach to the Development of Cognition and Action*. Cambridge, MA: MIT Press.

Whelton, W.J. (2001). 'Emotion in self-criticism.' Unpublished doctoral dissertation, York University, Toronto, Canada.

Whelton, W.J. and Greenberg, L.S. (2001). 'The self as a singular multiplicity: A PE perspective.' In J.C. Muran (ed.) *Self-relations in the Psychotherapy Process* (pp. 87–106). Washington, DC: American Psychological Association.

Zajonc, R.B. (2000). 'Feeling and thinking: Closing the debate over the independence of affect.' In J.P. Forgas (ed.) *Feeling and Thinking: The Role of Affect in Social Cognition* (pp. 31–58). New York: Cambridge University Press.

Chapter 8

The dialogical construction of coalitions in a personal position repertoire

Hubert J.M. Hermans and Els Hermans-Jansen

The film *Vivante* (2001), directed by Sandrine Ray, shows the moving story of a young student who was molested by four guys, who dragged her into a car, drove to a remote place, and raped her. The woman, very shameful about what happened, refused to share the event with anybody and tried to continue her life as if nothing had happened. When a nice young man invited her for a date, she refused in an aggressive way. Paradoxically, she had let herself be abused by other men she had never met before. Gradually, she lost contact with an increasing number of acquaintances and friends, who could not understand her capricious behaviour and suspicious attitude. Only one person, her brother, stayed loyal to her throughout this problematic period. He remained supportive and understanding despite her sudden mood changes and irrational behaviour, and prevented her from total alienation from others and from herself. At the end of the film she meets a new man, to whom she showed several drawings she had made. His sincere appreciation of her art and his interest in her as a person marked the beginning of a new and gratifying relationship.

The basic structure of this film, not unfamiliar to any psychotherapist working with traumatized clients, can be translated in terms of an organized repertoire of positions (voices or characters). By the sudden, traumatic rape, the woman was brought into a position ('I as raped') that became persistently dominant in her disorganized self. Not only was this position associated with extremely negative emotions (e.g. uncontrolled anxiety and anger), but also she shut herself off from a variety of contacts with significant others in her social environment. In terms of dialogical self theory (see Hermans, Chapter 1 in this volume), the traumatic event leads to the sudden emergence of a position ('I as raped') that becomes so rigidly dominant that it reduces the accessibility of other positions in the internal domain of the self (e.g. 'I as a sociable person who likes to make a date'). Correspondingly, the disorganizing event reduces the accessibility of significant positions in the extended or external domain of the self (e.g. 'my friends with whom I used to share things'). As a result of these changes, other positions may emerge that contribute to the further disorganization of the self (e.g. 'I as increasingly isolated').This disorganizing process can be stopped when the dominating position ('I as raped') and its associated positions (e.g. 'I as isolated') receive an adequate answer from one or more counterpositions in the self that are strong enough to reorganize the self in effective ways. In the film, the trusting brother and the understanding man functioned, in the external domain, as counterpositions to the devastating rapers, whereas 'I as a person who trusts people who deserve that trust' counteracted 'I as raped' in the internal domain. How does this process of positioning and counterpositioning work in psychotherapy? More generally, how can a dysfunctional positional repertoire be reorganized to a more healthy and adaptive one? Let's illustrate this with the actual cases of some clients. The purpose behind these case studies is to show that the construction of coalitions of positions is central to the reorganization of the self-system.

The process of positioning and counterpositioning: from stalking to accepting

In order to illustrate the therapeutic process of positioning and counterpositioning, we present a case study, discussed in more detail by Hermans (2003). The client is Leo, a 29-year-old man, who contacted a psychotherapist (Els Hermans-Jansen) after he was severely criticized by his superiors for his 'arrogant behaviour' and 'lack of empathy' in interactions with his colleagues. In the same period, his partner finished her relationship with him for similar reasons. In reaction, he wrote an extremely aggressive letter in which he accused her of being the cause of all of his problems. For his partner this letter was a good reason to refuse any further contact with him. Leo, however, could not stop thinking of her, and she increasingly became an obsession to him. He followed her and her new friend around all day and terrorized them with frequent nightly telephone calls. This stalking behaviour, the fear of its consequences, and the personal implications of his bad job evaluation, were reasons for Leo to contact a psychotherapist.

After listening to his story, the therapist proposed to Leo to explore his situation in terms of a position repertoire. This was done by constructing, together with Leo, a list of internal and external positions that were experienced by Leo as relevant to him (for details of the method, see Hermans 2001). One of the positions in the internal domain was 'I as a stalker' which was directly related to a central position in his external domain: his ex-partner Laura. The strategy of the therapist in this stage was to examine the meaning of Leo as a stalker by placing this position in the context of other positions of the repertoire. It was found that the relationship between the stalker and Laura was strongly influenced by the association between the stalker and the 'revenger' as two strongly related positions in the internal domain. In the external domain, it was found that his contact with Laura was meaningfully connected with another position in the external domain: his 'fantasy girlfriend'. As long as he experienced the relationship with Laura as satisfying, Laura and his fantasy girlfriend were almost identical. However, after Laura had ended the relationship with Leo, the two figures became highly divergent, with the fantasy figure functioning as a compensation for Laura's absence.

In further exploring the several parts of the internal domain of the self, the therapist and Leo discovered that there was a highly influential background position: the dreamer. Leo explained that this position was very important to his relationship with Laura, who always had been an ideal person for him. For the therapist this was reason to explore, together with Leo, the relationship between the revenger and the dreamer as two relevant context positions of the stalker.

In order to further articulate and deepen the two positions, the psychotherapist proposed to Leo to tell his story from the perspective of the revenger and the dreamer separately. This invitation leads the client to approach the positions as different voices each with a particular story to tell from a specific point of view. Telling and listening to those stories not only clarifies their specific memories, concerns and goals, but also provides a basis for understanding their mutual relationship.

The positions were explored by using some questions that are part of the self-confrontation method (Hermans and Hermans-Jansen 1995). This method invites clients to relate significant events or circumstances in their past, present and future, so that the specific historical perspective of each position can be examined. An example of a question about the past is this: 'Has there been anything of major influence in your past life which still continues to exert a strong influence on you?' Client and therapist read this question sitting side-by-side, taking spatial positions that symbolize a relationship of cooperation. The procedure invites clients to give their spontaneous associations which then leads, with the assistance of the therapist, to the formulation of some sentences that each refer to a significant experience in the client's life. These sentences are written down on small cards so that they can easily be taken up in a later phase in the therapeutic process and compared with other sentences. Similar questions are also asked about the client's present and future (Hermans and Hermans-Jansen 1995: 35).

Here are two sentences that Leo phrased from the perspective of the revenger:

When I have nothing more to lose, I can enjoy destroying somebody; I derive some pride from that.

When I have the feeling that somebody (my ex-partner) is not honest with me, and I discover this, I want to give a lesson to such a person, with verbal violence and with telephone calls. . . . I want to let somebody suffer.

As these sentences (written down 'utterances' from a specific voice) suggest, the revenger does not have a long history. The formulations are phrased in the present rather than in the past. When Leo told his story from the perspective of the dreamer, however, an entirely different voice is sounding, which brings us further into Leo's past:

> I was fantasizing that I would later get a rich and easy life; I practiced that with letter combinations.

> I am the reformer of the world, a well-known figure who traces criminals, a kind of private-detective, a hero who gets much admiration and attention.

A comparison of the formulations from the two positions led to the conclusion that, from the perspective of the revenger, Leo's stalking behaviour was an act of restoring his self-esteem threatened by Laura's decision to finish their relationship, and, from the perspective of the dreamer, this behaviour could be understood as a form of attracting Laura's attention. It became apparent that, although the dreamer was experienced by Leo as opposite to the revenger, the dreamer played an indirect, but nevertheless significant, role in his behaviour towards his ex-girlfriend. The discussion brought forth the insight that the stalker, the revenger and the dreamer functioned as a coalition in which the revenger was aroused in an effort to restore the threatened ideals of the dreamer. In the service of the unrealistic dreamer and the self-affirmative revenger, Leo became a stalker. An important implication for therapy was to develop a counterposition that was able to give an adequate response to the dreamer and the revenger who were some of the driving forces behind the stalking behaviour.

The cycle of attending, creating and anchoring

The formulation of positions and sentences is not to be seen as part of a diagnostic procedure in which the client is simply 'assessed' by the therapist. Rather, the client contributes significantly to the process by proposing positions, telling significant story parts, and formulating clarifying sentences. Throughout therapy the client is invited to participate in the discussion and interpretation of the results. In fact, the client is involved as a co-investigator during the entire process of investigation (Hermans and Bonarius 1991).

The construction of positions and associated storytelling is the first phase of the presented approach. The next phase in the therapeutic process is the 'validation/invalidation process'. Building on the insights emerging from the previous investigation, the client is encouraged to initiate specific actions in order to validate or invalidate parts of the existing position repertoire. This means that the repertoire has to pass, in terms of Kelly (1955), the test of lived experience.

Three subphases are part of the validation/invalidation process: attending, creating and anchoring. In the *attending* phase, clients are stimulated to pay attention to those experiences in their daily lives that are relevant to the positions and stories constructed in the stage of investigation. In this phase clients have an opportunity to find out which positions are dominant in their daily lives and which positions are lacking. In this stage, clients typically become aware of positions that are an obstacle for their future development and which ones are felt as possible expansions of their repertoire in the future.

A useful technique in the attending phase is a diary form which is based on the four Ws: what happened, where did it happen, when did it happen, and who was present? Clients typically focus on one or two specific situations in which a particular position is dominant and describe these situations in detail so that they can be discussed thoroughly in the next session with the therapist. When clients feel unable to fill in such a form, the therapist may ask the same or similar questions during the session.

During the attending stage, Leo became aware, not only of the impact of the revenger and the dreamer in his life, but also of a position that was hidden somewhere in the background of his repertoire. This position seemed particularly significant to his future development: 'I as accepting'. Leo and his therapist both felt that this position was valuable as an effective counterweight to the narrow-minded attitude of the revenger and the unrealistic ideals of the dreamer. At this point the attitude of the therapist became particularly crucial. Increasingly, the therapist had the feeling that behind Leo's incidental boasting and hero stories, there was an idealistic, but highly vulnerable, dreamer and she tended to respond to this with warm attention and a nurturing attitude with only a mild degree of confronting questions. Looking back at the therapeutic process as a whole, it seems that the accepting position of the therapist, who expressed her understanding of his rage and threatened ideals, helped Leo to become more aware and acceptant not only of his own vulnerability but also of the wishes, anxieties and goals of the people in his environment.

In the next subphase, entitled '*creating*', the client is encouraged to try out new behaviour and to act in a different way than before. Central to this phase is 'the principle of feasible steps'. Psychotherapist and client are aware that in the beginning of the process of change it is important that new actions should not exceed a certain level of difficulty or risk. Therefore, therapist and client carefully plan or reflect on new actions in such a way that the chances of a positive outcome are optimal (e.g. sharp and concrete formulation of action plans; no discouraging remarks; actively relating initiatives to the corresponding positions of the repertoire; making notes in a logbook). Only when the first try-outs are successful, actions of a more difficult or risky nature can be undertaken. In the creating subphase, several techniques can be used. A typical one is the 'validation ladder'. The client selects and describes, with the assistance of the therapist, a number of situations of increasing difficulty with regard to the selected position. Then, the client experiments with one or more situations at the lower end of the scale, with the advantage that the probability of success is increased.

In the creating phase, Leo started to experiment with accepting himself and others in various situations. It appeared that some situations were quite difficult to him (e.g. accepting that his new girlfriend had a talk with another man), whereas other situations were more easy (e.g. accepting that a colleague at work had a different opinion about a particular subject-matter). By discussing such examples in the sessions with the therapist, Leo gradually learned to become aware of the fact that other people had their own opinions, wishes and anxieties and that it was important, to others but also to himself, to take these into account.

The third phase of the validation/invalidation process aims at the *anchoring* of positions that are relevant from a therapeutic point of view. Whereas in the second phase the client has experimented with new or alternative positions by creating new events and constructing new stories, in the third phase these changes must be rooted as acquired and established parts of the repertoire. Even in those cases in which new actions are welcomed by therapist and client, the client may fall back to earlier modes of experience and action, because the new actions are not yet incorporated as stabilized parts of the repertoire. Therefore, the main activity in the third phase is practice. This is done by repeating actions, and inventing new ones as 'variations on a theme', long enough to transform them into 'new habits'.

During the anchoring phase, Leo was confronted with an event which was quite dramatic to him: his new girlfriend broke off her relationship with him. In fact, this event could be seen as the ultimate test of his acceptance. Would the same fierce aggression show up again? Would the avenger take precedence over all other positions? Leo discussed the new situation with the therapist and succeeded to keep himself under control. He and his girlfriend found a way to continue their relationship as friends but not as lovers.

Evaluation of therapy progress

In order to check if the process of change is going in the intended direction, it is recommended to examine if the new positions are playing a prominent role in the organized repertoire. Usually the changes are evaluated by making a comparison between the position repertoire in the beginning of the therapy and after some time when the therapy has arrived in the creating or anchoring phase (for a detailed procedure to examine the content and organization of the repertoire, see Hermans 2001). When, however, therapist and client do not want to perform an extensive investigation of the repertoire, it is recommended to give the client the opportunity to tell his or her story from the perspective of the new position and to discuss in depth the pros and cons of this position in the client's life situation. The therapist may assist the client in formulating some sentences on the basis of questions referring to the past, present, and future of the new character. In order to stimulate the dialogical contact between the old positions and the new one(s), it is useful to take the formulations from the old positions, and invite the client to give an answer to them from the perspective of the new position.

In Leo's case, such an evaluation session took place five months after the beginning of the validation process. In the meantime, the accepting position was so far developed that Leo was able to formulate some sentences from the perspective of this position. Here are some examples:

> When the accepting is not there, there are emotions: That attacking, short-sighted, reproaching kind of communication . . . then I give room to the revenger.

> Whereas Johnson [previous employer] reacted somewhat amused to my self-image (dreamer), I see now that I receive respect from Jackson [present employer], for example, my suggestions are followed and I receive respect from the administration.

In the first sentence, Leo refers explicitly to the revenger but he prefers to focus on moments when the accepting position is 'not there' and to criticize the revenger from the outside. The formulation suggests that he is aware of the narrow perspective of the revenger and somewhere accepts his responsibility for the emergence of this character ('. . . then I give room to the revenger'). In the second valuation, Leo establishes some kind of coalition between the accepting position and the dreamer. As this formulation suggests, the dreamer is no longer merely fantasizing and building air castles but becomes integrated into the accepting position which suggests that he is on his way to find a more realistic manner of receiving respect and attention.

In more general terms, the presented dialogical approach implies several criteria for therapy progress: (a) the inclusion of new positions, the foregrounding of existing positions, or the establishment of coalitions that function as an effective counterweight to the positions that previously ruled the self; (b) the sensitivity to see a clear connection between the previously dominating positions and the emerging counterpositions in the experiences of everyday life; (c) the ability and willingness to experiment with new behaviour in such a way that the desirable position is developed and strengthened; (d) the application of the counterposition in a variety of situations so that it becomes a new habit.

In summary, the procedure described aims at a gradual transition between assessment and change and is devised as a dialogical enterprise between client and therapist. The process is realized in a cycle with three phases: investigation–validation–investigation (IVI). The validation phase is, in turn, divided into three subphases: attending–creating–anchoring (ACA). Together, these cycles represent the dynamic process of positioning and repositioning (Harré and Van Langenhove 1991).

Coalition of positions: shifting loyalties in the self

It would be naive to assume that an organized position repertoire can be reorganized by simply 'introducing a new position'. (See also Dimaggio, Salvatore, and Catania, Chapter 12 in this volume.) The reason is that clients, and people in general, organize their repertoire in such a way that, instead of one position, a multitude of positions or voices are dominating the repertoire (Honos-Webb et al. 1999). Moreover, dominant positions usually have their companions, helpers, satellites and auxiliary troops that form stabilizing forces in the internal and external domains of the self. It is a therapeutic challenge to devise strategies for modifying existing coalitions into new ones that are more adaptive. In Leo's case, we could see the emergence of a new coalition. Whereas in the beginning of therapy, a coalition between the revenger and the dreamer was prevalent, later in the therapy the accepting position started to cooperate with the dreamer ones. In one of the statements of the accepting position, Leo said: 'I receive respect from the administration'. This phrase may well be considered a fusion or cooperation between a position that accepts the existence of a societal reality and, at the same time, a position that 'dreams' of getting recognition from the outside world.

At first sight, it may seem self-evident that, as therapists, we do a good job if we try to strengthen desirable positions and weaken undesirable ones, so that the former receive a more dominant place in the repertoire than the latter. Yet this is, in our view, not the best strategy to follow. The heart of the matter is in the question of how it is possible to make a constructive use of the potentials of 'undesirable' positions as contributions to more desirable coalitions. In other words, the matter of 'desirability' or 'positivity' is not to be located in a position per se, but in the team of positions to which it belongs in a particular situation and time. If it is possible to integrate old positions into new coalitions, we find a way to combine the continuity of the self, in teams of existing energies, with the discontinuity that is intrinsic to the therapeutic innovation of the self. Let's illustrate this with an example of a client.

The example is from Fred, a 50-year-old man, who exhibited burn-out symptoms after a long period of overdemanding himself in his work situation. Fred described himself as a 'persistent doubter', a phrase he used to indicate his anxiety to take decisions, particularly in situations in which he had to decide if a job was finished or not. The first author was his therapist during eighteen months and assisted him with the personal position repertoire (PPR) method that allows the study of not only the content of personal positions but also their organization (for a detailed description of the method and the presented case, see Hermans 2001). In Fred's case, three positions were particularly significant during the period of therapy: the doubter, the perfectionist and, somewhat in the background but very important to him, the enjoyer of life. The last position was certainly an enduring feature of his personal history, but seemed to be suppressed by the coalition between the doubter and the perfectionist, the latter position compensating for the anxiety aroused by the former.

After some sessions, client and therapist discovered that the perfectionist could be tackled by learning to delegate tasks to other people at the right moment. Instead of completing a task in full detail, Fred learned to contact other people in order to cooperate on some of the tasks and even to delegate some tasks before he started the job. After more than one year of practising this new style of working, it was decided to investigate his position repertoire again. The most significant finding was that there seemed to emerge a new coalition, between the perfectionist and the enjoyer: doing a 'good job' without making too many demands on himself. This coalition was strong enough to push the doubter to the background of the self-system. Whereas in the first investigation the perfectionist formed a coalition with the doubter, in the second investigation the perfectionist seemed to have changed camps and joined the enjoyer of life. This new coalition enabled Fred to work with more pleasure and to cooperate more easily with other people. This example suggests that it is, in principle, possible to dissolve a particular position (perfectionist) from an unproductive coalition (perfectionist and doubter) and combine it with another, more desirable position (enjoyer), with the result that the new coalition is even more beneficial than the desirable position (enjoyer) alone.

In order to study the last statement (about the most beneficial coalition) more in depth, it was decided to study Fred's repertoire on the basis of a position matrix in which the rows represent the internal positions and the columns the external positions. Each cell in such a matrix represents the extent to which a particular internal position is prominent in relation to a particular external position. One of the internal positions in Fred's case was 'I as deep-down inside', which was introduced into the matrix as a standard internal position in the repertoire of several clients. The investigation was organized in such a way that the separate positions (the perfectionist and the enjoyer apart) could be compared with their coalition (the perfectionist and the enjoyer together). The coalition showed a high correlation ($r = 0.81$) with 'deep-down inside', higher than the correlations of the separate positions with 'deep-down inside' ($r = 0.32$ and $r = 0.41$, respectively). This finding suggests that the coalition in Fred's case was not simply an addition of the separate positions but rather had the nature of a Gestalt with a surplus value above its constituents.

Meta-position as a linkage between a variety of positions

Although dialogical self theory acknowledges the relative independence of positions, they do not work in isolation from each other. In order to get more insight into the linkages between the several positions, a client may be invited to formulate the nature of their relationship in his or her own terms. In order to examine the relationship between the three positions (doubter, perfectionist and enjoyer) from the perspective of the client, the therapist proposed Fred to phrase his insight in their connection at the end of the second investigation. With the assistance of the therapist, Fred constructed the following formulation:

> I accept the perfectionist in myself; I'm convinced that this is something which has grown in me, probably as a result of fear of failure; at the same time, the enjoyer cannot exist without the perfectionist; however, I don't let the perfectionist destruct me any more; they should learn to deal with each other and to make compromises; when something is performed well, I can enjoy it.

In this formulation Fred not only emphasized the importance of a cooperation between the enjoyer and the perfectionist but also placed the several positions in the broader context of his personal history. Moreover, such a formulation is useful as a 'take-home message' for the client in the process of anchoring the insight and its associated behaviour in the everyday situation.

Fred's formulation can be considered the expression of a meta-position, a perspective from which the client phrases the linkages between several significant positions in a self-reflective way. Several researchers have proposed to introduce the notion of a meta-position or observing position as a welcome theoretical contribution to dialogical self theory (e.g. Dimaggio et al. 2003; Georgaca 2001; Leiman 2002; Watkins 1999; see also Hermans, Chapter 1 in this volume).

Fragmentation of the self: the case of the witch

Central in dialogical self theory is the assumption that each position provides a specific perspective on the person–environment interaction, has its own intentions, memories, motives and concerns, and, moreover, has a voice to communicate about this. Another assumption, of particular importance to therapeutic change, should not be neglected: crucial for the facilitation of the process of positioning and repositioning is the affective dimension (see also Hermans, Chapter 1 in this volume).

As part of a study on the affective dimensions of dysfunctional positions (Hermans and Hermans-Jansen 1995), we presented a detailed description of a client, Mary, who was close to suffering from a dissociative disorder. She had bad memories about her father, who was an alcoholic, and every time she saw a man who was drunk, she was overwhelmed by panic and disgust. In her adolescent years she joined a drug scene, where she was forced to have sex, sometimes even under armed threat. After leaving the drug scene, she tried to 'protect' herself by always wearing a tampon and she started to bathe excessively in order to 'clean herself'. The problems became acute after she married. When her husband was sleeping, she sometimes felt an almost uncontrollable urge to murder him. At those moments she felt like a witch, an alien experience that frightened her. She was scared to death, and felt sometimes literally strangled, by a power that was stronger than 'herself'.

After discussion of her personal history, we proposed to talk about her experiences from the perspective of two positions, one from her ordinary position as 'Mary', and the other from the position of 'the witch'. The rationale behind this proposal was that, given the split between the two positions, an improvement of her fragmented self was expected if (a) the two positions were to be clearly distinguished with regard to their specific wishes, aims and feelings, and (b) a dialogical interchange could be established between the two positions, so that the witch would have the opportunity to say what she wanted. The expectation was that Mary could take the needs of the witch into account and respond to them, without losing control of her vehement impulses.

As part of the self-confrontation procedure (Hermans and Hermans-Jansen 1995), we invited Mary and the witch to rate the affective meaning of the sentences that they constructed from both positions. For example, Mary said: 'I want to try to see what my mother gives me: there is only one of me.' This formulation was experienced by Mary in a very positive (pleasant) way. The witch, however, experienced the same sentence in a negative way and felt a fierce aggression toward the mother. One of the statements from the witch was: 'With my bland pussycat qualities I have vulnerable things under my control, from which I can derive power at a later moment (somebody tells me things that I can use later to get what I want).' For the witch this valuation was associated with a large amount of self-affirmative affect (e.g. strength, self-confidence, pride) and with a great deal of positive affect. In relation to the same statement, however, Mary felt a rather low degree of self-affirmative affect and a high amount of negative affect. In other words, Mary and the witch exhibited strongly contrasting affective responses regarding the same statement.

On the basis of this investigation, we discussed with Mary two ideas that would guide the validation/invalidation process. First, she was advised to exercise (e.g. by sport, cycling or walking), in order to expand her experience of space and to express the dammed-up energy of the witch. Second, we proposed that she keep a diary in which she could write her daily observations in order to sharpen her perception. In this way, Mary learned to make a clear perceptual distinction between her ordinary self and the witch. She learned not to respond with panic and to split away from the witch, but to be as alert as possible to her appearance and to the situations in which this happened. When the witch came up, Mary decided to take a break, walked first (movement was important to the witch), and negotiated with herself about what to do in the situation at hand.

One year after the first investigation, Mary performed a second one in order to evaluate the changes in herself. In this investigation we found an increased similarity between the affective responses from Mary and the witch. Strikingly, the formulations constructed by the witch in the first investigation were, in the second investigation, reformulated in such a way that they were incorporated into Mary's ordinary self. For example, in the second investigation, Mary said: 'When this hard side comes and I recognize it, I get in touch. I can look at it and examine where the signal is from. Then I make good use of it.' Such findings suggested that a more dialogical relationship had developed between the two positions, with Mary's position as more dominant than the witch.

One of the most striking findings in Mary's case referred to a statement, formulated in her first investigation, from her ordinary position as Mary: 'In my work I can be myself. I am planning from which angles I can enter. The trust that I receive gives me a foothold, more self-confidence.' As this formulation suggests, it was associated with a high degree of self-affirmative affect. When the same statement was rated by the witch, an affective pattern was found that was highly similar to that of Mary herself ($r = 0.74$). This high correlation, an exceptional finding in Mary's affective ratings, indicated that Mary and the witch agreed on its positive nature. Indeed, Mary could cooperate quite well with the witch in her work situation in which a certain hardness was very welcome. In the intimate relationship with her husband, however, this hardness was felt as extremely dangerous.

The finding of the similarity of the affective responses from Mary and the witch suggests the existence of a coalition between the two positions in *that* particular situation (work). Although the witch was experienced by Mary as strange, threatening and dangerous to her marriage, she could go along quite well with the witch in her work situation. This suggests that the witch was not 'bad' in all situations of her life but represented a force in herself that could be used in a constructive way in those situations in which a certain assertive behaviour was welcomed or even required.

In summary, indications of the emergence of coalitions between positions were found not only in Mary's case, but also in the cases of Leo (between the accepting and the dreamer) and Fred (between the perfectionist and the enjoyer of life), as discussed earlier in this chapter (for a fourth case study with similar findings, see Hermans 2001). Apparently, positions that are considered, at first sight, as undesirable or even destructive, can function as desirable or constructive forces, dependent on the coalition in which they participate. Apparently, a position can take a particular function or meaning

as part of a (changing) coalition and coalitions are formed in close correspondence with (changing) situations. An important implication for therapy and research of therapy is that the *organization* of the self-system is central to the study of meaning. Meaning is position-bound and is constructed by an extended self that is organized and reorganized in space and time. Therefore, the fit or misfit between an organized position repertoire and the life situation of the client is a central focus of a dialogical therapy.

Featuring a 'dialogical therapy': summary

The psychotherapy that we envision, takes dialogical self theory as its conceptual background. This approach, briefly labelled as 'dialogical therapy', has some central features: (a) it conceptualizes the self as a dynamic multiplicity of I-positions located in space and time; (b) the focus of the therapeutic process is on changing the nature of the dialogical interchange between positions with proper attention to their relative dominance; (c) the psychotherapist's goal is not in changing the separate positions but rather in the organization and reorganization of the repertoire. As part of this reorganization, the construction of strong and effective coalitions is paramount to therapy success.

The psychotherapist's role in the life of the client is not very different from the role of the brother in the film *Vivante*. As 'another I' in the dialogical self of the client, the therapist belongs temporarily to the family of positions, and has the challenging task to enhance the quality of the relationships between its members.

References

Dimaggio, G., Salvatore, G., Azzara, C. and Catania, D. (2003). 'Rewriting self-narratives: The therapeutic process.' *Journal of Constructivist Psychology*, special issue on the dialogical self, *16*, 155–181.

Georgaca, E. (2001). 'Voices of the self in psychotherapy: A qualitative analysis.' *British Journal of Medical Psychology*, *74*, 223–236.

Harré, R. and Van Langenhove, L. (1991). 'Varieties of positioning.' *Journal for the Theory of Social Behaviour*, *21*, 393–407.

Hermans, H.J.M. (2001). 'The construction of a personal position repertoire: Method and practice.' *Culture and Psychology*, special issue on culture and the dialogical self: theory, method and practice, *7*(3), 323–365.

Hermans, H.J.M. (2003). 'The innovation of self-narratives: A dialogical approach.' In J. McLeod and L. Angus (eds) *The Handbook of Narrative and Psychotherapy: Theory, Research and Practice*. Thousand Oaks, CA: Sage.

Hermans, H.J.M. and Bonarius, H. (1991). 'The person as co-investigator in personality research.' *European Journal of Personality*, *5*, 199–216.

Hermans, H.J.M. and Hermans-Jansen, E. (1995). *Self-narratives: The Construction of Meaning in Psychotherapy*. New York: Guilford.

Honos-Webb, L., Surko, M., Stiles, W.B. and Greenberg, L. (1999). 'Assimilation of voices in psychotherapy: The case of Jan.' *Journal of Counseling Psychology, 46*, 448–460.

Kelly, G.A. (1955). *The Psychology of Personal Constructs*. New York: Norton.

Leiman, M. (2002). 'Toward semiotic dialogism: The role of sign-mediation in the dialogical self.' *Theory and Psychology*, special issue on the dialogical self, *12*, 221–235.

Watkins, M. (1999). 'Pathways between the multiplicities of the psyche and culture: The development of dialogical capacities.' In J. Rowan and M. Cooper (eds) *The Plural Self: Multiplicity in Everyday Life* (pp. 254–268). London: Sage.

Chapter 9

Standing in the spaces

The multiplicity of self and the psychoanalytic relationship

Philip M. Bromberg

Perhaps in some measure due to Freud's fascination with archaeology, clinical psychoanalysis has tended to embrace an image of two people on a 'quest' – a journey to reach an unknown destination to recover a buried past. Despite the fact that I rather like the image, in my day-to-day work as a practising therapist, I seem to find my reality shaped more by Gertrude Stein than by Indiana Jones. Stein (1937/1993: 298) commented about the nature of life and the pursuit of goals, that when you finally get there, 'there is no there there'. My patients frequently make the same comment. The direct experience of 'self change' seems to be gobbled up by the reality of 'who you are' at a given moment, and evades the linear experience of beginning, middle and end. But linear time does indeed have a presence of its own – like the background ticking of a clock that cannot be ignored for too long without great cost – and it is this paradox that seems to make psychoanalysis feel like a relationship between two people each trying to keep one foot in the here-and-now and the other in the linear reality of past, present and future. Described this way, it sounds like a totally impossible process. If indeed 'everyone knows that every day has no future to it' (Stein 1937/1993: 271), then what sustains a person's motivation for analytic treatment? How do we account for the fact that a patient remains in a relationship with another person for the express purpose of dismantling what he experiences as his 'self' for a presumedly 'better' version that he cannot even imagine until after it has arrived? The answer, as I see it, touches what may be the essence of human nature – the fact that the human personality possesses the extraordinary capacity to negotiate continuity and change *simultaneously*, and will do so under the right relational conditions. I believe that this attribute is what we rely on to make clinical psychoanalysis, or any form of psychodynamic psychotherapy, possible. How we understand this remarkable capability of the mind, and what we see as the optimal therapeutic environment for it to flourish, are, I suggest, the fundamental questions that shape psychoanalytic theory and practice. What I want to talk about here is an outcome of this way of experiencing and thinking about the human relationship we call 'psychoanalysis'.

For example: a patient is engaged in a passionate sexual moment that she refers to, in session, as 'coming in diamonds'. She and her lover are 'lost' in each other and she, a woman who had entered analysis with 'gender confusion', has a visual experience that her lover's penis moving in and out, might be his or it might be hers. She can't tell 'whose penis it is, who is fucking whom', and 'it doesn't matter'. How does the analyst hear and process this 'loss of reality testing' at that moment?

Another patient reports having been reading a book in bed, looking down at the book, and noticing that it was wet. She realized she had been crying. What allows the analyst to comfortably conceptualize the fact that she didn't know she had been crying *when* it was happening? Does he think of such a mundane event as even interesting, analytically?

A patient, a woman with an eating disorder, is asked by her analyst to describe the details of last night's binge. She cannot do it. She insists, in a voice without affect, that she has no memory of the step-by-step experience of what she ate, how she ate it, and what she thought or felt as she was eating it. Resistance?

Psychoanalysis and the decentred self

A discernible shift has been taking place with regard to psychoanalytic understanding of the human mind and the nature of unconscious mental processes – away from the idea of a conscious/preconscious/unconscious distinction per se, towards a view of the self as decentred, and the mind as a configuration of shifting, nonlinear, discontinuous states of consciousness in an ongoing dialectic with the healthy illusion of unitary selfhood. Sherry Turkle (1978/1992), for example, sees Lacan's focus on the decentredness of selfhood as his most seminal contribution, and writes that

> for generations, people have argued about what was revolutionary in Freud's theory and the debate has usually centered on Freud's ideas about sexuality. But Lacan's work underscores that part of Freud's work that is revolutionary for our time. The individual is 'decentered'. There is no autonomous self.
>
> (Turkle 1978/1992: xxxii)

Other seminal figures such as Sullivan (1940, 1953), Fairbairn (1944, 1952), Winnicott (1945, 1949, 1960, 1971a, 1971b, 1971c), Laing (1960), Balint (1968) and Searles (1977), each in his own metaphor, have accorded the phenomenon of 'multiplicity of self' a central position in their work.

Winnicott's contribution to this area is, I feel, particularly far-reaching. Not only did he conceptualize primary dissociation as a psychoanalytic phenomenon in its own right and write about it in a manner that brought it directly into the basic psychoanalytic situation (Winnicott 1949, 1971a, 1971c), but also I would suggest that what we now formulate as psychological 'trauma' that leads to the pathological use of dissociation is the essence of what he labelled 'impingement'. Although not specifically elaborated by him in terms of dissociated states of consciousness, perhaps most significant of all was his vision of a true and false self (Winnicott 1960) which emphasized the *nonlinear* element in psychic structure. It is not unreasonable to suggest that Winnicott's nonlinear leap in psychoanalytic theory has been a major factor in encouraging postclassical analytic thinkers to re-examine their model of the unconscious mind in terms of a self that is decentred, and their concept of 'growth' as a dialectic rather than a unidirectional process.

In this context, a research study by Sorenson (1994) discusses the range of theories in which a formerly axiomatic presumption about the nature of human mental functioning is now being rapidly revised – the presumption of a linear, hierarchical, unidirectional model of growth, and that integration is necessarily or continuously superior to disintegration. Using Thomas Ogden's reformulation of Melanie Klein's developmental theory as an example, Sorenson says the following:

> Ogden (1989) has argued that Melanie Klein's theory of psychological development from the paranoid-schizoid position to the depressive position is too linear and sequential. Instead of Klein's phases which were developmentally diachronic, he proposed synchronic dimensions of experience in which all components play enduringly vital roles, at once both negating and safeguarding the contexts for one another. Unchecked integration, containment and resolution from the depressive position, for example, leads to stagnation, frozenness, and deadness; unmitigated splitting and fragmentation of the paranoid-schizoid likewise leads to fundamental discontinuities of self-experience and psychic chaos. The paranoid schizoid position provides much needed breaking up of a too-frozen integration . . . I believe we make an error to valorize integration and villianize disintegration, just as Ogden was reluctant to do the same to the depressive and paranoid-schizoid positions, respectively.
>
> (Sorenson 1994: 342)

Normal multiplicity of self

A human being's ability to live a life with both authenticity and self-awareness depends on the presence of an ongoing dialectic between separateness and unity of one's self states, allowing each self to function optimally without foreclosing communication and negotiation between them. When all goes well developmentally, a person is only dimly or momentarily aware of the existence of individual self states and their respective realities because each functions as part of a healthy illusion of cohesive personal identity – an overarching cognitive and experiential state felt as 'me'. Each self state is a piece of a functional whole, informed by a process of internal negotiation with the realities, values, affects and perspectives of the others. Despite collisions and even enmity between aspects of self, it is unusual for any one self state to function totally outside of the sense of 'me-ness' – that is, without the participation of the other parts of self. Dissociation, like repression, is a healthy, adaptive function of the human mind. It is a basic process that allows individual self states to function optimally (not simply defensively) when full immersion in a single reality, a single strong affect, and a suspension of one's self-reflective capacity is exactly what is called for or wished for.

As Walter Young (1988) has succinctly put it:

> Under normal conditions, dissociation enhances the integrating functions of the ego by screening out excessive or irrelevant stimuli. . . . Under pathological conditions . . . the normal functions of dissociation become mobilized for defensive use.
>
> (Young 1988: 35–36)

In other words, dissociation is primarily a means through which a human being maintains personal continuity, coherence and integrity of the sense of self. But how can this be? How can the division of self-experience into relatively unlinked parts be in the service of self-integrity? I suggest that the most convincing answer is based on the fact that self-experience originates in relatively unlinked self states, each coherent in its own right, and that the experience of being a unitary self (cf. Hermans et al. 1992: 29–30; Mitchell 1991: 127–139) is an acquired, developmentally adaptive illusion. It is when this illusion of unity is traumatically threatened with unavoidable, precipitous disruption that it becomes in itself a liability because it is in jeopardy of being overwhelmed by input it cannot process symbolically and deal with as a state of conflict. When the illusion of unity is too dangerous to be maintained, there is then a return to the simplicity of dissociation as a proactive, defensive response to the potential repetition of trauma. As one of my patients put it as she began to 'wake up', 'All my life I've found money on the street and people would say I was lucky. I've started to realize I wasn't lucky. I just never looked up.'

Slavin and Kriegman (1992), approaching this issue from the perspective of evolutionary biology and the adaptive design of the human psyche, write the following:

> Multiple versions of the self exist within an overarching, synthetic structure of identity [which] probably cannot possess the degree of internal cohesion or unity frequently implied by concepts such as the 'self' in the self psychological tradition, the 'consolidated character' in Blos's ego psychological model, or 'identity' in Erikson's framework. . . . [T]he idea of an individual 'identity' or a cohesive 'self' serves as an extremely valuable metaphor for the vital experience of relative

wholeness, continuity, and cohesion in self-experience. Yet, as has often been noted, when we look within the psyche of well-put-together individuals, we actually see a 'multiplicity of selves' or versions of the self coexisting within certain contours and patterns that, in sum, produce a sense of individuality, 'I-ness' or 'me-ness'. . . . Although the coexistence of 'multiple versions of the self' that we observe introspectively and clinically may thus represent crystallizations of different interactional schemes, this multiplicity may also signal the existence of *an inner, functional limit on the process of self-integration* . . . The cost of our human strategy for structuring the self in a provisional fashion – around a sometimes precarious confederation of alternate self/other schemas – lies in the ever-present risk of states of relative disintegration, fragmentation, or identity diffusion. The maintenance of self-cohesion . . . should thus be one of the most central ongoing activities of the psyche . . . [but] the strivings of such an evolved 'superordinate self' would emanate . . . *not primarily from a fragmentation induced by trauma or environmental failure to fully provide its mirroring (self–object) functions.* Rather, its intrinsic strivings would emanate from the very design of the self-system.

(Slavin and Kriegman 1992: 204–205, italics added)

The implications of this are profound for the psychoanalytic understanding of self and how to facilitate its therapeutic growth. I've proposed (Bromberg 1993, 1998) that health is the ability to stand in the spaces between realities without losing any of them – the capacity to feel like one self while being many. 'Standing in the spaces' is a shorthand way of describing a person's relative capacity to make room at any given moment for subjective reality that is not readily containable by the self he or she experiences as 'me' at that moment. It is what distinguishes creative imagination from both fantasy and concreteness, and distinguishes playfulness from facetiousness.

Some people can stand in the spaces better than others. Some people can't stand in the spaces at all, and in these individuals we see the prototype of a psyche organized more centrally by dissociation than by repression. The key quality of a highly dissociated personality organization is its defensive dedication to retaining the protection afforded by the separateness of self states (their discontinuity), and minimizing their potential for simultaneous accessibility to consciousness, so that each shifting 'truth' can continue to play its own role without interference by the others, creating a personality structure that one of my patients described as 'having a whim of iron'.

When pathological dissociation is operating, whether it is central to the personality or an isolated area of serious trouble in an otherwise well-functioning individual, the issues of a person's shifting experience of time and how the analyst regards the phenomenon of timelessness are especially important here. Bollas (1989) and Ogden (1989) have in fact each developed the idea of *historical consciousness* as a mental capacity that must be achieved. Ogden writes that

> it is by no means to be assumed that the patient has a history (that is, a sense of historicity) at the beginning of analysis. In other words, we cannot take for granted the idea that the patient has achieved a sense of continuity of self over time, such that his past feels as if it is connected to his experience of himself in the present.
>
> (Ogden 1989: 191)

Until then, what we call 'resistance' to interpretation is often simply evidence that some dissociated voice is experiencing the analyst's words as disconfirming its existence.

In order for authentic therapeutic growth in personality to take place, the inherent decentredness of the self and the inherent nonlinearity of its development must be fully accepted by the analyst. This in turn will allow the analyst to recognize and work with dissociation as a phenomenon that is fundamentally perceptual and secondarily cognitive; in other words, dissociation as a *process* must be addressed as a here-and-now interpersonal event in order for intrapsychic dissociative *structure* to be altered.

Dissociation as an interpersonal process

Dissociative processes operate in both patient and analyst as a dynamic element in the therapeutic relationship, an observation that traditionally has been made only with reference to the treatment of extreme psychopathology or severe dissociative disorders. I am suggesting however, that this statement is true as a general phenomenon of human behaviour and relevant to any therapist working with any patient within an analytically informed frame of reference, regardless of theoretical persuasion.

Peter Fonagy and his associates (Fonagy 1991; Fonagy and Moran 1991; Fonagy and Target 1995) have offered a perspective on the relationship between conflict and dissociation that places both phenomena within a clinical model that incorporates developmental and cognitive research, object relational thinking, and a postclassical interpersonal sensibility. Fonagy writes:

> We take the position that the greater the unevenness in development, the less effective will be a technique which relies solely upon intepretations of conflict, and the greater will be the need to devise strategies of analytic intervention aimed to support and strengthen the child's capacity to tolerate conflict.
>
> (Fonagy and Moran 1991: 16)

Similarly, and even more to the point:

> Interpretations may remain helpful but their function is certainly no
> longer limited to the lifting of repression and the addressing of distorted
> perceptions and beliefs. . . . *Their goal is the reactivation of the patient's*
> *concern with mental states, in himself and in his object.*
>
> (Fonagy and Target 1995: 498–499, italics added)

Pathological dissociation is a defensive impairment of reflective capacity
brought about by detaching the mind from the self – what Winnicott (1949)
called the 'psyche soma'. In the analytic relationship, such patients (individuals dedicated to the avoidance of reflection) are in need of 'recognition'
rather than understanding, but if an analyst is to help someone who is dedicated to the avoidance of reflection, it is necessary for him or her to accept
that the 'act of recognition', both developmentally and therapeutically, is
a dyadic process – a 'two-way street' of mutual regulation (Beebe and
Lachmann 1992; Beebe et al. 1992). Consider what Fonagy and Target (1995)
have to say about this:

> We believe that the developmental help offered by the active involvement
> of the analyst in the mental functioning of the patient, and *the reciprocal*
> *process of the patient becoming actively involved in the analyst's mental*
> *state*, has the potential to establish this reflection and gradually to allow
> the patient to do this within his own mind. . . . *The critical step may be the*
> *establishment of the patient's sense of identity through the clarification of*
> *the patient's perception of the analyst's mental state.* . . . It seems
> that gradually this can offer a third perspective, opening up a space for
> thinking between and about the patient and the analyst.
>
> (Fonagy and Target 1995: 498–499, italics added)

A space for thinking *between and about* the patient and the analyst – a space
uniquely relational and still uniquely individual; a space belonging to neither
person alone, and yet, belonging to both and to each; a twilight space in
which 'the impossible' becomes possible; a space in which incompatible
selves, each awake to its own 'truth', can 'dream' the reality of the other
without risk to its own integrity. It is above all an intersubjective space which,
like the 'trance' state of consciousness just prior to entering sleep, allows both
wakefulness and dreaming to coexist. Here in the interpersonal field
constructed by patient and analyst, such a space is opened in the service of
therapeutic growth, and the implacable enemies, 'hope and dread' (Mitchell
1993), because they can each find voice, can potentially find dialogue. How is
this phenomenon possible? My answer, in its most general and oversimplified
form, is that the reciprocal process of active involvement with the states of
mind of 'the other' allows a patient's here-and-now perception of self to

share consciousness with the experiences of incompatible self-narratives that were formerly dissociated.

What is the analyst's role in this asymmetrical dyadic process that permits such a space to open? Because of the way dissociation functions interpersonally, unsymbolized aspects of the patient's self are routinely enacted with the analyst as a separate and powerful channel of communication in the clinical process – a channel that is multifaceted and continually in motion. One dimension of analysts' listening stances should therefore be dedicated to their ongoing experience of the here-and-now at the same time that their focal attention may be elsewhere. That is, no matter how 'important' the manifest verbal content appears to be at a given moment, analysts should try to remain simultaneously attuned to their subjective experience of the relationship and its shifting quality. Optimally, they should try to be experientially accessible to (a) the impact of those moments in which they become aware that a shift in self state (either their own or their patients') has taken place and (b) *the details of their own self-reflection* on whether to process this awareness with their patients or to process it alone – and if with their patients, when and how to do it. Are analysts reluctant to 'intrude' upon their patients at that moment? Do they feel protective of their patients' need for safety and vulnerability to traumatization? Do they feel pulled in two directions about whether to speak? Do they feel strangely paralysed by being unable to move in both directions simultaneously, as if they must somehow choose between their own self-expression and their patient's vulnerability? If so, can they find a way to use this very experience of their felt constriction of freedom? Would the act of sharing this entire sequence of thought, along with the moment that led to it, be a useful choice in this instance? I believe that, at any point in time, the questions themselves are of greater value than the answers as long as analysts remain open to exploring the impact of their choice rather than seeing their choice as either correct or wrong. In my own work, I find that even when I choose not to openly share my experience with my patient, my conscious *awareness* of the shift in the intersubjective field, because it changes my mode of processing what is being heard, is invariably picked up by my patient and eventually becomes 'usable' because I am no longer hearing the patient's words and my own in the context I was hearing them before the shift. I am now experiencing their meaning being shaped by the participation of another aspect of the patient's self that has been engaged with an aspect of my own self in enacting something beyond what the words had earlier appeared to be conveying.

Dissociation and self-reflection

From my perspective, the capacity for self-reflection is a matter of the degree to which self states are dissociated from one another. What I call the structural shift from dissociation to conflict is clinically represented by the increasing capacity of the patient to adopt a self-reflective posture in which one aspect of the self observes and reflects (often with distaste) upon others that were formerly dissociated. There are always self states that are enacting their experience because they are not symbolized cognitively as 'me' in the here-and-now of a given moment. For the most part this creates no problem within normal, healthy human discourse. It is where these self states are experienced as 'not-me' and are discontinuous with other modes of defining self and reality that the trouble occurs. For most patients, though to different degrees, I see the goal as being able to first accept, as a valid mental state in itself, the experience of observing and reflecting upon the existence of other selves that it hates, would like to disown, but can't. In some patients this initial shift in perception is dramatic, and involves a major personality reorganization. In its most extreme form this transition is paradigmatic in the successful treatment of severe dissociative disorders, but the basic transition is one that I have encountered in every analysis during all phases. If the transition is successfully negotiated, an opportunity has been provided for an internal linking process to take place between a patient's dissociated self states by broadening his or her perceptual range of reality in the transference/ countertransference field. In the linking process, fantasy, perception, thought and language each play their part, providing the patient is not pressured to choose between which reality is more 'objective' (Winnicott 1951) and which self is more 'true' (Winnicott 1960, 1971a, 1971b).

For example, after a session with one of my own patients that began with an uncharacteristically lengthy silence, broken by her saying quite matter-of-factly, and without any discernible anxiety or defensiveness, 'I'm having three different conversations with you today.' I replied, 'Different in what way?' My question was followed by another silence, this one more obviously organized by self-reflectiveness. 'Good question!' she stated.

> First I thought that the *topics* were different. But when you asked that question I started to realize that I didn't want to answer because there are really three different moods all at the same time, and I don't know which one I want to answer you from.

There could be no more clear evidence than this moment, to show that dissociation is not principally a mode of self-protection (even though it serves as such in the face of trauma). It can be seen here in its intrinsic form as the basis of creativity, playing, illusion and the use of potential space to further self-growth. It was shortly after this session that, following a typically unsatisfying phone conversation with her father, she described looking at herself in the mirror, hating her father, and watching her face while she was hating – playing with the facial expressions (cf. Winnicott 1971c), trying them out, enjoying the hateful feelings, but, as she put it, 'still feeling like "me" all the way through it'.

Standing in the spaces

As an enactment begins, an analyst will inevitably shift his or her self state when the patient shifts his or hers, but the phenomenon is always a two-way street. An enactment can just as easily begin with the analyst. Dissociation is a hypnoid process, and inasmuch as analyst and patient are sharing an event that belongs equally to both of them – the interpersonal field that shapes the immediate reality of each and the way they experience themselves and the other – any unsignalled withdrawal from that field by *either* person will disrupt the other's state of mind. Thus, when an enactment begins (no matter by whom it is initiated), no analyst can be immediately attuned to the shift in here-and-now reality, and the analyst inevitably becomes part of the dissociative process, at least for a period of time. Analysts are often in a hypnoid state qualitatively similar to that which their patients are in and sometimes become fixated, concretely, upon the verbal content of the session; the words begin to take on an 'unreal' quality, and this is frequently what 'wakes analysts up' to the fact that something is 'going on'. They have been hypnoidally dissociated from that part of themselves that was participating in the enactment, but once they regain access to it they will no longer be 'asleep' to the fact that their patients, although using words, are equally 'asleep' to the here-and-now *experience* between them. A dissociated self state of the patient holding another reality – one that sometimes is fiercely opposing the one being talked about – may then start to gain a voice.

Transference and the 'real' relationship

Analysts, guided by their patients and by their own experience of personal authenticity, allow themselves to form relationships with each of the patient's selves or self states to the degree that each patient allows it, and in each relationship analysts have an opportunity to creatively utilize a range of their own states of consciousness. Often, a particular self state of the patient has never before been drawn out in its own terms so that it can, without shame, communicate to another human being its unique sense of self, purpose, personal history and personal 'truth'. In my own work, this experience has at times led directly to the source of a symptom or behaviour pattern that has been until then 'resistant' to change, as for example, in the case of a patient who had suffered many years with an eating disorder, and then revealed one day that she finally discovered why she binged. 'I do it,' she said,

> because I feel my brain trying to switch to another consciousness and I want to stop it – so I eat or drink something cold to stimulate me in the moment. I need to stay awake, to stay grounded, and sometimes, when I'm afraid I'm not going to be able to, I eat something heavy like pasta or bagels.

The interplay between confrontation and empathy is interesting and especially relevant when working from the perspective of *multiple real relationships* rather than 'a real relationship and a transferential relationship'. Each of the patient's dissociated self states does what it does because it sees a single 'truth' that it tries to act upon, but on the other hand each has its own reason for existing and will not rewrite its reality to suit an analyst's personal belief system of what defines 'growth'. The optimal analytic stance is in this light a negotiated dialectic between attunement and confrontation, or (to express it in a slightly different frame of reference) between 'empathy and anxiety' (Bromberg 1980). There is no way that one's personal narrative of 'who I am' ever changes directly; it cannot be cognitively edited and replaced by a better, more 'adaptive' one. Only a change in *perceptual* reality can alter the cognitive reality that defines the patient's internal object world, and this process requires an enacted collision of realities between patient and therapist. Analysts' struggles with their own confusion – their ability to make creative use of contradictory realities within a single analytic field without unduly inflicting their need for clarity of meaning upon their patient–play as much of a role in the analytic process as does empathy or interpretation individually. In other words, for patients to develop confidence in their growing ability to move from dissociation to intrapsychic conflict they must engage with their analyst in what I have elsewhere (Bromberg 1991) called the 'messy' parts of the analytic relationship. As the analyst furthers the capacity of the patient to hear in a single context the voices of other self states holding alternative realities that have been previously incompatible, the fear of traumatic flooding of affect decreases along with the likelihood that opposing realities will automatically try to obliterate each other. Because there is less opposition between aspects of self, there is less danger that any individual self state will use the gratification of being empathically supported in its own reality simply to further its individual sense of 'entitlement' to priority within the personality. Translated into the traditional metapsychology of 'pathological narcissism', a patient's investment in protecting the insularity of a so-called 'grandiose self' diminishes as the need for dissociation is surrendered and replaced by increased capacity to experience and resolve intrapsychic conflict.

Fonagy (1991: 641) labels the capacity to symbolize conscious and unconscious mental states in oneself and others as the capacity to 'mentalize', and writes that

> 'wholeness' is given to objects only through an understanding of the mental processes that provide an account of the object's actions in the physical world. Before mental states are conceived of, the mental representation of the object will be, by definition, partial, tied to specific situations . . . since the vital attribution of mental functioning is absent. . . . [Consequently], the distortion of mental representations of objects

through projection is unavoidable at this early stage. . . . Until the point is reached when mental states may be confidently attributed to the object there can be no capacity to limit this projection.

(Fonagy 1991: 641–642)

In individuals where the capacity to mentalize is severely impaired, dealing with this aspect of the transference may be considered a precondition of analytic treatment . . . failure to achieve this may lead patients to treat interpretations as assaults and analytic ideas as abusive intrusions.

(Fonagy 1991: 652, italics added)

Psychoanalysis is at its core a highly specialized communicative field, and what constitutes a psychoanalytically meaningful moment is constantly in motion with regard to one's experience of both reality and temporality. The shifting quality of time and meaning reflects the enactment of self states in both patient and analyst that define the multiplicity of relationships that go on between the patient's selves and the analyst's selves, only some of which are being focused on at any given moment. As an analyst opposes, is opposed by, affirms and is affirmed by each dissociated aspect of the patient's self as it oscillates – in its cycle of projection and introjection – between his or her own inner world and that of the patient, the energy the patient has used in sustaining the dissociative structure of his or her mind will be enlisted by the patient in vitalizing a broadening experience of 'me-ness'. Because this less dissociated configuration of selfhood is *simultaneously* adaptational and self-expressive, certain self states do not have to continue to remain unable to participate in living except as 'on call' watchdogs that suddenly and unexpectedly seem to become possessed by an 'irrational' need to make a mess.

Used judiciously, I have found that an approach which addresses the multiplicity of self is so experience-near to most patients' subjective reality, that only rarely does someone even comment on why I am talking about them in 'that way'. It leads to a greater feeling of wholeness (not *dis*integration) because each self state comes to attain a clarity and personal significance that gradually alleviates patients' previously held sense of confusion about who they 'really' are and how they came, historically, to be this person. And for therapists, it is not necessary to work as hard to figure out what is going on, what has gone on in the past, and what things 'mean'. They engage in a dialogue with that self that is present at the moment, and find out from that self, in detail, its own story, rather than trying to approximate it. All told, it facilitates an analyst's ability to help his patient develop increased capacity for a life that includes, in Loewald's (1972: 409) language, a past, a present and a future as mutually interacting modes of time.

Acknowledgements

Modified version of 'Standing in the spaces: the multiplicity of self and the psychoanalytic relationship, *Contemporary Psychoanalysis* (1996). 32:509–535 reprinted by permission of Contemporary Psychoanalysis © 1996 Contemporary Psychoanalysis.

References

Balint, M. (1968). *The Basic Fault*. London: Tavistock.
Beebe, B. and Lachmann, F.M. (1992). 'The contribution of mother–infant mutual influence to the origins of self- and object representations.' In N.J. Skolnick and S.C. Warshaw (eds) *Relational Perspectives in Psychoanalysis* (pp. 83–117). Hillsdale, NJ: Analytic Press.
Beebe, B., Jaffe, J. and Lachmann, F.M. (1992). 'A dyadic systems view of communication.' In N.J. Skolnick and S.C. Warshaw (eds) *Relational Perspectives in Psychoanalysis* (pp. 61–81). Hillsdale, NJ: Analytic Press.
Bollas, C. (1989). *Forces of Destiny: Psychoanalysis and the Human Idiom*. London: Free Association.
Bromberg, P.M. (1980). 'Empathy, anxiety, and reality: A view from the bridge.' *Contemporary Psychoanalysis*, *16*, 223–236.
Bromberg, P.M. (1991). 'On knowing one's patient inside out: The aesthetics of unconscious communication.' *Psychoanalytic Dialogues*, *1*, 399–422.
Bromberg, P.M. (1993). 'Shadow and substance: A relational perspective on clinical process.' *Psychoanalytic Psychology*, *10*, 147–168.
Bromberg, P.M. (1998). *Standing in the Spaces: Essays on Clinical Process, Trauma and Dissociation*. Hillsdale, NJ: Analytic Press.
Fairbairn, W.R.D. (1944). 'Endopsychic structure considered in terms of object-relationships.' In W.R.D. Fairbairn (1992). *Psychoanalytic Studies of the Personality* (pp. 82–132). London: Routledge.
Fairbairn, W.R.D. (1952). *An Object Relations Theory of the Personality*. New York: Basic Books.
Fonagy, P. (1991). 'Thinking about thinking: Some clinical and theoretical considerations in the treatment of a borderline patient.' *International Journal of Psycho-Analysis*, *72*, 639–656.
Fonagy, P. and Moran, G.S. (1991). 'Understanding psychic change in child psychoanalysis.' *International Journal of Psycho-Analysis*, *72*, 15–22.
Fonagy, P. and Target, M. (1995). 'Understanding the violent patient: The use of the body and the role of the father.' *International Journal of Psycho-Analysis*, *76*, 487–501.
Hermans, H.J.M., Kempen, H.J.G. and van Loon, R.J.P. (1992). 'The dialogical self: Beyond individualism and rationalism.' *American Psychologist*, *47*, 23–33.
Laing, R.D. (1960). *The Divided Self*. London: Tavistock.
Loewald, H.W. (1972). 'The experience of time.' *Psychoanalytic Study of the Child*, *27*, 401–410.
Mitchell, S.A. (1991). 'Contemporary perspectives on self: Toward an integration.' *Psychoanalytic Dialogues*, *1*, 121–147.

Mitchell, S.A. (1993). *Hope and Dread in Psychoanalysis*. New York: Basic Books.

Ogden, T.H. (1989). *The Primitive Edge of Experience*. Northvale, NJ: Jason Aronson.

Searles, H.F. (1977). 'Dual- and multiple-identity processes in borderline ego functioning.' In P. Hartocollis (ed.) *Borderline Personality Disorders* (pp. 441–455).' New York: International Universities Press.

Slavin, M.O. and Kriegman, D. (1992). *The Adaptive Design of the Human Psyche*. New York: Guilford.

Sorenson, R.L. (1994). 'Therapists' (and their therapists') God representations in clinical practice.' *Journal of Psychology and Theology, 22*, 325–344.

Stein, G. (1937/1993). *Everybody's Autobiography*. Cambridge, MA: Exact Change.

Sullivan, H.S. (1940). *Conceptions of Modern Psychiatry*. New York: Norton.

Sullivan, H.S. (1953). *The Interpersonal Theory of Psychiatry*. New York: Norton.

Turkle, S. (1978/1992). *Psychoanalytic Politics: Jacques Lacan and Freud's French Revolution*, rev. edn. New York: Guilford.

Winnicott, D.W. (1945). 'Primitive emotional development.' In D.W. Winnicott (1958). *Collected Papers: Through Paediatrics to Psycho-Analysis* (pp. 145–156). London: Tavistock.

Winnicott, D.W. (1949). 'Mind and its relation to the psyche-soma.' In *Collected Papers: Through Paediatrics to Psycho-Analysis* (pp. 243–254). London: Tavistock.

Winnicott, D.W. (1951). 'Transitional objects and transitional phenomena.' In *Collected Papers: Through Paediatrics to Psycho-Analysis* (pp. 229–242). London: Tavistock.

Winnicott, D.W. (1960). 'Ego distortion in terms of true and false self.' In D.W. Winnicott (1965). *The Maturational Processes and the Facilitating Environment* (pp. 140–152). New York: International Universities Press.

Winnicott, D.W. (1971a). 'The location of cultural experience.' In *Playing and Reality* (pp. 95–103). New York: Basic Books.

Winnicott, D.W. (1971b). 'The place where we live.' In *Playing and Reality* (pp. 104–110). New York: Basic Books.

Winnicott, D.W. (1971c). 'Dreaming, fantasying, and living: A case-history describing a primary dissociation.' In *Playing and Reality* (pp. 26–37). New York: Basic Books.

Young, W.C. (1988). 'Psychodynamics and dissociation'. *Dissociation, 1*, 33–38.

Chapter 10

The psychodramatic 'social atom method' with children

A developing dialogical self in dialectic action

Leni M.F. Verhofstadt-Denève, Let Dillen, Denis Helskens and Mariska Siongers

This chapter describes the construction of a semi-structured protocol of the action sociogram for 6- to 12-year-old children. The first section outlines the basic characteristics of a development-oriented theory, the Phenomenological-Dialectic Personality model (Phe-Di PModel). The second section demonstrates how – within this theoretical framework – the psychodramatic social atom can be applied to school-aged children. The social atom enables the children to devise a spatial scene in which they use puppets to represent themselves in relation to significant others. This action method makes it possible to externalize the child's multiple self-constructions and the internal self-dialogues. Moreover, we think that the action sociogram can be understood as an intense situational-affective experience of dialectic oppositions, in which emotions, actions, cognitions, language and effective learning can be integrated.

A development-oriented therapeutic theory

The Phenomenological-Dialectic Personality model

The Phe-Di PModel – as constructed by Verhofstadt-Denève (2000, 2003) on the basis of practical work – aims to describe, explain and stimulate developments occurring in the course of a lifetime. The core idea is that personal oppositions can effect qualitative changes via inherently dialectic processes and that the content of these processes is characterized by existential themes.

The *phenomenological aspect* refers to the content which individuals design about themselves, significant others and their surroundings (Verhofstadt-Denève 2000, 2003). The model describes the person as a dynamically developing relation between I and Me, the I as the subject pole (see James's 'self-as-knower') being able to reflect on the Me, the object pole (see James's 'self-as-known').

The reflection of I on Me generates six fundamental questions, leading to six phenomenological self-constructions or dimensions of the self:

- Who was I, am I and will I be with my shortcomings and my potential in this world? Answers reflect the *Self-Image*.
- This Self-Image is continuously compared with the perception that we have of other people. The answer to 'Who are the others in their world at this moment, in the past or in the future?' constitutes the *Alter-Image*.
- If one tries to form an idea of how one's own person is viewed by the others ('What perception and/or expectations do the others have of me and my world at the different time dimensions?') one is constructing the *Meta-Self*.

These three dimensions are counterbalanced by their corresponding ideal-images:

- Who would I like to be in a world I would like to live in? The *Ideal-Self*.
- What should the others be like in a world they should like to live in? *Ideal-Alter*.
- How should the others perceive me and my ideal world? *Ideal-Meta-Self*.

The I–Me reflection encompasses more than the conventional self-reflection, since the object pole comprises subjective interpretations not only of the self but also of the social and object world. The Me can be seen as the objectified result of a 'multivoiced' self with six parts that can interact or conflict with each other.

The same basic structure applies to each of the six constructions: differentiation between personality characteristics and conditions, a time dimension with past, present as well as future situations, a distinction between internal aspects (what we feel and think) and external aspects (how we act towards the outside world) and different levels of awareness, ranging from unaware to fully aware.

While the dimensions of the self constitute the content of the personality model, the moving force of the development process is *dialectics*. It is the very nature of dialectic processes that a higher synthesis is achieved through double negation (for concrete examples: see protocol). The synthesis – or *Aufhebung* – comprises at once the preservation, the annihilation and the raising to a higher level of conflicting but complementary poles (Verhofstadt-Denève 2000). This view has a significant effect on the positive interpretation of oppositions,[1] as a conflict is seen as a potential for change. The Phe-Di PModel assumes that the six constructions can be dialectically opposed so that development becomes possible.

The dialogue between the multiple selves connected to the different phenomenological dimensions is the basis for stimulating personality development into the greatest possible actualization of the self, all the while maintaining a harmonious relationship with significant others. The interrelational activity, between the self and others,[2] is the primary requirement for this kind of personality development.[3] Action and drama techniques can stimulate these self-dialogues in a secure atmosphere through concrete-spatial action.

Origin and development of I–Me dynamics

In view of the adaptation of the protocol, the question is raised to what extent the primary-school children (6–12 years)[4] can use their cognitive and social-emotional skills to integrate self-reflection and self-knowledge (Self-Image), reflection on and empathy with the other (Alter-Image and Meta-Self) and reflection on the world, including possible divergences between subjective constructions and 'objective' reality. At the core is the general problem of the development of children's understanding of mind.

According to Piaget's early writings this development runs parallel to general cognitive development; mental phenomena are highly confusing to young children because of their non-substantial nature. This difficulty in understanding mental states is extended into *middle childhood*. Although the child learns to organize experienced reality systematically and is capable of taking several dimensions into account within a given situation, (social) cognitive understanding remains largely dependent on the tangible representation of reality. It is for instance assumed that the child does not develop role-taking skills until the age of 7–8 and that profound hypothetical thinking is impossible until adolescence.[5] Within this frame of reference, the incipient reflection on and differentiation of the self (Self-Image) and others (Alter-Image) is situated at the age of 7–8, when the transition from egocentrism to decentration takes place. Indeed, the dialectics of assimilation and accommodation create a transition from external to internal I–Me dynamics, which makes an incipient form of self-reflection possible.

Recent studies within the *theory of mind* tradition have qualified Piaget's claims. For instance, children are assumed to acquire an understanding of the relations between their own mental states, the world and action even during the first years of their lives (Scholl and Leslie 2001). The possession of a 'theory of mind' implies the use of someone's convictions and desires in order to understand, explain and predict his or her behaviour. Such a reasoning carries the possibility for the simultaneous comparison of representations of mental states of themselves and others, as well as representations of the world and an understanding of the relation between these mental representations of the world and the resulting convictions (Templeton and Wilcox 2000). In contrast with Piaget's views, the *early competence theory* proposed by Leslie and colleagues states that theory-of-mind acquisition takes place universally, rapidly and at a very early stage (Scholl and Leslie 2001). Even at the age of 2, children are believed to acquire our mental terminology and use it appropriately in daily life (Perner, Frith, Leslie and Leekman 1989). The age between 3 and 5 is assumed to be characterized by a developing power of reflection on others' minds and a rapidly changing understanding of the psychic basis of human actions (Dunn, Brown, Slomkowski, Tesla and Youngblade 1991). Studies suggest a shift from an understanding of desire and emotions to an understanding of beliefs, thoughts and knowledge (Wellman 2002). The initial explanation of human action on the basis of the actor's wishes, desires, hopes and intentions is complemented at the age of 4–5 by a contemplation of human action in terms of representational mental states, such as thoughts, representations and knowledge. At this age, children start comprehending something of the subjectivity and consequently the diversity of thoughts. This suggests that they can differentiate between the perspective of themselves on the one hand and the perspective of someone else on the other. It also indicates that the young school-age child is capable of contemplating more than one representation simultaneously (Templeton and Wilcox 2000). At around the age of 6, children are assumed to have representational skills that are similar to those of adults and they start developing the capacity for second-order belief attributions ('Mary thinks that John thinks that . . .') (Perner et al. 1989). These metarepresentational skills, together with the understanding of interpretative diversity, will be developed fully around the age of 8 (Taylor, Cartwright and Bowden 1991).

Results within this research tradition enable us to situate the different reflection capacities at an early stage in childhood. This early psychological conceptualization is largely confined to emotional and situational attributions and the still developing capacity for contemplating different representations simultaneously. In other words, the Self- and Alter-Images will be construed mainly by means of emotions, desires and concrete information. From the age of 6 or 7 onwards, the child will learn to fully appreciate the interpretative nature of representations.[6] In other words, there is an enrichment of the phenomenological images. The internal aspect of the Self-Image and the Alter-Image can now be supplemented with representational information. In addition, children acquire the capacity for attributing second-order beliefs, which makes the construction of the Meta-Self possible.

Ideal Images are formed on the basis of early comparisons of Self-Image, Alter-Image and Meta-Self. During childhood the different – possible contradictory – features of the self-constructions are joined together.[7] According to Harter (1998), the capacity for bidirectional thinking installs the incipient possibility of coexisting positive and negative self-evaluations, which creates a more accurate Self-Image and more general self-evaluations.

Although the building blocks of the Phenomenological-Dialectic Personality model are present at the end of primary school age, the organization of the whole still has to be achieved (mainly during adolescence).[8]

Dialectic action: psychodrama and the social atom

Development of psychodrama and the social atom

In 1920 Moreno created *psychodrama* – 'the science to explore the truth by dramatic methods' (Moreno 1946). The concept is intrinsically linked with Moreno's basic philosophy, which regards man as a social interacting being (Marineau 1989). Our social matrix influences and guides our actions and self-perceptions and underlies our personal identity (Davies 1987). As social relations were seen to be so important, a central theoretical and procedural psychodrama construct was developed, namely the *social atom theory* (Taylor 1984), a theory of relations constituting a psychological, social and cultural framework in order to describe and explain how people build up and maintain long-term relationships (Remer 2001).

The social atom is the diagram of 'the smallest nucleus of all individuals with whom a person is related in a most significant manner constituting negative and positive emotional bonds' (Moreno 1934). The therapeutic impact of the social atom is enhanced by means of the *spatial* activation of the social atom in the action sociogram (Anderson-Klontz, Dayton and Anderson-Klontz 1999). The action sociogram is a psychodramatic method which allows the protagonists to portray their significant others (via group members or objects) spatially in a rational-affective distance to themselves and to each other. The protagonists are thus able to enter upon a dialogue between the self and his significant antagonists. The I constructs a 'multi-voiced' world in which the individual can talk not only *about* a variety of imaginary others (antagonists), but also *with* them as a relatively independent parts of a wider self (Hermans 2003). The action sociogram is distinctive in that the dialectic makes for an intense integration of emotions, cognitions, language, action and effective learning.

In view of the current interest in accountability and evidence-based pro-ceeding, psychodramatists need to concentrate on weaknesses, unambiguous conceptualizations, protocols and reporting on techniques (Kane 1992) and on a more solid personality theory (Kellermann 1987a, 1987b; Kipper 1978, 1997, 1998). This chapter is part of the attempts to update psychodrama. It tries to found the action sociogram on a development-oriented theory of psychotherapy to make this technique adapted for the work with children, and to facilitate the evaluation of effects by means of clearer descriptions in the protocol.

Construction of a semi-structured protocol for children

The scenario of the action sociogram for adults (Verhofstadt-Denève 2003) served as the basis for this study, the same multistage *structure* being used to find out what adaptations were necessary to suit the primary school children.

In a first stage, phenomenological reality is exteriorized via the puppets (stage A). The second stage offers the opportunity to explore the ideal images (stage B). Further stages (C and D), though relevant, are not considered in this chapter. The practical work showed that the following adaptations had to be made.

Individual sessions

Although the original scenario called for a group setting, preference was given to individual one-hour sessions, because of the children's attention span and motivation.

Addition of pet animals and fantasy figures

Practice showed that the introduction of pet animals and fantasy figures was essential. They are part and parcel of the child's phenomenological reality.

From chairs to puppets

Initially we used chairs to represent him- or herself in relation to significant others. Puppets were substituted for chairs for four reasons: first, children found the chairs dull and boring. Second, speaking through the puppets acts as a buffer against reality, which the child may find threatening. The director and the co-director also used puppets as symbols for themselves through which they addressed the I-puppet and other puppets directly. When chairs were used, the children seemed to have difficulties with the transition from the Self-Images to Alter-Images and Meta-Selves. We noticed that using puppets instead of chairs facilitated this transition. Third, the puppets constitute projection screens since (a) they create distance ('they are not my family, they are merely puppets') and (b) their connotations are not threatening, they have a human shape and they can be manipulated by putting clothes on them. Fourth, the puppets introduce curiosity, playfulness and unpredictability.

The children create their phenomenological reality on the stage; they choose which puppet is going to play, clothe the puppets and represent the concrete image they have of themselves and the others.

Avoidance of lengthy proceedings

Children's limited attention span requires some further changes in the scenario. First, rigidity and standardized questions need to be avoided. If children are to remain motivated, it is important to deal with each situation creatively. Second, a change in the order of role-taking turned out to be necessary. Initially, the first step was to have all the puppets take a role, after which each puppet's Meta-Self was investigated. This procedure was laborious; the children's attention quickly waned and information on the Meta-Self was scarce. We therefore questioned the Alter-Image and the Meta-Self at the same time. Third, the sessions were reduced to one hour instead of four hours. Fourth it is recommended to deal with stages A and B in separate sessions in order to avoid confusion.

Transition from the concrete to the abstract

The construction of ideal-images requires abstract thinking, the ability to make simultaneous comparisons of self-images and an effective capacity for mutual role-taking. These are skills which, although they are potentially present in the latency child, are not fully developed until adolescence. This difficulty became apparent in stage B. Although the children were well able to stage an ideal reality with the aid of the puppets, the transfer to everyday reality proved to be laborious. This could be rectified by phrasing the questions in such a way that reality was strongly emphasized: 'The way things are at home, what would you like to change?' Likewise, the question of how to stage ideal reality needed to be tackled in a different way, for the children's answers did not go beyond the concrete level (e.g. 'move the chairs closer'). This can be solved by means of doubling by the co-director. In doubling, the co-director verbalizes what he or she thinks the person is thinking or feeling or what information is possibly lacking. Such doublings enable the co-director to make third-person information more explicit.

Probing the Self-Image through questions in specific areas

Children younger than 8 find it difficult to achieve overall self-evaluations and instead focus on specific areas. Therefore questions about overall self-evaluation ('What do you think of yourself?') are replaced with questions about specific areas. Later in the chapter all these recommendations will be illustrated.

Clinical work

Illustration of the semi-structured protocol for children

We will now describe and comment on a few episodes from our clinical work with an 11-year-old boy. John was referred to a psychiatric centre because of oppositional and aggressive behaviour. After an assessment period the following diagnosis was proposed:

- Axis I: Disorganized attachment disorder and post-traumatic stress disorder as a result of a history of multiple abuses. John has been sexually abused by his maternal grandparents, uncle and great-uncle. His mother

forced John to make sexual advances on his sister and his stepfather beat
him several times.

- Axis II: Light mental retardation (mental age estimated at 6–7 years).
- Axis III: Epilepsy and nocturnal enuresis.
- Axis IV: Problems within primary support group: neglect, maltreatment,
  sexual abuse.

This co-morbid diagnosis legitimized a long-term residential therapeutic programme in which the social atom method was introduced because of its
potentials in the field of self-appreciation, relationships with significant
others and self-insight.

Sessions comments

Cast of characters:

- P = Protagonist (John): the protagonist is the person whose life (or
  aspects of his life) is explored in the psychodrama session. It is the protagonist who determines the pace of the session and the themes dealt
  with.
- DR = Director (Denis): the DR follows the patient's pace and theme; he
  does not prod, he stimulates (Meillo 1984). Yet the DR should use his
  questions to structure the session.
- CO = Co-director (Mariska): the CO forms an extension of both the
  Protagonist (expressing the protagonist's images, cognitions and affects)
  and the Director (exploring and steering).

Session 1 stage A: concretizing of phenomenological reality

After an initial warming-up exercise the social atom is introduced. The child
dresses every puppet and gives it a mouth and a wig. The protagonist starts
with a puppet for himself; next, he dresses his mother, brother and sister. The
director and co-director also make a puppet for themselves (Figure 10.1).
When John has dressed up a puppet for himself, his mother, brother and
sister, the director asks the following question:

DR: Wonderful! Who else is there in your family?
P: The bad one.
DR: The bad one?
P: My dad is too weak, you know!
DR: What does your dad look like?
P: I'm going to dress him in the filthiest clothes I can find.

Selecting and dressing a puppet is a first action-oriented exploration of the
external aspects (and projections of internal aspects) of the Self-Image and

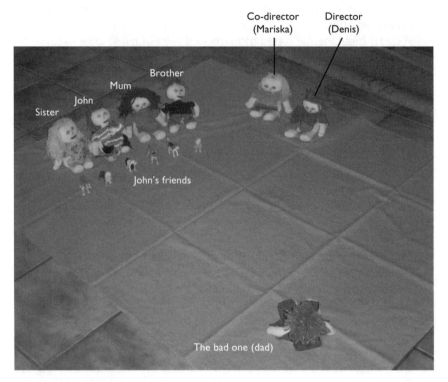

Figure 10.1 The puppets in session 1

Alter-Image. The filthy clothes refer to an external aspect of the Alter-Image and are coloured by the negative feelings towards the father puppet. This Alter-Image is explored through questions.

P constructs his father as a bad person (internal Alter-Image). His mother – in contrast – will get an absolutistic all-good meaning for John (see further). Because of intense emotions and conflict, traumatized children fail partially to integrate different modes of relating internal experiences to the external situation (Fonagy and Target 1997). Disorganization of attachment leads to multiple, conflicting representations (Nicolai 2001a, 2001b). Familial abuse is seen as interacting with the domain- and situation-specific restrictions upon reflective function. John possesses the beginning ability to be reflective in general, but shows minimal reflectiveness in the familial context or relationships which activate the same schemata.

A blanket is spread on the ground and serves as the stage on which John is going to present his family.[9] From now on, the puppets are addressed directly. The director and co-director also sit down on the edge of the blanket, each with their puppet. First John introduces a puppet for himself, which he enacts (Self-Image):

DR: Hi John! You can stand or sit anywhere you like.

P (as John): Ah! (Places his puppet on the left side of the room)

DR: Is this where you want to be? Do you feel comfortable there?

P (as John): (nods).

DR: OK. Now John. . . . if your friends were asked 'what is John like . . .', what would they say?

P (as John): I don't know.

DR: What do you like?

P (as John): I like playing with my teddy bears; I'll show them to you (smiles, takes the dogs and places them on the blanket in front of him).

The question concerning the Meta-Self ('What would your friends think of you?') appears too difficult because of insufficient role-taking capacities, insufficient metarepresentational skills and an insufficient capacity for hypothetical thought. And yet, John's doubt can be construed as a first step towards reflection on the Meta-Self.

Next, aspects of the Self-Image (thesis) are probed. 'Who are you?' is replaced by 'What do you like?' (cf. difficulty of overall self-evaluation with 7 year olds). The protagonist installs the dogs at the metaphorical level in his internal Self-Image (i.e. interests) and gives them a protective and aggressive function (John will indicate later during the session that he needs these dogs for his protection). During the session John often 'growls'.

After introducing himself (Self-Image), John also stages the other family members. And that's when the puppets can start talking. Before a new puppet is brought into the room, we always return to the Self-Image (I-puppet).

DR: Fine, John. I suggest that we ask someone else of your family to come in. Who would you like to come in?

P (as John): My dearest, dearest mum!

DR: Ah, there's mum! Hi mum, do come in. Tell us: who are you, mum?

P (as mother): I am a mother of three children.

DR: Is there something you don't like?

P (as mother): I like almost everything, except when my darling is having a row.

DR: And John, what do you think of him?

P (as mother): He's a great boy. If a bad guy threatens me, John defends me, he is strong.

DR: Well, in that case John must like you very much.

P (as mother): Oh yes, he loves me. But his father? I don't know, we'll find out later.

DR: John, did you hear what your mum said?

P (as John): Yes, that's nice.

DR: Does this make you feel good?

P (as John): Yes, because my mother always likes me.

This passage illustrates the concrete probing of characteristics and conditions of the Alter-Image. Starting from the introduction of the Self-Image (thesis), the protagonist negates this Self-Image in moving to his internal Alter-Image ('my dearest, dearest mum'). This role-taking in the mother puppet comprises the dialectical antithesis stage, since the protagonist – by becoming his mother (Alter-Image) – ignores himself (Self-Image).

At the same time we see the internal (nice) and external (defence) Meta-Self: what mother thinks of John, according to the protagonist. In contrast with the first attempt to grasp the Meta-Self, the questioning and role-taking make the articulation of the Meta-Self possible.

Before the introduction of another puppet, there is a short reflection from the I-puppet – as a synthesis of the dialectic process. From the I-puppet, it is examined what John thinks of what mother has said. In doing so, John ignores the Alter-Image (i.e. his role-taking of his mother) and becomes himself again (Self-Image).

Now John is asked to give his mother a place on the stage. The emotional-affective distance is important here: someone who is important is placed nearby the I-puppet; someone who is less important or whom the protagonist has a conflictual relationship with, is kept at a greater distance. John places his mother close beside his I-puppet. Next, his brother and sister are introduced and are placed nearby the I-puppet as well.

The determination of the affective-emotional distance emphasizes the spatial dimension proper to the dynamic within a dialogical self. Mother is placed nearby, indicating that she is an important figure to John (social condition of the Self-Image).

The significant others and accessory self-constructs underscore the 'multi-facetedness' of the self, the action and enacting the 'multivoicedness' of the self. The different selves or I-positions are given an affective-situational concreteness by means of the puppets, which makes it possible to exteriorize internal dialogues into action.

DR: OK, John. Who can come in now?
P growls, barks and takes the dogs.
DR: Who are you, little dogs?
P (as dog): We are John's friends!

John places the dogs in a semicircle around himself, his mother, brother and sister.

DR: What are you doing, why are you standing there?
P (as dog): We are protecting John and the others . . .
DR: Who else have we forgotten?

P growls softly.
P (as John): The father.
DR: How do you call father?
P (as dad): The bad one.
DR: John, I'm now going to ask your dad.
P (as John): That's what he himself says, doesn't he?
DR: You think you're bad. Why?
P (as dad): Mum doesn't want me any more.
DR: And do you get on with your son John?
P (as dad): He is mean to me.
DR: What do you think John?
P (as John): Bad.

This enactment represents the internal Alter-Image (the bad one). At the same time, the fragment illustrates how difficult it is for John to enact the aggressor (when there is no mediation by the dogs). He initially doesn't speak from the father role but from himself; that is why the director 'repeats' the question. The Alter-Image and the Meta-Self ('John is mean to me') imply an antithesis *vis-à-vis* the Self-Image.

The return to the Self-Image comprises the synthesis in which an *Aufhebung* is reached via a double negation. Given John's serious traumatic anamnesis, the *Aufhebung* process is achieved only partially. The difficulty of reconstructing meaning may be part of (a) black-and-white thinking in which contrasts can only sporadically be offset and integrated (cf. mental age 6–7 years), (b) the insufficient capacity for real role-taking behaviour, and (c) the partially problematic reflective function caused by the disorganized attachment style. Given this background, the process as launched in the social atom, can only be a first realization for a further reconstruction of meaning within a longer therapeutic process.

At the end of this psychodrama session, the social atom is checked from above and John is given the opportunity to say something to every member of his family.

DR: Do you have something in mind? Are you going to say it loud or
           silently?
P (as John): I'm going to whisper.
P whispers something to the 'I-puppet', to his mother, brother and sister.
DR: You can also say something to your father.
P (as John): FUCK YOU!!!

The protagonist talks not only *about* but also *to* and *with* significant others (externalization of self-dialogues). After desymbolizing the puppets ('This is no longer John, it's just a puppet'), a short scene concludes the psychodrama.

The protagonist has the final say. Then the session is closed explicitly ('And this ends our puppet play'). Finally, it is checked whether the protagonist is in the here-and-now again by asking concrete questions, so that he doesn't remain fixed to the object projections.

Session 2 stage B: concretizing of the ideal phenomenological image

A connection is made with the previous session by reinstalling the actual phenomenological situation (stage A). John makes no major changes. Next, it is checked again from above whether this is the 'real' situation. This is followed by the move to the desired situation:

DR: This is the situation at home as it is now. Supposing you had magic power, what would you change at home?
P (as John): Remove Roger.
DR: Who is Roger? Dad?
P (as John): Yes.

Figure 10.2 The puppets in session 2

DR: OK, you can now do with the puppets whatever you like.

P (as John): I can do whatever I like?

DR: You can do whatever you like.

P (as John): Roger: throw away!

DR: That's OK. Do you want to throw him away?

P growls and barks.

P (as John): I can undress the puppet as well, can't I?

DR: You can do whatever you like. You can undress it.

P growls, barks, shouts. The dogs tear the clothes off the Dad- puppet and the
        puppet is thrown into a box which serves as jail (Figure 10.2).

P (as dad): Help!!!

DR: OK. Now we'll listen first. I'm first going to ask John what he
        thinks . . . John?

P (as John): Yes?

DR: Did you see what happened?

P (as John): Yes.

DR: And what do you think?

P (as John): Better.

DR: If this were to be the case, would you feel better?

P (as John): Well, the father is gone, isn't he?

DR: How does that make you feel?

P (as John): Me? He did mean things. He hit my mother and had a fight with
        her. Don't you understand?! Can't you get this into your head?
        Can't you get this into your head, stupid?

CO (doubles John's puppet Figure 10.2): I think that my father should be
        punished for all the bad things he's done. That's why I'm very
        angry with him.

P (as John): Right.

DR: Right. So Mariska is right?

P (as John): Yes.

DR: Could you say this in your own words?

P (as John): I'm saying that he should be sent to jail.

This passage illustrates the search for ideal constructions and 'possible selves'
as components of the 'multivoiced' self (Hermans 1996). Everything is
checked from above again to see whether this new situation is better for the
protagonist. After this general reflection, John and the other members of the
family are asked how they feel about this new situation. The I-puppet (Self-
Image) is constantly returned to in order to probe his thoughts and feelings.

CO (doubles John's puppet): I'm wondering whether dad is missing us, now
        that he's gone.

DR: Could John think this?

P laughs.

DR: Could John think that dad misses them? Do you think dad misses
           you?
P (as John): No . . . I don't know . . . He was mean; he hit my mother.

After every doubling, the protagonist should be asked whether the 'doubled'
statement is correct. The protagonist should then reformulate it in his own
words – the protagonist thus becomes co-investigator of his own phenomenological truth. The above doubling illustrates that storytelling is a co-
construction between the storyteller and the listener (Hermans 1996).
Doublings may include slight provocations/contradictions to stimulate the
reconstruction of meaning. With John as well, we see that after an initial 'no',
the doubling stimulates doubt ('I don't know') or a rudimentary type of
integrative reflection process.

Finally, John is allowed to say or whisper something to everyone, after
which the puppets are desymbolized and there's a short closing scene. Stages
C and D of the experimental version of the protocol are currently being
elaborated and are not illustrated in the present case.

Discussion

Our clinical work with John illustrates the first steps of a reflection process in
which meanings are reconstructed. This case study shows how the action
sociogram, if duly adjusted, can support and intensify the dialogical self-
processes even in children. The children are given the chance of actually
moving from one I-position to other positions (Hermans 2003), becoming
and meeting the antagonists in a concrete space and time (Verhofstadt-
Denève 2003). Moreover, the emotional-cognitive exploration of the
problem, via affective-situational actions, intensifies the learning process
(Verhofstadt-Denève 2003). Nevertheless, it proved difficult to launch an
explicitly dialectic process of reconstruction of meanings in just a few
sessions. This may be explained as follows.

First, the age of 7 is a major milestone in cognitive development. The
egocentric features gradually weaken, so that reflection on the (more objective) knowledge of the self, the others and the world grows. Before that age, the
child is limited to unidimensional or black-and-white thinking; before the age
of 6 or 7, children find it hard to cope with multirepresentationality or the
simultaneous contemplation of several conflictual representations (Templeton
and Wilcox 2000). In addition, children around this age develop an incipient,
clear understanding of interpretative diversity that needs to be consolidated
(Taylor et al. 1991). Now although John's biological age is 11, his mental age
of 6 to 7 years can partly explain the momentous breakthroughs of unidimensional and egocentric self-constructions and the difficulties he shows
with the second-order belief attributions.

Second, John has to cope with *severe psychic problems*, which affect his potential for reflection. Bowlby (1969) postulated a clear link between attachment disorders and psychic problems in later life. Attachment is a mental state or representation which organizes information about emotions and cognitions regarding the self and others, integrates affects and cognitions and makes memories accessible. Recent research has specified this link to Self-Image disorders and the processes which trigger the integration of Self-functions. Children with a disorganized attachment style are thought to have problems developing the reflective function, which comprises the ability to react to the behaviour of others and to conceive an idea of their beliefs, wishes, pretensions, plans and feelings. Evaluation and appreciation of significant others is a major determiner in the growth of a positive feeling of self-esteem (Harter 1998); the internalization of standards and evaluations of significant others co-determines the content of self-constructions. As a result, children growing up in dysfunctional families are more liable to develop negative perceptions, with all the accessory feelings of worthlessness, impotence and badness. This means that damage could occur in the Me (inter alia, greater discrepancies between the real and ideal selves, lower self-esteem, self-accusation) as well as in the I (inter alia, damaged self-coherence, diminished agency). This could be why traumatized children find it so much harder to achieve the integration of positive and negative self-evaluations (cf. all-or-nothing thinking or lack of reflexive function). We recognize all these limitations in John, as illustrated, for instance, in his inability to immerse himself in his father without the help of mediators.

These theoretical considerations lead to a number of issues to be examined. The first question that is raised is whether the laborious explicit *Aufhebung* of oppositions, as witnessed in John, is a major consequence of his insufficient cognitive development, a major consequence of his psychopathology, or an interaction of the two.

Second, the case study proves the practicability of the action sociogram in working with school-aged children. Stages A and B (i.e. the construction of phenomenological reality and the ideal situation, respectively) can be worked through, on condition that proceedings are based on concrete questions and direct spatial action and backed up by doubling.

NOTES

1 Yet, not all oppositions have a constructive effect (Verhofstadt-Denève 2000).
2 This importance of the interrelational activity between the self and others is also emphasized by Bakhtin. Indeed, it is in the actual interaction of a dialogue with others that we can know the third person's view of who we are. Without this perspective, our view of ourselves would remain incomplete. In addition, the inherent interpretation differences between two speakers of the same action makes that self and other are essentially in dialogue with each other (both at the interpersonal and intrapersonal level) (Barresi 2002).

3   The phenomenological constructions and internal dialogues constitute the basis
     for therapeutic work, and this goes for psychodrama too: 'The subject must act
     out "his truth" . . . Enactment comes first, retraining comes later' (Moreno and
     Moreno 1975/1959: 234).
4   This age limit serves as a guideline only and should not be taken too strictly.
5   In Selman's social perspective-taking model, we see that children acquire a rudi-
     mentary form of perspective-taking capacity at an early age. However, Selman
     suggests that in the period between ages 7 and 12, there is no self-reflective role-
     taking. A 5 year old already recognizes the subjective singularity of preferences
     and feelings and also realizes that others may have different feelings. However,
     only between ages 7 and 12 does the child begin to recognize that others make
     inferences about his or her thoughts and feelings. However, these stages have been
     criticized on the grounds that the research method has led to an underestimation
     of children's capacities.
6   Before this age, children do have the capacity for thinking about diversity through
     emotional responses but not through interpretative representations.
7   Up to middle adolescence, the multiple, situational selves remain compartmental-
     ized; they coexist alongside each other (Kunnen and Bosma 2000).
8   Research into the development of the dialogical self also suggests that – in spite
     of the fact that multiple selves occur in early childhood (Fogel, de Koeyer,
     Bellagamba and Bell 2002) – reflections on and dialogues between the different
     voices are not fully possible until late adolescence. The compartmentalization of
     the multiple selves then shifts to a higher level of integration.
9   The stage is the place where the psychodrama is enacted. Cuvelier (1993) clarifies
     that – irrespective of the use of a real stage – the creation of a symbolic space by
     the protagonist is the essence. The blanket concretizes a symbolic spatial
     delimitation.

References

Anderson-Klontz, B.T., Dayton, T. and Anderson-Klontz, L.S. (1999). 'The use of
    psychodramatic techniques within solution-focused brief therapy: A theoretical
    and technical integration.' *International Journal of Action Methods*, *52*(3),
    113–119.
Barresi, J. (2002). 'From "thought is the thinker" to "the voice is the speaker": William
    James and the Dialogical Self.' *Theory and Psychology*, *12*(2), 237–250.
Bowlby, J. (1969). *Attachment and Loss*, Vol. 1. Harmondsworth: Pelican.
Cuvelier, F. (1993). 'Groepspsychotherapie en drama: Een protagonist staat voor de
    groep [Group psychotherapy and drama: A protagonist in front of the group].' In
    P.J. Jongerius and J.C.B. Eyckman (eds) *Praktijkboek voor groepspsychotherapie*
    [Practice Book for Group Psychotherapy] (pp. 277–290). Amersfoort: Academische
    Uitgeverij Amersfoort.
Davies, M.H. (1987). 'Dramatherapy and psychodrama.' In S. Jennings (ed.)
    Dramatherapy: Theory and Practice 1 (pp. 104–123). London: Routledge.
Dunn, J., Brown, J., Slomkowski, C., Tesla, C. and Youngblade, L. (1991). 'Young
    children's understanding of other people's feelings and beliefs: Individual
    differences and their antecedents.' *Child Development*, *62*(2), 1352–1366.
Fogel, A., de Koeyer, I., Bellagamba, F., and Bell, H. (2002). 'The dialogical self in
    the first two years of life: Embarking on a journey of discovery.' *Theory and
    Psychology*, *12*(2), 191–205.

Fonagy, P. and Target, M. (1997). 'Attachment and reflective function: Their role in self-organization.' *Development and Psychopathology*, *9*, 679–700.

Harter, S. (1998). 'The development of self-representations.' In W. Damon (ed.-in-chief) and N. Eisenberg (vol. ed.) *Handbook of Child Psychology, Vol. 3, Social, Emotional and Personality Development* (pp. 553–618). New York: Wiley.

Hermans, H.J.M. (1996). 'Voicing the self: from information processing to dialogical interchange.' *Psychological Bulletin*, *119*(1), 31–50.

Hermans, H.J.M. (2003). 'The construction and reconstruction of a dialogical self.' *Journal of Constructivist Psychology*, *16*(2), 89–130.

Kane, R. (1992). 'The potential abuses, limitations, and negative effects of classical psychodramatic techniques in group counselling.' *Journal of Group Psychotherapy, Psychodrama and Sociometry*, *44*(4), 181–189.

Kellermann, P.F. (1987a). 'A proposed definition of psychodrama.' *Journal of Group Psychotherapy, Psychodrama and Sociometry*, *40*(2), 76–80.

Kellermann, P.F. (1987b). 'Outcome research in classical psychodrama.' *Small Group Behaviour*, *18*(4), 459–469.

Kipper, D.A. (1978). 'Trends in the research on the effectiveness of psychodrama: Retrospect and prospect.' *Journal of Group Psychotherapy, Psychodrama and Sociometry*, *31*, 5–18.

Kipper, D.A. (1997). 'Classical and contemporary psychodrama: A multifaceted action-oriented psychotherapy.' *International Journal of Action Methods*, *50*(3), 99–107.

Kipper, D.A. (1998). 'Psychodrama and trauma: Implications for future interventions of psychodramatic role-playing modalities.' *International Journal of Action Methods*, *51*(3), 113–121.

Kunnen, E.S. and Bosma, H.A. (2000). 'A developmental perspective on the dialogical self.' Paper presented at the First International Conference on the Dialogical Self, Nijmegen, June.

Marineau, R.F. (1989). *Jacob Levy Moreno 1889–1974: The Father of Psychodrama, Sociometry and Group Psychotherapy*. London and New York: Tavistock/Routledge.

Meillo, J. (1984). 'Adolescent, weerstand en psychodrama [Adolescent, resistance and psychodrama].' *Kind en Adolescent* [Child and Adolescent], *5*(3), 204–212.

Moreno, J.L. (1934). *Who Shall Survive? A New Approach to the Problem of Human Interrelations*. Washington, DC: Nervous and Mental Disease Publishing.

Moreno, J.L. (1946). *Psychodrama, Vol. 1*. New York: Beacon House.

Moreno, J.L. and Moreno, Z.T. (1975/1959). *Psychodrama, Vol. 2*. New York: Beacon House.

Nicolai, N. (2001a). 'Hechting en psychopathologie: Een literatuuroverzicht [Attachment and psychopathology: An overview].' *Tijdschrift voor Psychiatrie* [Journal of Psychiatry], *43*(5), 333–342.

Nicolai, N. (2001b). 'Hechting en psychopathologie: De reflectieve functie [Attachment and psychopathology: Reflective functioning].' *Tijdschrift voor Psychiatrie* [Journal of Psychiatry], *43* (10), 705–714.

Perner, J., Frith, U., Leslie, A.M. and Leekman, S.R. (1989). 'Exploration of the autistic child's theory of mind: knowledge, belief, and communication.' *Child Development*, *60*(3), 689–700.

Remer, R. (2001). 'Social atom theory revisited.' *International Journal of Action Methods*, *54*(2), 74–83.

Scholl, B.J. and Leslie, A.M. (2001). 'Minds, modules, and meta-analysis.' *Child Development*, *72*(3), 696–701.

Taylor, J.A. (1984). 'The diagnostic use of the social atom.' *Journal of Group Psychotherapy, Psychodrama and Sociometry*, *37*(2), 67–84.

Taylor, M., Cartwright, B.S. and Bowden, T. (1991). 'Perspective taking and theory of mind: Do children predict interpretive diversity as a function of differences in observers' knowledge?' *Child Development*, *62*(6), 1334–1351.

Templeton, L.M. and Wilcox, S.A. (2000). 'A tale of two representations: The misinformation effect and children's developing theory of mind.' *Child Development*, *71*(2), 402–416.

Verhofstadt-Denève, L. (2000). *Theory and Practice of Action and Drama Techniques: Developmental Psychotherapy from an Existential-Dialectical Viewpoint*. London: Jessica Kingsley Publishers.

Verhofstadt-Denève, L. (2003). 'The psychodramatic "social atom method": Dialogical self in dialectical action.' *Journal of Constructivist Psychology*, *16*, 183–212.

Wellman, H.M. (2002). 'Understanding the psychological world: Developing a theory of mind.' In U. Goswami (ed.) *Blackwell Handbook of Childhood Cognitive Development* (pp. 167–187). Malden, MA: Blackwell.

Part III

Reconstructing dialogical processes in severely affected patients

Chapter 11

Performing the self:

Therapeutic enactment and the narrative integration of traumatic loss

Robert A. Neimeyer and Marla Buchanan-Arvay

Social life abounds with the telling of stories. In the most literal sense, spouses and partners commonly give accounts of the events of their day when they return home from work and friends entertain one another and seek support by relating humorous or troubling episodes from their daily lives to what they hope will be a responsive audience. Surrounding and sustaining these (inter)personal processes of narration are all manner of social and cultural discourses, also structured in narrative terms, in forms ranging from time-honoured origin myths and parables to contemporary television shows and films (Neimeyer and Levitt 2001). It is hardly surprising, then, that when people's life stories become too chaotic to understand, too restrictive to be sustained, or too painful to bear privately, they often seek the counsel of culturally sanctioned healers whom they trust will be able to hear what others cannot, and provide valued perspective and direction for how a problematic life story might be lived differently. Our work is premised on the assumption that this seemingly ubiquitous narrative impulse carries profound implications for the study and practice of psychotherapy (Hermans 2002).

Our intention in this chapter is to advance this goal in two ways. First, we will sketch an emerging model of life transition as a process of *meaning reconstruction* (Neimeyer 2001), which can be usefully understood and facilitated in narrative terms. As we will see, this perspective is enriched by a conceptualization of *identity as a narrative achievement*, one that is fashioned, challenged and reconstructed at intrapersonal, interpersonal and broadly social levels. Second, we will illustrate some of these principles as they apply to an intensive therapeutic episode, emphasizing the dialogical and dialectical quality of narration and performance in the integration of loss. Our hope is that this effort will make a modest contribution to the aims of this volume, and to the larger field of narrative psychology of which it is a part.

Identity and disruption of the self-narrative

In a constructivist perspective, the co-construction of identity in a social field involves the development of a *self-narrative*, defined as an overarching cognitive-affective-behavioral structure that organizes the 'micro-narratives' of everyday life into a 'macro-narrative' that consolidates our self-understanding, establishes our characteristic range of emotions and goals, and guides our performance on the stage of the social world.

(Neimeyer 2004)

As such, the self-narrative is (typically) both more stable and coherent than our moment-to-moment performances in discrete social episodes, and more fluid and shifting than is implied by the 'essentialist' terminology of traits, personality, or character. Instead, self-narratives can be usefully viewed as a kind of 'sedimentation' in the flow of events, an attempt to establish a sense of lived continuity in one's experience over time (Neimeyer 1995).

At times, however, the meaningful assimilation and direction of experience provided by the self-narrative are severely challenged. Three such disruptions concern narrative disorganization, dissociation and dominance. Here we will consider each in turn, summarizing and extending a germinal taxonomy of narrative disruption developed elsewhere (Neimeyer 2000, 2004) to set the stage for the case study to follow.

Disorganized narratives

Disorganized narratives commonly result from traumatic loss, in which life events that are radically inconsistent with the person's prior self-narrative profoundly challenge its form and function (Neimeyer 2000). The resulting disruptions can be felt on virtually every level of narrative activity, from the organization of a coherent *plot structure* for life experiences (Neimeyer and Stewart 1998), through the underlying *themes* of the person's assumptive world (Kauffman 2002), to those overarching *goals* that conferred on the earlier self-narrative its distinctive teleology and direction (Neimeyer 2000). When the trauma is associated with a human cause (e.g. the murder of a loved one, violent assault or torture, sexual abuse by a member of the family), the *characterization* of specific actors in one's life narrative – or even of people in general – can also be deeply affected (Sewell 1997). Finally, even seemingly benign features of the *setting* of one's life story can be contaminated by the trauma, as previously neutral sights, sounds, smells and sensations associated with the loss event become 'triggers' for subsequent traumatic re-experiencing (Horowitz 1997). The unique biology of traumatic memories (van der Kolk and van der Hart 1991), being encoded under conditions of high neurophysiological arousal, results in a fragmented, intrusive and ruminative recall of the relevant events, fused with the intensive emotions and embodied sensations (e.g. anxiety, helplessness, nausea) that initially accompanied them. Consequently, catastrophic events can remain in this sense pre-narrative, persisting as fragmentary perceptual modules that are difficult to integrate into a consistent micro-narrative of the traumatic experience, much less into the broader macro-narrative of the survivor's life story.

As Hermans (2003) observes, this struggle to integrate conflictual emotional episodes may be especially acute for persons whose relationships with caregivers during development provided insufficient empathic attunement to stimulate the maturation of brain centres necessary for the transcendence of distressing experience. As a result, the traumatized individual is handicapped in shifting from immersion in the problematic experience to alternative internalized perspectives or I-positions that offer the prospect of self-solace. Unable to construct transitions or meaning bridges between highly negative and positive states of mind, the individual's sense of self-continuity is jeopardized, contributing to the disorganization of the self-narrative. This view is compatible with the general argument that insecure attachment during critical developmental periods complicates later adult efforts to construct a coherent self-representation in the face of conflictual experience (Schore 1994). It also accords with the specific argument that the traumatic disorganization of the self-narrative following the loss of a loved one is especially likely for bereaved persons with problematic developmental histories, predisposing them to complicated grief following the loss of a stabilizing attachment (Neimeyer et al. 2002).

Dissociated narratives

Dissociated narratives are 'silent stories', accounts of loss or trauma unvoiced to others, and often even to the self (Neimeyer 2004). As such they commonly involve dissociation in two senses, disrupting the link between narrator and audience, as well as the communication between I-positions within the self (Hermans 2002). The result is a breakdown in sociality, as well as subtle or profound dissociation in the classical psychodynamic sense, such that critical incidents in one's self-narrative are segregated and compartmentalized in an attempt to control the pain or guilt that would come with their fuller integration into the public or conscious story of one's life. As in Stiles' (1999) assimilation theory, dissociated experiences can be seen as ranging from those that are warded off from conscious acknowledgement, through those that are acknowledged, but actively avoided, to those that are painfully known, but denied expression. Incongruous micro-narratives that threaten an individual's image in the eyes of relevant others are particularly likely to be held in this silent, unvoiced fashion, such as histories of abuse, marital infidelity, and hidden addiction. Even the losses of loved ones through stigmatizing death (e.g. of a son through AIDS) can be dissociated in this manner, depriving the bereaved of the social support – but also safeguarding him or her from the social censure – that might come from an unabridged account of the circumstances of the death (Neimeyer and Jordan 2002). Thus, a particularly pernicious consequence of dissociated narratives is that they disrupt processes of account-making that promote transcendence of trauma (Harvey 1996).

Dominant narratives

Dominant narratives, as the term implies, can disempower and marginalize alternative accounts of self, conferring problem-saturated identities on those subject to them (White and Epston 1990). As such, they typically have their roots in larger societal or cultural discourses, such as professional discourses of psychopathology that subordinate an individual's unique challenges and resources to the dominant narrative of his or her psychiatric diagnosis, or narratives of ethnic, gender or racial inferiority that colonize the individual's self-narrative and that justify oppression.

Dominant narratives underscore the role of larger social and cultural processes in our narration of self, which necessarily draws on the terms and discourses of our historical place and time as we strive to attribute meaning to our own life experiences (Neimeyer 2000). When such discourses are pre-emptive and hegemonic, they can eclipse alternative accounts of the person submerged in them, such that all experience is assimilated into a 'grand narrative' that makes totalizing claims on people subjected to it. Thus, dominant narratives (a) often arise within broad social systems, (b) structure the self-narratives of individuals, and (c) confer a good deal of meaning on experience, at the expense of (d) obscuring alternative accounts of the individual's life and identity.

Relearning the world: psychotherapy as meaning reconstruction

What implications does this narrative conceptualization hold for psychotherapy? As diverse answers to this question have been pursued at length elsewhere (Neimeyer 2001; Neimeyer and Mahoney 1995; Neimeyer and Raskin 2000), we will simply introduce here a framework for intervention that has special relevance to the enactment-based therapy to be illustrated in the subsequent extended case study.

A tenet of constructivist therapy is that problems are defined, lived and resolved at the level of meaning, not at the level of behaviour alone (Neimeyer and Bridges 2003). This implies that it is less the life one has lived than the significance attributed to that life that counts (Kelly 1955/1991), and accordingly, that mastering a problematic life story entails reaffirming or reconstructing a world of meaning that has been challenged or that has become in some way constraining (Neimeyer 2001). With major disruptions of life narratives such as the patterns of disorganization, dissociation or dominance described above, individuals are faced with the task of 'relearning the self' and 'relearning the world' (Attig 1996), as they struggle to revise their previous life stories to render them more adequate to the circumstances in which they live.

But what form does this 'relearning' take? A clue is provided by a model of adult learning formulated by Kolb (1984), who suggests that genuine learning entails two dialectical dimensions, one of which involves 'prehending' or taking in information in the form of concrete experience or abstract conceptualization, and the second of which involves 'transforming' it through reflective observation or active experimentation. Thus, formulated as a cycle, learning might be seen as anchored in emotionally vivid life experiences, which are processed reflectively to yield understandings of important patterns, which in turn suggest fresh possibilities for action. Because active experimentation in turn generates new concrete experiences, a recursive cycle of further learning is stimulated as the learner observes and reflects on these new patterns and acts upon them. Phrased in narrative terms, this movement might be viewed as one of immersion in the experience of compelling elements of plot, which are then interpreted to winnow out the abstract themes that underpin it. Once formulated, the learner is in a position to experiment actively with alternative performances that cohere with rather different goals. Such experimentation generates novel experiences calling for further reflection, and so on, in a cycle of narrative consolidation, revision or replacement. Just such a model of learning is implied by the major new psychotherapeutic method to which we will now turn, that of *therapeutic enactment*.

Performing the self through therapeutic enactment

New approaches to trauma repair accord with a dialogical perspective that emphasizes the active, social and embodied nature of the self (Hermans 2003). Thus, these emerging trauma therapies are focusing on the integration of mind and body, moving beyond traditional treatment approaches into models that are action based, participatory, and attuned to bodily experience. One such approach is therapeutic enactment (TE: Westwood et al. 2002), a performance-based method of trauma repair that evolved from the work of Marvin Westwood and Patricia Wilensky at the University of British Columbia. Like the broader field of psychodrama (Moreno and Elefthery 1982) from which it emerged, TE enables the client or protagonist to devise a spatial structure within which critical relationships among facets of oneself, or between the self and relevant others, can be re-enacted and reconstructed (Westwood et al. 2003). Westwood and his associates (2002: 226) contend that 'reliving through physical action is central to the facilitation of the participant's experience of change' and accordingly have found TE to be of value in the treatment of complicated bereavement, traumatic loss, military combat, sexual assault, homicide and child abuse.

Westwood and his colleagues (2003) delineated a five-phase approach to therapeutic enactment. First comes the *assessment phase*, as the director evaluates the client's (or lead's) level of distress and life functioning, and determines the client's preparedness for the trauma work. A story script or trauma narrative is then provided by the client, who is encouraged to bring concrete resources in the form of friends or family members to the enactment to provide support, as well as meaningful objects (articles of clothing, masks, photographs, special jewellery, mementos) to assist in the performance of the trauma memory.

Phase two is the *group-building phase*. Westwood usually involves several assisting practitioners who have expertise in group process (and who have participated in therapeutic enactments previously) to help build group cohesion. These helpers sit among the group of fifteen or more witnesses and are called upon occasionally to assist witnesses who may become distressed. Group norms are discussed before the enactment and a check-in begins the group-building phase. The witnesses in the enactment are told about their role in the session – to watch, listen, serve as a container for the performance to unfold and potentially to perform a role for the lead.

Phase three is the *enactment phase* – the performance of the trauma narrative, which will be explained and illustrated in detail in the case study to follow. In this phase, the director of the enactment uses various techniques to facilitate the change process such as *doubling, role reversal, mirroring, immediate feedback* and *sensing into the body processes*.

Phase four is the *processing phase*, in which the completed enactment is discussed from the perspective of each of its witnesses and participants. Processing begins with the actors who were called upon to be in the enactment, then the responses of the witnesses who watched the performance, and finally the lead, who responds to those who provided feedback. This sharing of all participants' reactions helps consolidate the lead's experience and provide validation for the work that has been done.

Finally, the enactment moves toward the *integration phase*. Integration begins immediately upon the completion of the enactment during the group processing phase, but continues as the lead and assistants meet later in the day or evening to check-in on the lead's physical and emotional state of being. The lead is contacted three to four days later by telephone, and again after one month, to check-in again to see if the new insight, learning or sense of being is holding in everyday life. Clients are encouraged to call the director with any concerns at any point following completion of their enactment.

In summary, TE offers a systematic, experientially intense and safety-enhancing procedure for narrative scripting, performance, reflection and revision. Its structure naturally incorporates each of the components of Kolb's (1984) model of learning, as it accesses and transforms both abstract life themes and concrete traumatic experiences through reflective observation and active experimentation with alternative meanings and responses. Likewise, it articulates with a dialogical conception of the self, as different I-positions and relationships with critical others are given voice and prompted to enter into emotionally charged, but ultimately healing dialogue. We turn now to a case study of its use to foster profound narrative revision in a young man struggling with long-term effects of an abusive childhood.

Brent's enactment: performing a child's trauma story

Participants arrive early at a secluded lodge to set the stage for the therapeutic enactment scheduled for this rainy evening in October. Marvin Westwood, his co-facilitator, and the lead for this evening are tucked away in one of the cabins going over the script one last time before entering the great hall. One of the assisting directors builds a fire and others place the chairs and couches into a large circle. Approximately twenty-five people are in attendance. It is foggy outside, rain drizzling off the porch eaves. Everyone waits as the director calls Brent into the centre of the circle. The experienced witnesses have a strong sense of anticipation – mixed feelings of excitement and dread. Brent is 35 years old, an attractive man, married, with a newborn son. Brent has brought with him his mother and sister, who have been fully briefed on the TE procedure, and several symbolic objects, including a heart-shaped amulet to symbolize hope, a box of childhood keepsakes to represent his past, and a photograph of himself as a young child. He tells us that he wants to do this enactment to get rid of some of his anger at his abusive father. He fears that his anger will affect his relationship with his new son. He wants to be a different kind of father than his own. He wants to end the cycle of violence.

Marv: You've been waiting a long time to tell this story, so let's begin.[1]

Brent explains the significance of the symbolic objects, and shows a picture of himself at 8 years of age, passing it around for everyone to see. He chooses a group member to be 'Little Me'. This group member, shy at first, walks with Brent around the inner circle while Brent describes his 8-year-old self to this stand-in.

Marv: What do you want us to know about him?
Brent: He is adorable, so lovable, so precious. He is funny and cute and so sweet. (As Brent says this he hugs the man he has selected to be Little Me.)
Marv: I want to know what you love about him. Tell him 'When I hold you like this I remember . . .'
Brent: I remember how badly I wanted to be held like this, but I don't remember it.
Marv: 'And feeling held like this gives me . . .'
Brent: It gives me strength, certainty, knowledge that I am okay.
Marv: And notice where you feel it in your body . . .

They remain in a locked embrace for about five minutes until Marv says, 'I really don't think you want to let go of him, do you? And that is the reason why we are here tonight, isn't it?' Brent gently leads Little Me back to the outer circle and instructs him to watch, not to be afraid, but to watch, because 'Big Brent is going to go back and get what he needed.' Next Brent selects a double to play himself at the age of 17. The double is a tall, strong, young man who eagerly joins Brent in the centre of the circle.

Marv: Tell him why you chose him to be you. Tell him what you would like him to be able to do tonight for you.
Brent: I need you to be me at 17, to go back and enact a scene where I was beaten up by my father, and later to be me at a football game where my father berated me and let me sit with a serious knee injury for the whole game before taking me to the hospital.
Marv: How should he walk and hold himself? What would he be saying? What is he like? Show us.

Brent walks with his double, talking to him, coaching him in how he spoke and acted at the age of 17. After he is satisfied that this part is properly instilled in the actor, he puts this 17-year-old self to the side and then selects four people to play four different parts of himself. In this section of the enactment, Brent is using his resources that he brought with him in the form of friends. He selects one person to be a hypervigilant self: 'She watches carefully, always looking out for danger, assessing the escape routes, being my alarm signal.' Next he chooses a man to be his entertainer self: 'He likes to be the centre of attention, he is humorous, and it gets him a lot of praise, but he hides behind this self.' Brent then selects another actor, stating: 'This is the caretaker self – this part notices everyone else's needs and keeps giving himself away. He can get all used up.' Finally, he makes one last selection, explaining, 'This is the counsellor self, who knows the lens of the counsellor's world. It's exhausting because I am always seeing the multiplicity of lives and trying to make meaning out of everything.'

Marv: So say to these parts of self that they need to stay out of the way and just watch; that you don't need rescuing tonight, right?
Brent: Right, I am not going to fall upon these parts of self tonight. I am going to do this in a new way.
Marv: Say, 'I need to put you all away so that I can go back to the most painful part of my life and get something. I don't want you to rescue me tonight.' (Brent repeats these sentences.)[2]
Marv: Why are your sister and mother here tonight?
Brent: They need to witness that I can do this. They need to see the victory so that maybe they could do this for themselves some day.
Marv: Who else needs to be here tonight?

Brent: My father John.
Marv: Who is he?[3] We need to be introduced to the guy who caused this.

Brent gestures toward the man from the witness group who has agreed to play his father and as they walk in the circle, he describes his father as liked by everyone, quick witted, a volunteer fireman but a man who has a lot of wounds of his own inside him.

Marv: We really need to see him – show him how he walks and talks, move with him.

Hesitantly at first, Brent begins coaching the father on his vocal characteristics and movements. Next Marv moves Brent into a previously scripted scene in which his father is beating him for drinking a sip of the father's Coca-Cola. Marv instructs the stand-ins (17-year-old self and father) through the choreographed scene with Brent's help: 'Tell the actors what happened next and tell the double how he feels.' Marv now moves Brent into the scene, asking him to notice the boy on the ground at the bottom of the stairs after his father has beaten him and pushed him down there. Brent, overcome with compassion for his double, turns to the father, face reddening, trembling. Marv then instructs Brent: 'Say to your Dad – "What is it with you Dad? How could you do this to me?" '

Brent starts to tell him off, first in a calm voice, then getting louder and angrier: 'How could you do this to a defenceless boy? How could you do this to him for just sipping your pop? What is wrong with you?'

The father replies that he deserved it. This infuriates Brent. He is now very angry and aggressively attacks the father. Marv and another male member of the group restrain Brent as he yells at his father and struggles to get a bear-hold on him. Brent releases his anger toward his father and his pain.

Once Brent has finished yelling, Marv moves him into the father role.

Marv: Speak for your father.[4]
Brent: I did it because I needed respect and you disobeyed me.
Marv: I don't believe him Brent. Say, 'The reason I beat you was . . .'
Brent (as his own father): The reason I beat you was . . . you reminded me of
            everything I dislike about myself and that is why I beat you up, you
            were just there.

Marv has the 17-year-old double step in and confront Brent (as his father). 'Do it forcefully, tell him why this answer doesn't cut it.'

Brent hears his double confront his father and Brent finally replies, in his father's voice: 'You came between my young wife and me; you were more loving, faster, and smarter than me and that's why I beat you up.'

Marv: 'And the other reason I put you down and shamed you was . . .'

Brent: I had so much anger in me for what I didn't get and I resented that you were getting all the attention. Then it just became a habit to take all my stress out on you, because you loved me and were starving for my attention.

Marv: OK, your father is now going to watch this scene. Your father's role here tonight is to witness what he has done, in silence, because you are going to go back to that day at the football match and get the father you deserved. Right?[5]

Marv has Brent tell the story about being at the football stadium, during the last game of the season, and he is tackled and shatters his knee. The pain is excruciating and as he lies on the ground he hears his father tell the coach, 'Oh, he's just faking it, ignore him. He just wants attention.' The coach wants to call an ambulance but the father insists that he is okay and waits until the end of the game (two hours later) to take him to the hospital. Marv has Brent's double enact the scene as Brent watches. Brent coaches his double about the pain that he is in and what his father is saying to him.

Marv: How does he feel right now? What is he thinking? What does his body want to do?

Marv instructs Brent to take his double's place. 'Let's do this now, Brent. You're in your body now. What needs to be done?' Brent starts to cry, and sobbing begins to struggle to crawl across the floor. Then he is silent, frozen, contorting with a somatic memory of the pain as it springs through his body. Brent starts to gag and experiences dry heaves. Marv comes down on the floor beside Brent and tells him to let it out.

Marv: You hear your father telling the coach that you are faking it. Give this a voice, Brent.

Because Brent had mentioned several times during the enactment that he wished he had told his father how he felt and wished that he had voiced his opinion, the director encourages Brent to speak, to break the silence that robs him of voice. Brent lets out a great roar from deep inside; it sounds so old, so deep, filled with anger, fear and shame. Marv moves a new participant into place, the 'Caring Father', carefully selected by Brent earlier before the enactment began. He puts this Caring Father into place beside Brent to console him.[6]

Marv: Tell him you'll always be there for him; tell him how proud you are of him.

Caring Father: I'm here, Brent. Don't move, hold my hand, and give me your pain. Squeeze my hand as hard as you can and give me your pain. I can take it. I'm here for you. The ambulance is on the way. If I could take your pain away, I would. Keep squeezing my hand, son. I love you.

Still crying and writhing, Brent starts to gag, dry heaving up all his pain.

Marv: That's it Brent, let it all come, let it out.
Caring Father: That's okay, son, let your pain out. I'm here for you, with you in your pain.
Brent: Don't leave me, dad.

Caring Father holds him tightly in his arms and kisses his forehead saying, 'You're my boy. You're going to be okay. That kiss right there is for you son. That kiss is meant for you to feel forever. I wish I could take your pain away, but I am here now and forever. Feel me holding you and know that this love for you will last forever.'
    There is a long pause while they keep embracing until his sobbing stops.

Brent: It's over. It's over. (He means the surging feelings rushing through his body.)

Caring Father begins to tell him stories, remembrances of him as a small boy and how much joy he brought him. He tells Brent how precious he was when he was little. They re-story the father for Brent to feel and hear. Marv cues the Caring Father into this narrative, then turns to Brent.

Marv: Tell this dad, 'If I have you like this, then . . .'
Brent: Then I know that I am worthy. I am a good person.
Marv: Are you getting what you need and deserve right now? Do you know what this feels like now?
Caring Father: I am holding you like this forever. Feel it in every cell of your body and know what a father's love is.
Marv: You need to know this. You need this for your own son.

Brent and Caring Father are lying on the floor in each other's arms.
    Now Marv brings the 8-year-old boy into the scene. The 8-year-old lies between Brent's legs facing forward toward the witness group, holding the picture of himself. The three men make a sculpture, a sitting sandwich, lying wrapped in each other's arms, leaning back on Brent's double, who is backing the Caring Father for support.

Marv: When you are ready, Brent, speak out what you are noticing now. What are you experiencing?

Brent:	Nothing can stop me now. I know what it feels like to have a father's love.
Marv:	Tell them (meaning address Little Me and 17-year-old self), 'I am going to take you both with me because . . .'
Brent:	I am going to take you both with me because . . . I need both of you to be whole.

Brent is now directed to speak to his other father who watches from the side: 'I hope you saw that and now we'll just be . . . each his own man. You never got it (unconditional love from a father figure), but I did.'[7]

Now the director, Marv, brings the four parts of self back into the body sculpture. They surround Brent, Caring Father and Little Me on each side, top and bottom. Marv allows Brent to soak it in and they remain that way on the floor together for another several minutes.

Upon completion of the performed narrative, Marv asks everyone to join the large circle – all actors return to the outer circle, including Brent. Marv asks the participants in the enactment to come to the centre to form an inner circle in order to de-role. Forming a tight circle in front of the other witnesses, each person who played a part in Brent's enactment states, 'I am not——[role in the enactment], I am——[real name]', and takes a step back. Back now in the outer circle, Marv first invites the participants to speak about the experience of playing the role for Brent and what they learned, first in their respective roles, and then as themselves. Each does so briefly and poignantly, often describing their feelings and sense of profound respect for Brent and hope for his future. Then Marv invites every witness to speak into the circle whatever they wish to say (an awareness, experiences that resonated for them, their feelings, and validation for the 'lead' but no judgements). This takes about 45 minutes, bringing the total time for the enactment to nearly three hours, but the director does not rush it. He has promised the lead that they will all stay until it is finished, no matter what the time. Lastly, Brent, having listened to the witnesses and having had time to reflect on their words, speaks into the circle. He summarizes his own experiences, recounting what is important to him to carry forward with him. He expresses great release and a joyful weariness. He thanks the group and the participants for their caring support through this difficult passage. The director and co-facilitator call Brent the next day to check in. They also call a week later, and approximately four to six weeks later to follow-up on his progress. At each check-in point the powerful integrative effects of the enactment are holding, and new insights regarding Brent's sense of self and trans-generational patterns continue to percolate into consciousness and into his processing with his wife, his mother and sister, and intimate friends.

Healing the disruption

TE integrates mind and body through the reconstruction of the self-narrative in the act of performing the trauma story. In this embodied narrative approach, painful chapters of the self-narrative are relived and revised in action, and new constructions of identity, relationships and beliefs are created through an enactment that externalizes and realigns the dialogical relationships among multiple I-positions. The effects can be seen in all three of the domains of narrative disruption detailed earlier, a consideration of which will bring our discussion to a close.

Narrative disorganization

In Brent's life story, his schema for the father–son relationship was disrupted by his father's physical and emotional abuse. Through the re-enactment of the plot of traumatic childhood and adolescent micro-narratives, Brent was able to re-access these somatic memories in a safe environment that permitted their exploration and re-authorship. At a thematic level, Brent questioned his own ability to be a loving father, given that he had never had the experience of being loved by his own. The director helped Brent to reconstitute a new self-schema using the body as a somatic marker to embody the experience of being loved by a father (performed by the Caring Father figure in the enactment). Brent had to feel the experience and 'know' it deeply to transform the belief that he was unworthy of a father's love. The enactment also gave Brent the opportunity to identify, differentiate and ultimately reintegrate various I-positions within himself that had served important defensive functions, but that also had kept him from confronting his pain more directly. Through the enactment, Brent was able to perform, view and reflect on a new and more coherent self-narrative, and establish new goals and strategies for fathering his own son. The result was a powerful integration of the traumatic micro-narratives into the macro-narrative of his life, at cognitive, affective and somatic levels.

Narrative dissociation

The unspoken tale of abandonment and abuse experienced by Brent was voiced and released in the performance of his trauma narrative. Brent had never disclosed his 'secret' to friends or colleagues because of the fear of being judged. Shame is a common experience in survivor tales. Rothschild (2000) explains that many who have suffered traumatic experiences feel a terrific sense of guilt and shame for freezing or 'going dead' during the trauma moment. Brent felt ashamed for not fighting back, not voicing his anger toward his father and not taking a stand against his father's rage. In the enactment, the director was able to recreate the fear response through an actor, enabling Brent to bear witness to his own powerlessness and have it exposed in a safe community of witnesses. For Brent, recreating his own powerlessness as a child allowed him to understand that the freezing response was automatic, that the shame was not warranted, and that he could forgive himself for his voicelessness and disempowerment. Alternating between the role of actor and audience, Brent was able to give public expression to the silent story of his abuse, and to find acceptance of himself in the sphere of his own feelings. As a result, a more mature and competent voice emerged in his community of self, which seemed to carry over to the follow-up contacts.

Narrative dominance

The dominant narratives in Brent's story deal with life scripts and the discourse of fathering. The good father/bad father dichotomy was at the heart of this performance. The actors who were called upon used normative markers of the good father (who held, comforted and kissed his son, and promised always to be there for him) and the bad father (who was distant, physically abusive and mocking). In both words and actions, they performed the discourse of fathering, in both of its extremes. Another discourse was also in play in this enactment – the good son/bad son. Brent was encouraged to deconstruct these life scripts by embodying their meanings through action. Brent physically and verbally confronted his father. He embraced his good father emotionally and physically. He was able to re-experience and reconstruct and differentiate the position of son through the roles of Little Me and the 17-year-old self, each of which was positioned within the trauma narrative and the new, emergent story of knowing a father's love. Thus, Brent's story illustrates how dominant discourses shape the kinds of tales we tell ourselves, and how TE can provide a setting within which clients can elaborate their self-narratives in more hopeful directions.

Conclusion

As creatures that seem intrinsically drawn to 'storying' experience, human beings construct a sense of both self and world in narrative terms. It is not surprising, then, that profound experiences of trauma and loss have the capacity to shake this world of meaning, often shattering the coherence of our life stories, silencing our narration of critical experiences, and imposing constricting and dominant accounts of who we are and what we have suffered. In detailing these effects, we have tried both to clarify their influence on survivors, and to suggest the potential for transforming disrupted self-narratives by assisting in their re-accessing and re-authorship. We have also drawn on some of the many contributions of a dialogical model of self (Hermans 2002) in conceptualizing disruptions in the self-narrative, as well as the processes by which these are redressed in a performative psychotherapy.

In particular, the process of 'relearning the self' in the wake of traumatic loss can be facilitated by the application of a contemporary understanding of adult learning, which emphasizes the importance of anchoring meaning-making in concrete, here-and-now emotional experiences, processing these through reflective observation, distilling new understandings, and experimenting with these in the domain of action. We have suggested that therapeutic enactment represents one especially promising method for implementing such relearning, promoting as it does the integration, disclosure and elaboration of self-narratives that had been disorganized, dissociated and dominated by loss. We hope that other researchers and clinicians will join us in exploring and using this and similar methods, so that the power of trauma in human lives might be counterbalanced by the power of transformation.

NOTES

1   The authors wish to express their appreciation to Marvin Westwood for his permission to draft this case study of therapeutic enactment derived from his work with Brent, whose identifying information has been altered to protect his identity. We have used Westwood's familiar nickname as a gesture of respect for his figural role in the enactment.
2   Note that, in order to allow for the fuller voicing of initially silent or marginalized I-positions in the enactment, Brent must also create space for them by quieting others who typically pre-empt them. This careful articulation and representation of multiple relevant positions through the use of group members permits Brent to 'externalize' his internal complexity, and 'set the stage' for the transformative dialogue to follow.
3   The perpetrator roles are always selected beforehand. The lead and the director decide who would be a suitable person to play the role and check with the person before the enactment, describing the part and ascertaining whether the witness/participant would feel comfortable playing this difficult role.
4   The director uses role-reversal paradoxically to encourage the client to see his father's indifference and to experience his father in an embodied way.
5   An important aspect of therapeutic enactment is the reconstitution of the self-narrative. By replacing the old narrative with a restorative and reparative narrative, a new, authoritative self-as-narrator can emerge or be transformed.
6   Again, the director is installing a reparative experience – the embodied experience of being held during this extremely painful and traumatizing moment.
7   Note that what emerges here, spontaneously, is something close to the I–Thou or I–I form of dialogue between initially quite antagonistic I-positions, as recommended by Cooper (2003). It is commonly our experience in TE that this form of realignment, in which each position displays greater respect and empathy for the subjective integrity of the other, emerges from successful enactment.

References

Attig, T. (1996). *Grieving: Relearning the World*. New York: Oxford University Press.
Cooper, M. (2003). ' "I–I" and "I–Me": Transposing Buber's interpersonal attitudes to the intrapersonal plane.' *Journal of Constructivist Psychology*, *16*, 131–153.

Harvey, J.H. (1996). *Embracing their Memory*. Needham Heights, MA: Allyn and Bacon.

Hermans, H.J.M. (2002). 'The person as a motivated storyteller.' In R.A. Neimeyer and G.J. Neimeyer (eds) *Advances in Personal Construct Psychology*, Vol. 5 (pp. 3–38). Westport, CT: Praeger.

Hermans, H.J.M. (2003). 'The construction and reconstruction of a dialogical self.' *Journal of Constructivist Psychology*, *16*, 89–130.

Horowitz, M.J. (1997). *Stress Response Syndromes*, 3rd edn. Northvale, NJ: Jason Aronson.

Kauffman, J. (ed.) (2002). *Loss of the Assumptive World*. New York: Brunner-Routledge.

Kelly, G.A. (1955/1991). *The Psychology of Personal Constructs*. New York: Routledge.

Kolb, D.A. (1984). *Experiential Learning*. Englewood Cliffs, NJ: Prentice Hall.

Moreno, J.L. and Elefthery, D.G. (1982). 'An introduction to group psychodrama.' In G.M. Gazda (ed.) *Basic Approaches to Group Psychotherapy and Group Counseling*. Springfield, IL: Charles C. Thomas.

Neimeyer, R.A. (1995). 'Client-generated narratives in psychotherapy.' In R.A. Neimeyer and M.J. Mahoney (eds) *Constructivism in Psychotherapy* (pp. 231–246). Washington, DC: American Psychological Association.

Neimeyer, R.A. (2000). 'Narrative disruptions in the construction of self.' In R.A. Neimeyer and J. Raskin (eds) *Constructions of Disorder: Meaning-Making Frameworks for Psychotherapy* (pp. 207–241). Washington, DC: American Psychological Association.

Neimeyer, R.A. (ed.). (2001). *Meaning Reconstruction and the Experience of Loss*. Washington, DC: American Psychological Association.

Neimeyer, R.A. (2004). 'Fostering posttraumatic growth: A narrative contribution.' *Journal of Psychological Inquiry*, *15*, 53–59.

Neimeyer, R.A. and Bridges, S.K. (2003). 'Postmodern therapies.' In A. Gurman and S. Messer (eds) *Essential Psychotherapies*, 2nd edn (pp. 272–316). New York: Guilford.

Neimeyer, R.A. and Jordan, J. (2002). 'Disenfranchisement as empathic failure.' In K. Doka (ed.) *Disenfranchised Grief* (pp. 97–117). Champaign, IL: Research Press.

Neimeyer, R.A. and Levitt, H. (2001). 'Coping and coherence: A narrative perspective.' In C.R. Snyder (ed.) *Stress and Coping* (pp. 47–67). New York: Oxford University Press.

Neimeyer, R.A. and Mahoney, M.J. (eds) (1995). *Constructivism in Psychotherapy*. Washington, DC: American Psychological Association.

Neimeyer, R.A. and Raskin, J. (eds) (2000). *Constructions of Disorder: Meaning-making Frameworks for Psychotherapy*. Washington, DC: American Psychological Association.

Neimeyer, R.A. and Stewart, A.E. (1998). 'Trauma, healing, and the narrative employment of loss.' In C. Franklin and P.S. Nurius (eds) *Constructivism in Practice* (pp. 165–184). Milwaukee, WI: Families International.

Neimeyer, R.A., Prigerson, H. and Davies, B. (2002). 'Mourning and meaning.' *American Behavioral Scientist*, *46*, 235–251.

Rothschild, B. (2000). *The Body Remembers: The Psychophysiology of Trauma and Trauma Treatment*. New York: Norton.

Schore, A.N. (1994). *Affect Regulation and the Origin of the Self*. Hillsdale, NJ: Lawrence Erlbaum Associates.

Sewell, K.W. (1997). 'Posttraumatic stress: Towards a constructivist model of psychotherapy.' In G.J. Neimeyer and R.A. Neimeyer (eds) *Advances in Personal Construct Psychology*, Vol. 4 (pp. 207–235). Greenwich, CT: JAI Press.

Stiles, W.B. (1999). 'Signs and voices in psychotherapy.' *Psychotherapy Research*, 9, 1–21.

Van der Kolk, B. and van der Hart, O. (1991). 'The intrusive past: The flexibility of memory and the engraving of trauma.' *American Imago*, 48, 425–454.

Westwood, M.J., Black, T.G. and McLean, H.B. (2002). 'A re-entry program for peacekeeping soldiers.' *Canadian Journal of Counselling*, 36, 221–232.

Westwood, M.J., Keats, P.A. and Wilensky, P. (2003). 'Therapeutic enactment: Integrating the individual and group counselling models for change.' *Journal for Specialists in Group Work*, 28(2), 122–138.

White, M. and Epston, D. (1990). *Narrative Means to Therapeutic Ends*. New York: Norton.

Chapter 12

Strategies for the treatment of dialogical dysfunctions

Giancarlo Dimaggio, Giampaolo Salvatore and Dario Catania

Impoverished dialogues

'Let me tell you what happened and you'll be able to understand my problem.' Sabrina has just sat down. This is her first appointment with her therapist (GD). Patient and therapist already know that it is not going to be possible to do therapy together. The session has an assessment function and is preparatory to Sabrina being seen by another therapist. Sabrina goes on:

> I bought myself a pair of shoes. Once home, I put them on. There was a long nail inside one of them. I risked hurting myself. I returned to the shop. I showed them the shoes and asked for them to be exchanged. The shopkeeper was arrogant and maintained that the shoes were all right; the shop assistants didn't want to get involved. But the nail really was there. You see? It's always like that: I can never manage to get people to take me seriously. [Sabrina breaks into tears.] I can't go on like this. I feel like a piece of dirt. I'm not worth anything and my ideas don't count. I'd like to just disappear.

The therapist is worried as he listens to her words. The reason is that the story contains a dialogue between a character (the shopkeeper) dominating and causing harm to another one (Sabrina as victim), who suffers as a result. The former is insensitive to the latter's protests and pays no heed to her distress. The submissive character gets trampled on, tries to make her voice heard but does not manage to. All the episodes related during this session have almost invariably the same cast of characters and dialogical relationship pattern. A humiliating character hurts a humiliated one, who protests in vain and, as a result, feels useless and would like to withdraw from any sort of relationship.

Various authors maintain that the interpersonal schemas in narratives drive people's relationships. Each of us enters a relationship moved by a goal and by a representation of self, of other, of how other will respond to self's desires and of what self's reaction will be to that, actual or foreseen, response.

The interaction foreseen in the schema triggers how one then behaves in reality (Baldwin 1992; Hermans 1996; Horowitz 1998). A man considering himself unattractive may long for a woman's love and imagine getting rejected. The rejection he expects makes him feel disappointed. Being driven by such a schema, he avoids courting the woman or does it in a half-hearted manner, thus probably provoking the rejection he fears.

Each character in a text can take control of the action: a victim can become a tyrant and a character that is rejected can contemptuously repel another. In view of this, the therapist hypothesizes that Sabrina could take on the role of tyrant too. He therefore asks her if she has ever experienced angry reactions. She reveals that she got someone to write a letter protesting about a teacher who, according to her, had called her a prostitute. On that occasion Sabrina insisted, to no avail, that the teacher be punished, and therefore took on a threatening nature. The shoeshop saga has an ending in line with this other story: Sabrina, in a search for justice and revenge, as with her teacher, returned to the shop accompanied by her mother, whom she felt supported her, and the shopkeeper reimbursed her money. Sabrina felt disappointed as she would have liked to have got satisfaction by herself, without being under her mother's wing. Thus, a character capable of asking for and getting justice – although this is not enough for the injured character – appears.

The session finishes as follows: the therapist explains to Sabrina that the chief reason for her distress is her unbearable feeling of being humiliated and treated as if she did not exist, and that the prime goal of therapy will therefore be to tackle this distress. He finishes by saying that he needs a few days to decide which of his colleagues is the best for her. The two stand up and the therapist tells her the cost of the session. Sabrina's expression alters and she shouts angrily: 'You're joking! I'm supposed to pay just to get someone's name? If you don't mind, when I call you, just give me the name, okay?'

The therapist realizes that his fears were justified. The two characters, one dominating and the other submissive and injured are there, face to face with each other. His intervening now can decide whether this relationship pattern will take over the stage or not. His emotions make him swing between the two positions in the schema: a fear of having problems, which drives him to accept giving her the name without getting paid, thus taking on the submissive position, and anger at the patient's arrogant attitude, which incites him to force her to pay, as he feels he is right.

The therapist realizes that he has entered a cognitive-interpersonal cycle (Safran and Muran 2000), which he can reinforce. After mastering his emotions internally without enacting them, he leaves the cycle, by bringing a third character on stage. He says:

> Sabrina, I'm sorry you feel treated badly. I consider what I've been doing an assessment operation. Without it I wouldn't have known what your problems were, if psychotherapy was the right treatment and which

therapist was best for you. It's therefore part of my work and that's why I believe I should be paid. But I'm also concerned that you don't leave here feeling mistreated, because that's exactly what is causing your suffering. And so you are free to not pay me and look for another therapist, and in that case I'll consider myself no longer obliged to look for one for you.

Sabrina's tone of voice changes and she agrees to pay. A few days later she telephones for the colleague's name. The call is friendly and Sabrina starts her therapy, the course of which we describe below.

Let's hypothesize that Sabrina has, temporarily, experienced the option of getting out of a stereotypical dialogical pattern, thanks to the therapist, who has embodied a character that refuses to get into an argument and is prepared to give up something if this means each other's point of view being respected.

As well as tackling her difficult humiliating/humiliated relationship pattern, the therapist has another problem: Sabrina's narratives concentrate almost exclusively on the stereotyped dialogue between these humiliating and humiliated characters and we shall see that her mental life is focused on understanding whether another is offending her and how she can overturn this situation. Even although only 25 years old, her life has already suffered: she has interrupted an interesting university course and is thinking about resigning from work, as she cannot stand her colleagues.

What goes on when patients relate, and enact, narratives in which the characters participating in the dialogue are few and the relationship between them only dwells repetitively on the same topics? We are dealing here with impoverished dialogues (Dimaggio and Semerari 2001; Lysaker and Lysaker 2001). The challenge is not only to solve the narrative content problem, but also to help patients to get involved in new forms of dialogue, embody new characters, and experience a variety of life goals rich enough to allow them to tackle the complexities of relationships.

Disorganized dialogues

With other patients the problems are completely different: their mind's theatre is inhabited by a multitude of characters, each chaotically occupying centre stage and begging urgently to speak, without waiting for the question posed by another to be solved or the latter's desires to be attained. This is the disorganized dialogue zone (Dimaggio and Semerari 2004). This extract from the third session with Linda (L), 25 years old and asking for therapy because she suffers panic attacks, is an example.

L: I've not been well the last few days. . . . As soon as I got the underground with my father, I thought: I've got to shake off these groundless fears. At least when I'm with my father I don't need to be afraid. And this seemed positive to me. Then I got an attack because I thought about having to take public transport even when I'm afraid. . . . And I remembered some other problems with my grandmother . . . I can't take criticism. At night I'm thinking people are criticizing me . . . I don't know how to defend myself . . . I've no longer got the strength to react positively . . . present myself to others with a smile, try to be like my mother would like me to be. I just want to cry.

T: You can if you want.

L: Yes and in fact that's what I've been doing these last few days, including last night, with my brother next to me . . . he was disturbed by my crying and couldn't get to sleep.

T: Oh, so you woke up crying? Tell me about it.

L: No, I saw a film on the television, but that wasn't the problem. I mean that everything went okay in the film. But then I started getting my usual thoughts again and I started . . .

T: Sorry, what thoughts?

L: My thoughts about the fact that I'm not well and in a situation I can't get out of straight away merely because I want to . . .

T: Were you thinking that you couldn't solve the problem or were you thinking about one particular situation?

L: . . . I'm afraid of relationships with others.

T: Tell me now slowly: what relationships were you thinking about?

L: I don't know, because I get confused between what I was thinking about yesterday evening and what I've been thinking about continuously over these last few days.

T: Try . . . I just want to get an idea.

L: . . . The relationship I find particularly unbearable is with my grand-mother, because she lives with us and, although she's very kind and willing, she's always criticizing and loves to poke her nose into other people's business. I get annoyed when I find her always around whatever I'm doing and I get irritated by her continual interfering . . .

T: Give me an example.

L: . . . I'm getting myself something to eat and she says, 'Oh, what are you eating?' . . . I used to clean my bedroom a bit more, but now I feel I'm obliged to and I no longer feel like it . . . and so every so often she comes and gives it a tidy but when she tidies it she moves my things around . . . I can't find some letters any more.

T: And what happens in such circumstances, for example with the letters?

L: . . . it's one of those things that deep down annoy me . . .

T: Last night you woke up crying . . .

L: Well, I couldn't get to sleep. I was thinking about my mother and how she'd like me to perhaps make a slight effort and try to behave normally, so as to not burden others too much with my problems. I was thinking that I'm not up to that and that I only wanted to burst into tears or else perhaps sink into the arms of someone willing to take me but without judging me. I compared to myself to a little girl who cries and wants only affection . . . I was thinking about going to wake up my parents or else going to the sitting room. Next door to the sitting room is my grandmother's bedroom. She'd have heard me and I didn't know how I'd have reacted if I'd had to face my grandmother.

T: What were you frightened of? What would they have done?

L: My parents would have got irritated because I'd woken them up too and so there would have been some criticism . . .

T: . . . Do you mean they'd have got angry?

L: . . . They'd have been annoyed because I'd woken them up. It's a situation I don't know how to tackle.

Linda's story is similar to Sabrina's: a weak character experienced as self and other characters, experienced as external, criticizing and intruding, like the dominators in Sabrina's story. However, the problem to be tackled by the therapist is different: a multitude of characters crowding on stage in rapid succession, each with its own different point of view, and with none of them remaining long enough for it to be possible to grasp its problem, discuss it and try to solve it. A *self-confident* character in a meta-position, i.e. capable of observing the actions of other parts of the self (Hermans and Hermans-Jansen, Chapter 8 in this volume), starts the story and describes what the *frightened self* does. Her *father* supports the frightened self. Later in the text the *frightened self* becomes the main character: it fears being forced to overcome its fears. Another sudden change, as described in the text, and the focus of the story becomes the relationship between the self *subject of a negative opinion* and *critical and intrusive others* ('I remembered some other problems with my grandmother . . . I can't take criticism. At night I'm thinking people are criticizing me'). The self swings between feeling squashed and wanting to rebel (like Sabrina). The judged self, moreover, *wants to please* others and be how they'd like it to be: *strong and independent*.

At this point the reader probably feels confused and overwhelmed by this army of characters crowding one after another into the story, and is unable to make any sense of the session extract. This is exactly what the therapist felt at that moment! Moreover, in the final part of the transcript things get even worse: weak characters, in need of help and so on, appear on, the stage.

According to dialogical self theory, the self is composed of various different characters, some perceived as self, while others belong to the self's external domain (Hermans 2003). These characters weave narrative plots, with each of them bringing its own point of view, and hold a dialogue with each other, thus creating a *polyphonic novel* (Hermans, Chapter 1 in this volume). Linda's narrative is an example of this variety of characters and of the dialogue between different parts of the self, but the tune that results is difficult to grasp. Which of these characters should the therapist listen to? What should the therapy be aimed at? Calming the panic attacks? Promoting autonomy? Validating her need for help and for someone to listen to her? Further investigation of Linda's anger?

Problems common to dialogical dysfunctions

The extract from Linda's session demonstrates how therapists dealing with disorganized dialogues find themselves with a clinical problem that goes beyond the question of narrative content. When they listen to dialogues with voices all crowding each other out with emotional urgency, there is the risk that they get confused and driven to choose only one among the various voices seeking help, thus neglecting the others, or to operate in a confused manner, without any guiding principles, jumping from one relational scenario to another. We would urge here that therapy be directed not only at the contents of a patient's narratives, but also the dialogical form that they take. In the case of disorganized dialogues the main purpose should be to bring order to chaos (Dimaggio and Semerari 2004).

In impoverished narratives the problem is the opposite: in addition to problematic contents, patients suffer because they are obliged to move around among a limited number of self-positions (Dimaggio et al. 2003). They do not have the tools to operate in a world in which they are required to take on a variety of different roles: caregiving, assisting, struggling to be independent, courting a possible partner and so on. Even in her romantic relationships, for example, Sabrina swung between feeling she was dominated by her partner and reacting angrily in an attempt to assert her rights; the outcome was always that the relationship broke up. Therapists will sense that outside such stories there is a vacuum, and so, as well as finding new endings to problematic situations, they should also aim at filling patients' narratives with new characters that have the potential to give a more adequate response to relevant life situations.

The theory we are expounding here is that a therapeutic strategy depends on the form of dialogue. Sabrina and Linda tell the same story: a struggle against a tyrant, as Linda also demonstrates during therapy. For their therapists the problems are different: in one case there is the need to enrich a poor scenario, and in the other to put some order in unmanageable chaos.

How to enrich impoverished dialogues

To illustrate treatment strategy, we are going to use some passages taken from a diary that Sabrina wrote during psychotherapy. The first text illustrates the problem her stories have as regards structure. Following on from this, we describe the rationale of the therapeutic strategy. Further passages show how Sabrina represented her relationship with her new therapist (GS). In the last extract one can see the first signs of change. Sabrina wrote the first extract after her third session.

> 8:30 a.m. Two colleagues of about my age invite me to have a coffee. This time in the morning there's nobody in the office. They take a break every two hours but I get left out the other times. The first days I was very tense. I said to myself: 'Just keep quiet and listen. Speak only if you have something intelligent to say.' I've been living a double life for a very long time: one person doing things and the other observing harshly. Those two are the only contact I have in my work environment. I'm completely isolated, except for my relations, which I keep to the absolute minimum, with the people in my section, who mob me. I've requested to be transferred. Since I made the request they've not given me any work; I'm in disgrace. The boss avoids me. My section head doesn't believe me but tells me to exercise self-criticism, while taking me for a ride. He says they haven't got it in for me. Then why do they leave me without any work for two months? The managing director shows his animosity when he sees me . . . I just feel lost and useless. . . . To go back to the coffee break: on one occasion Tony made me trip up so I stumbled and he could hold me up with a hand on my stomach so that I didn't fall. I told him 'You did that on purpose! Don't do it again'. Right at that moment I wasn't absolutely sure but then he started to court me. Today he tried to give me a hug. I pushed him away and said to him to be good. Jokingly, not as if I was annoyed. I don't like it. Does he think I'm ready to jump into bed with him? OK, I feel lonely, but this seems too much to me. Do they think I'm a tart?

The characters in this first extract are the same as in the scene with the nail in the shoe. All her work colleagues have a *malicious, rejecting and deceiving* position *vis-à-vis* self, which is *weak, humiliated and yearning for isolation*. In another dialogical pattern *self is seeking a relationship* but is under the gaze of a self-observing character (a meta-position), which is *mercilessly critical* ('Speak only if you have something intelligent to say'). Her young colleagues, even if *sexually attracted by her*, nevertheless take on *scornful* characteristics ('Do they think I'm a tart?'). The self's reply to this depreciating sexual interest is the *threatening anger* ('Don't do it again') that had already surfaced during assessment.

There is this same narrative pattern in almost all the texts written during the first two months of therapy. It is because there is no variation in subject matter and there are always the same characters that we define such dialogues as impoverished.

In other extracts one can note how her mother has the same characteristics as the meta-position, i.e. *tyrannical and scornful*. In the presence of this character self is characterized by *negative self-esteem and doubts about its own thoughts*. Her father is an exception: Sabrina loves him and considers him intellectually above her but unable to be of assistance. She sees herself as being tyrannical towards her parents. There is no relational context in which she uses different yardsticks in her interactions with others. As a result, in real life others either exclude her or deride her.

In treating this pattern, the therapist bears in mind that Sabrina has no other constructs to give meaning to her relations. He therefore asks her for feedback about the treatment and explains that, if she feels treated badly or cheated, she can be quite frank about this (Safran and Muran 2000). He tries to always maintain a neutral tone and is careful not to say anything that might sound like criticism. On this basis he pinpoints the main character in her narratives as being the *criticized and humiliated* one and helps her in recognizing this. He therefore validates her emotions: 'I can understand your being distressed; living continuously with the feeling that you're not worth anything and with others constantly confirming this must be awful.' These observations are effective and result in Sabrina feeling understood, while at the same time the atmosphere in the therapeutic relationship is good. At this point the therapist becomes an idealized figure, like her father and a former partner. There is nevertheless an ever present risk that the ideal character devalues herself.

> Marco [*former boyfriend*] behaves like you [*therapist*]. He has a kind ring to his voice and pays attention to everything I say. You can feel he's always making an effort. I've tried to reassure myself and to be less fearful. He always does so much for me. If he were to hurt me, I'd suffer. He keeps a certain distance. He's afraid too. Like you. I mustn't think he's laughing at me. Firstly, because it's a thought that has come to obsess me and, secondly, because I too can laugh at myself. But if you too say that when I'm seized by such a strong emotion I don't evaluate things correctly, this is like saying that you agree that I can't trust what I feel or think. However, I can suspend judgement and wait.

The patient construes the therapist as being kind and she feels welcome and loved, even if the dominant pattern appears in the background ('If he were to hurt me, I'd suffer'). And there is another novelty: Sabrina realizes that the therapist, as he has always remarked jokingly during her sessions, is afraid of her. This is the first sign that it is possible to make some progress; Sabrina is acquiring a self-reflective awareness that she herself contributes to eliciting the rejection that she fears.

The last extract is a good example of the proposition that impoverished narratives require their own attention. The therapist is in fact questioning Sabrina's perception that others are all malicious towards her, by making it hypothetical. Sabrina, however, does not have other positions from which to observe the world: she swings between confusion and her basic position where she *sees herself as worthless* ('you agree that I can't trust what I feel or think').

Pattern-breaking on its own is therefore not enough in the treatment of such patients. The next step that the therapist must take is to use the traces of new voices, emotions that are poorly articulated, as the foundations for new narratives. Kelly (1955), Stiles (1999) and Whelton and Greenberg (Chapter 7 in this volume) state that patients need to be assisted in expressing constructs or characters from their internal stage which have been hidden or not acknowledged until now (Hermans 2003). The first signs we see of them are often poorly expressed emotions, or vague sensations or fragments of speech not acknowledged as being the patient's own.

A further step is to identify these sensations better and create 'meaning bridges' between the new voices and the others that dominate the patient's inner community (Stiles, Osatuke, Glick and Mackay, Chapter 6 in this volume; Osatuke, Gray, Glick, Stiles and Barkham, Chapter 15 in this volume). Sabrina expresses this process, based on the Piagetian assimilation of new fragments of inner experience, in her own words: 'So I can suspend judgement while I seek out new information'.

A few sessions later we see how this process of constructing new characters takes place by way of a sort of learning through action. The extract starts with a reference to the last session:

> We met yesterday for a session. When I left, I felt so enthusiastic.

Already in this first line Sabrina reveals a part of her self that has been absent until now, and enters a mental state of joy. She carries on as follows:

> I'll try and make a summary to establish what we said and see if I've understood properly. My fears about others get manifested in my behaviour and my facial expressions. This can provoke a feeling of extraneousness, unease and remoteness in another person and he does not know what is causing it. However, on the basis of this sensation he tends to move away.

Sabrina has therefore constructed a meta-position together with the therapist, who interprets her difficulties in relationships in a different way. This is the pattern-breaking part of the therapy. What she writes below illustrates what meaning-construction involves.

> Well, I'd decided to keep a happier face and to be more self-confident. I was now aware of a process that was going on. I looked happy but I felt stupid. [Referring to her two colleagues] I tried to shake them off but, instead, they greeted me with such smiling faces that I felt I was welcome. I wanted to do the same sort of thing for them but I'm so awkward. I

make myself look awkward. But that's not how I am. I'm not going to commit suicide today either.

With these acquisitions, Sabrina explores her new position – *self-confident and accepted* – that, however, has not been assimilated. The fact that the accommodation process has barely started is evident from her remarks: 'I felt stupid'; 'I make myself look awkward'. Sabrina does not identify the emerging facets as being self. Her final comment, 'I'm not going to commit suicide' is ironical in tone and a sign that Sabrina is less despairing.

How to restore order to chaos

A therapist tackling disorganized narratives needs to take a number of actions. We present them systematically and give them a rationale, based on how Linda's therapist reacted to the last session extract and to what happened next in the session, as described later. In the first part the therapist tried to tune in with the various characters in Linda's dialogue as they surfaced, with the aim of getting to know them better. He therefore let himself be carried along by the various fluctuations that there were in her discourse. He asked for more information about the *incapable* character's sensitivity to criticism from a *stern and intrusive* grandmother, the relationship between the *weak* character suffering panic attacks and the *reassuring* father, her crying at night and so on.

This is the first step for a therapist to take when listening to a disorganized dialogue: try to tune in with all the characters surfacing. Excluding any of them would probably provoke a protest on their part. It is, however, an action with the limitation that it gives a therapist a feeling of confusion and overwhelming. 'Who is this? What am I doing?' is the typical reaction in such a situation. At this point a therapist has two options: stop tuning in with each individual character and try to show the patient how chaotic the latter's dialogue is, by helping him or her to observe him- or herself with detachment and select the questions that are really important. The therapist should say something like: 'I feel confused when we're dealing with all these different questions. I imagine that you must be experiencing the same sort of confusion with this whirl of emotions. In such instances I find it useful to stop a moment and not attempt to tackle everything all at once. Do you think we could give it a try?' (Dimaggio and Semerari 2004). Comments like this generally bring relief and, in particular, make a session easier to manage; patients will try, at least temporarily, to put some order in their discourse.

The second action that can be taken is illustrated in the next extract, where the therapist selects the symptomatic voice. He addresses himself, therefore, to the character suffering from panic attacks and asking to be cared for, and tries to calm it down and validate its mastery skills.

T: You'd like to be looked after in a really physical way . . . like when you feel the need to hug someone . . .

L: Yes and you also ought to know that yesterday evening I wasn't quite sure what I wanted . . .

T: What things were you not sure about?

L: I told you earlier: waking my parents up, getting myself spoilt a bit, perhaps going to sleep with them in their bed.

T: . . . You have the sensation of having to deal with situations in which you don't feel up to it and you have instead a very strong need for protection.

L: . . . During the current period I've been thinking that deep down these are problems that I've had since I was born . . .

T: Well done! Sure. Of course, when we're born, this is a problem we all have . . .

The therapist validates Linda's desire to be looked after and observes that it is universal (Bowlby 1969–1982).

L: There you are . . .

T: Because, given that we're all little and defenceless *vis-à-vis* the world, we all have the need, in a strange environment and in the situations we have to deal with, for someone who makes us feel protected and safe.

L: . . . Given that I've had it since I was born and until now, I reckon that it must be typical of me . . . I've also seen a link between these facts and the fear I have of taking public transport . . .

T: Well done!

L: Because I've no longer been thinking about my fear of movement but about that of finding myself in a strange environment . . .

T: Good! You've grasped the whole question (smiles).

L: I've grasped the whole question (smiles). Yes, what I'm afraid of is finding myself in a strange environment, where there's nobody to help me if I don't feel okay.

T: Very good! This is your underlying fear. Finding yourself in a strange environment, which then takes this particular form.

Here Linda sets up some meaning bridges (Stiles 1999) between the fragmented parts of self surfacing in the first part of the session: the frightened self and the one seeking someone to look after it without finding them, now communicate with each other. She feels strengthened, her mood alters and she is in tune with the therapist (they smile by mutual agreement).

It needs to be stated that the goal of all the actions described above is to foster communication between characters and make what the patient says *during sessions* coherent (Semerari, Carcione, Dimaggio, Nicolò and Procacci, Chapter 14 in this volume). Disorganized dialogues are in fact a serious pathological signal and, after a short period of integration, the bridges that have been built fall to pieces and leave the stage free again for confusion. In Linda there is also an activation of sexual desires making her temporarily enter delirious states, in which the therapist and her parents become characters in a conspiracy designed to make her have sexual relations.

A therapist therefore needs to have the building of meaning bridges between characters as a goal. The hypothesis is that a therapist's integrating voice gets slowly assimilated into a patient's landscape, where it has the ability to make sense of the multiplicity of voices and to self-soothe distressful emotions (Fonagy and Target 1996; Hermans 2003; Semerari et al., Chapter 14 in this volume).

The last tool that a therapist has for building more organized forms of dialogue is to divide up the setting. The following example is a good illustration of this proposition. After three years of therapy Linda's delirious episodes are becoming less common, but she is still terrorized by the idea of having sexual relations, even if she desires them. The therapist realizes that Linda is still going to feel too threatened by people of her own age to be able to have any sentimental relationships and, as he is worried about a relapse, he urges her to be cautious about this. Moreover, his internal *markers* are signalling to him that Linda's relationship with him, a man, excites the patient too much. He therefore decides to entrust Linda at the same time to a woman therapist. In this second setting a new *cheerful* voice, *with a desire for sentimental relationships without being frightened by them*, surfaces. The new character thus surfacing finds a therapist who sees Linda as being ready for sexual feelings. The therapist therefore creates a sort of fun atmosphere, in which Linda feels able to start integrating the voice expressing ego-syntonic sexual desires into her community of voices.

Conclusion

If therapists were to concentrate only on the contents of the narratives related during therapy, many underlying clinical problems would not get solved. As we have seen, Linda and Sabrina had a common core theme: being criticized, dominated and invalidated by malicious or contemptuous characters. However, the two patients handled this theme differently: Sabrina's inner and interpersonal dialogue is monotonous and stereotypical, whereas Linda's is confused and disorganized. Their therapists, once they have identified which dysfunctional dialogue form is involved, implement different types of treatment. We now describe the rationale common to the two treatment strategies, the differences and the problems left unsolved.

In both cases the therapeutic relationship is problematical and weakened not only by the contents of the stories, but also by the *form* the stories take. As a result of the repetitive nature of impoverished dialogues a therapist is obliged to embody stereotypical and often unpleasant characters – in Sabrina's case, tyrant and victim – which are difficult to keep up for very long. More generally, the sensation is one of moving about in a vacuum and with limited margins for manoeuvre.

In disorganized narratives a therapist can get confused on finding that he or she embodies one character after another. The result is that the therapist can easily get irritated, become inappropriately domineering or want to get out of the relationship.

A weak therapeutic alliance indicates a bad prognosis (Henry et al. 1986). The first step to take, therefore, is the regulation of the alliance in order to overcome any problems or ruptures. Therapists are often required to reveal their own state of mind and their own point of view about what is going on in order to help a patient to build up a new character and then, subsequently, internalize it. Sabrina's therapist, for example, realized that he was afraid of offending her and, after modulating this fear, then confided this internal process to her in an ironical tone (Aron 1996; Safran and Muran 2000).

The second common element is the *absence* of characters facilitating adaptation to relationships and subjective well-being. In *impoverished dialogues* this absence is widespread. As a result, one of the objectives of therapy should be the introduction of new characters or the foregrounding of one or more background characters. Stiles and colleagues (see Chapters 6 and 15) maintain that during therapy new voices surface and, with the therapist's assistance, get identified, validated and integrated into the dialogue with the other characters making up a patient's self. Such a process hardly ever occurs *tout court* and spontaneously. Patients undergoing therapy produce non-integrated fragments of their experiences. A therapist should aim to identify and validate these fragments, and integrate them into patients' mental landscapes, thus promoting the process of assimilation of new parts of self from poorly articulated emotional traces. Severe patients need to learn afresh new ways of being, discover new areas of the world and incorporate them into their cognitive schemas.

In disorganized dialogues there are no characters in a meta-position able to integrate the various parts of self, recognize constancy when relationships change and modulate distressful emotions. In both dysfunctions, therefore, a key part of the treatment is the introduction of new characters.

The therapeutic operations we have just described are time-consuming: assimilating new information, putting order in the chaos surrounding the characters and soothing the distress require time and there is still a high risk of relapse. Therapists finding these dysfunctions should, therefore, be aware that they are going to be involved in a process keeping them occupied for a long period.

The next step is to give this approach an empirical basis by researching into individual cases, with the aim of verifying, first, the existence of the dialogical dysfunctions we have hypothesized, and second, the change process that actually does take place in cases with a successful outcome and what happens, on the other hand, in cases with a negative outcome. Our hypothesis is that in the negative examples it is possible that therapists get stuck in patients' narratives, thus contributing involuntarily to the repetition of old stories. In the examples with a good outcome, on the other hand, therapists probably manage to get out of the dysfunctional interpersonal processes in which they find themselves – by, for example, taking on persecutory roles (with Sabrina) or lapsing into confusion (with Linda) – and then encouraging patients' ability to observe themselves and find new forms of dialogue.

References

Aron, L. (1996). *A Meeting of Minds: Mutuality in Psychoanalysis*. Hillsdale, NJ: Analytic Press.

Baldwin, M.W. (1992). 'Relational schemas and the processing of social information.' *Psychological Bulletin, 112*, 461–484.

Bowlby, J. (1969/1982). *Attachment and Loss, Vol. 1*, 2nd edn. London: Hogarth Press.

Dimaggio, G. and Semerari, A. (2001). 'Psychopathological narrative forms.' *Journal of Constructivist Psychology, 14*, 1–23.

Dimaggio, G. and Semerari, A. (2004). 'Disorganized narratives: The psychological condition and its treatment.' In L. Angus and J. McLeod (eds) *Handbook of Narrative and Psychotherapy: Practice, Theory and Research* (pp. 263–282). Thousand Oaks, CA: Sage.

Dimaggio, G., Salvatore, G., Azzara, C., Catania, D., Semerari, A. and Hermans, H.J.M. (2003). 'Dialogical relationship in impoverished narratives: From theory to clinical practice.' *Psychology and Psychotherapy, 76*(4), 385–410.

Fonagy, P. and Target, M. (1996). 'Playing with reality I: Theory of mind and the normal development of psychic reality.' *International Journal of Psychoanalysis, 77*, 217–233.

Henry, W.P., Schacht, T.E. and Strupp, H.H. (1986). 'Structural analysis of social behaviour: Application to a study of interpersonal process in differential psychotherapeutic outcome.' *Journal of Consulting and Clinical Psychology, 54*, 27–31.

Hermans, H.J.M. (1996). 'Voicing the self: From information processing to dialogical interchange.' *Psychological Bulletin, 119*, 31–50.

Hermans, H.J.M. (2003). 'The construction and reconstruction of a dialogical self.' *Journal of Constructivist Psychology, 69*, 89–127.

Hermans, H.J.M. and Kempen H.J.K. (1993). *The Dialogical Self: Meaning as Movement*. San Diego, CA: Academic Press.

Horowitz, M.J. (1998). *Cognitive Psychodynamics: From Conflict to Character*. New York: Wiley.

Kelly, G. (1955). *The Psychology of Personal Constructs*. New York: Norton.

Lysaker, P.H. and Lysaker, J.T. (2001). 'Psychosis and the disintegration of dialogical self-structure: Problems posed by schizophrenia for the maintenance of dialogue.' *British Journal of Medical Psychology, 74*, 23–33.

Safran, J.D. and Muran, J.C. (2000). *Negotiating the Therapeutic Alliance: A Relational Treatment Guide*. New York: Guilford.
Stiles, W.B. (1999). 'Signs and voices in psychotherapy.' *Psychotherapy Research*, *9*, 1–21.

Chapter 13

Dialogical transformation in the psychotherapy of schizophrenia

Paul H. Lysaker and John T. Lysaker

By the late 1970s, interest across the United States in psychotherapeutic treatments for schizophrenia had waned. Institutionally, the academic–private hospital partnerships that had provided the primary support for the psychotherapy of schizophrenia had undergone dramatic reorganization (Silver 2002). Psychotherapeutic approaches to schizophrenia were also undercut theoretically as its long-time legitimizing discourse, psychoanalysis, lost much of its standing as a valid form of science (Drake and Sederer 1986). However, at present, there is renewed interest in psychotherapy's potential to help people confront the challenges that schizophrenia poses for the conduct of their lives (e.g. Fenton 2000; Holma and Aaltonen 1995, 1998; Sensky et al. 2000).

One force that may be driving this recent interest in the psychotherapy of schizophrenia is an evolving interdisciplinary concern with how persons construct meaning in their lives, and how those constructions affect recovery from illness. Regarding multiple medical and existential issues, some have suggested that the most meaningful movements toward health may occur at the level of how persons understand and tell the story of their lives (Crossley 2000; Kleinman 1988; Neimeyer and Raskin 2000). Regarding psychiatric disabilities, it has been proposed from a rehabilitation perspective, that increased coherence in narratives of self and illness might enhance the abilities of disabled persons to critically examine and articulate beliefs and emotions, and embrace a realistic sense of agency (Davidson and Strauss 1992; Lysaker and France 1999; Williams and Collins 1999).

With an increasing emphasis on the reconstruction of self or meaning as a central aspect of mental health, it thus seems natural that practices like psychotherapy would attract theorists and practitioners concerned about schizophrenia. Most integrative accounts define psychotherapy as a process that facilitates reflection upon and change among personal narratives. At its root, psychotherapy is also a dialogue that can challenge, nurture and enliven clients' conversations both within themselves and between themselves and others. Psychotherapy is a process that can help reshape a person's narratives by addressing narrative at the level of the dialogues from which it emerges and evolves. Put another way, it seems a matter of intuition that from psychotherapy may come richer dialogue and from richer dialogue richer narratives and movements towards health, well-being and adaptation, even among the most disabled.

It is the contention of this chapter, however, that assisting persons with schizophrenia to make their way towards a more adaptive life by helping them to talk to themselves and others in different ways, raises a number of crucial questions at a finer level of analysis. For instance, how would we know when such a narrative change has occurred? What are possible markers? What types of transformations take place? For instance, is a once 'lost' narrator 'found', as the popular notion of awakenings suggests? Are groups of negative voices that previously dominated the telling of a life story silenced? Ultimately, these questions need to be answered if the field is to be able to pose the even larger questions; namely can such changes be empirically linked to healthy outcomes?

To examine these issues, we shall begin with a review of literature that bears on the possible descriptive and elemental qualities of the dialogical self and resultant narrative that might change as psychotherapy progresses. Next, we shall offer a content and thematic analysis of the dialogical and narrative qualities of a single client with schizophrenia that occurred over two and a half years of psychotherapy. Last, we will use this analysis to formulate hypotheses for future study.

Potential elements of narrative and dialogical transformation

Thinking about personal narratives and the dialogues that animate them, there seem several possible changes that might be detectable during the psychotherapy of schizophrenia. First, a narrative's content might change. It has been suggested, for instance, that recovery may necessitate the development of a coherent, future-oriented identity (Davidson and Strauss 1992; Roe and Ben-Yaskai 1999). Thus a story might evolve as driven by a voice seeking to assert control over destiny. It has also been suggested that uncertainty and a sense of overwhelming loss often result when formal symptoms are reduced and persons perceive their lives more accurately (Duckworth et al. 1997). Narrative transformation at the level of content might also involve the emergence of explicit grief. Literature on stigma and mental illness also has bearing on this. Given widespread, public belief that persons with mental illness are helpless and dangerously unable to control their behaviour (Martin et al. 2000), narrative change in schizophrenia could be construed to be manifest as the rejection of stigma.

Beyond changes in content, however, there might also be more global changes concerning the existence of any narrative at all. Holma and Aaltonen (1998: 263) have suggested that in acute psychosis, narrative has 'failed or collapsed' leaving only a 'pre-narrative' that fails to sufficiently capture the qualities of personal experience, thus leaving 'the present and especially the future . . . unstructured'. Consistent with the descriptions of many others (e.g. Young and Ensign 1999), Holma and Aaltonen (1995 1998) suggest that in a pre-narrative state one is left with a diminished sense of agency, reflexivity and temporality. For these authors, transformation may be characterized as a movement from a lack of narrative (or a pre-narrative state), to a narratively organized story wherein the narrator's self-portrayal presents someone who is a plausible participant in a historically grounded world.

These authors also suggest that being trapped in a pre-narrative state may be the result of affectively laden or traumatic events that the person has had difficulty successfully interpreting (Seikkula et al. 2001). In the larger sense it is implied here that the movement from pre-narrative to narrative often occurs when a mentally ill person is able to articulate particular traumatic events in a manner others can understand. This seems consistent with earlier psychoanalytic writings that stress that there may be particular difficulties that need to be clarified or resolved before story elements can cohere (e.g. Searles 1965; Singer and Wynne 1966). Distinct from trauma models, this view suggests not the creation of parallel or walled off aspects of being following trauma, but the total collapse of the story itself. Holma and Aaltonen thus also expect changes at the level of content in the process of narrative recovery: something previously secret comes to the fore, and the narrator's ability to acknowledge and make sense of it empowers and enables greater self-coherency.

Apart from changes in content and the global re-emergence of personal narratives, one might also look for changes in another sense, in the quality and manner of a narrative. Or, more precisely, one might look for changes in the organizing aspects of a narrative. As noted earlier and illustrated broadly throughout this volume, narratives are the product of ongoing conversations both within the individual and between individuals and others (Hermans 1996; Wortham 2001). Accordingly, stories are created when different aspects of the self interanimate each other or bring significance to one another through their interaction or dialogue (Bakhtin 1981, 1983). This perspective stresses that while narratives lend unity to the experience of daily life, they do so not only through the interpretation of worldly events, but through dynamic, multilayered and heterogeneous conversations that occur within persons (Crossley 2000; Hermans et al. 1993; Neimeyer and Raskin 2000).

With specific regard to schizophrenia we have argued (Lysaker and Lysaker 2001, 2002, 2004) that narratives in schizophrenia are compromised because the ability to maintain internal conversations has been disrupted given the decline in neurocognition present with the onset of the illness. In other words, as it becomes more difficult to connect thoughts together, perhaps it becomes increasingly difficult for the afflicted person to initiate and maintain the heterogeneous conversations necessary to produce and sustain an integrated life narrative. Specifically we have hypothesized that such a disturbance in the ability to sustain internal conversation could result in at least three forms of narrative disturbance: first, cacophonous stories wherein the narration is composed of animated self-positions occurring continuously without sufficient organizing structures, second, barren stories wherein self-positions are few and mostly isolated, and third, monological stories wherein self-positions and life experiences are dominated by a usually external, singular, tyrannical force (Lysaker et al. 2001). These suppositions may be seen to parallel observations that there are at least three major domains of psychopathology in schizophrenia including disorganized behaviour and speech (cognitive symptoms), the absence of affect, volition and interest (negative symptoms), and the domination of thought and behaviour by bizarre beliefs and/or sensory experiences (positive symptoms: Bell et al. 1994). These suppositions may also be seen as consistent with larger observations that persons with schizophrenia in general often have difficulties constructing meaningful accounts of the dilemmas they face (Amador et al. 1995) and may experience translating subjective experience verbally (Danion et al. 2001).

From this perspective, narrative and dialogical transformation in schizophrenia could involve movement from an inadequately generated narrative (i.e. one riddled by insufficient dialogue), to one wherein multiple self-positions and the social relations they entail converse and interanimate one another. Put another way, maybe narrative transformation in schizophrenia involves the development of increasingly complex and diverse internal conversations, which at a distance could be described as a movement away from a monologue or cacophony and towards dialogue. Such changes might be reflected in a concrete increase in the numbers of characters available within the narrative (both in terms of self and other presentations), and the number and manner of the interactions among these characters. With more persons available to relate to and with more self-positions to generate narrative, perhaps it will be easier to produce and revise narratives such that they are less monological, cacophonous or barren. Thus, in contrast to the assumptions of an awakenings model wherein a once absent narrator reappears, this model suggests that improved narrative coherence in schizophrenia may proceed incrementally, deepening as internal dialogue deepens. The dialogical model, therefore, should also be contrasted with the model that predicates transformation on the resolution of particular issues or dilemmas (Lysaker et al. 2003b). In other words, it may be that the cessation of dialogue is at issue for psychotherapy here, not the failure to resolve particular issues. Put another way, perhaps it is more important that conversation is reanimated than that a particular conclusion is reached.

In summary, narrative transformation in schizophrenia could move along several possible axes. Some would involve shifts in content, tied to matters of grief, increased agency, and the rejection of social stigmatization. Other axes might include a more global movement from a 'narrativeless' to a narrated life possibly with a missing narrator being recovered and possibly with this process linked to the resolution of trauma. It is lastly possible, and this is our view, that enriched dialogical exchanges among heterogeneous self-positions could be seen to emerge as psychotherapy progresses.

Case analysis of narrative transformation: methods

Case selection

To examine the extent to which some of the hypothesized changes in narrative can be observed, we have analysed the transcripts of a person with schizophrenia who was enrolled in individual psychotherapy over a two-and-a-half-year period. In choosing this case, we wished to avoid the common criticism that if improving, the client either did not have schizophrenia or had only a mild case (Harding et al. 1992). We thus purposefully sampled (Denzin and Lincoln 2000) someone with significant symptoms, neurocognitive deficits and psychosocial impairments. We were also concerned that the client's changes should not be measured from a particularly 'low' point. Thus the second criterion for selection included clinical stability at the onset of psychotherapy.

Context

The psychotherapy under examination was voluntary and provided under routine conditions in an outpatient psychiatric clinic. It was integrative in orientation with interventions derived from cognitive-behavioural, psychodynamic, humanistic and postmodern backgrounds (Lysaker and France 1999; Lysaker et al. 2001). Sessions were weekly, and at the client's request, lasted thirty minutes. The psychotherapist was a clinical psychologist with over fifteen years of experience working with persons with severe mental illness. The therapist's orientation emphasized the avoidance of authoritarian relationships and the provision of a supportive environment enabling the client to reflect. Objective aspects of mental illness were recognized as well as the processes of transference and countertransference. Thus the therapy was not explicitly dialogical in orientation. It was instead our interest to investigate dialogical and other narrative changes that might occur as a result of integrative psychotherapy.

Ralph: background information

Ralph is an unemployed, never-married male in his forties with multiple deficits and sources of social disadvantage.[1] His symptoms began in late adolescence and the course of his illness was associated with over twenty inpatient hospitalizations, episodes of homelessness, polysubstance

dependence and legal problems, including many instances of verbal aggres-
siveness at the medical centre where he was treated. On the Positive and
Negative Syndrome Rating Scale (Bell et al. 1994), prior to the onset of
psychotherapy he had severe levels of positive symptoms (i.e. symptoms such
as hallucinations and delusions), moderate levels of negative symptoms (i.e.
symptoms such as blunted affect and lack of interpersonal interest) and
moderately severe levels of cognitive symptoms (i.e. symptoms such as conceptual disorganization). On the California Verbal Learning Test (Delis et al.
1987), a test of verbal memory, and the Wisconsin Card Sorting Test (Heaton
et al. 1993), a test of flexibility in abstract thinking, Ralph demonstrated
significantly impaired performance of more than 1.5 standard deviations
below his age-expected score. Prior to the onset of his illness he was an above-
average student in school; he had been sexually abused in early adolescence
and struggled with substance abuse thereafter.

Analyses

To determine how Ralph's narrative and internal dialogues may have
changed over time we parcelled hand-written psychotherapy transcripts,
taken verbatim during session, from a two-and-a-half-year period into five
groups: months 1–6, 7–12, 13–18, 19–24 and 25–31. The choice of six months
was deemed desirable since it would allow for multiple sessions within each
block and might avoid our being misled by spurious movements.

We read and reread each group of hand-written transcripts and considered
the patient's speech within every session as a sample of how he was narrating
his life. As each segment was read we had the goal of identifying: (a) the
characters that tended to populate the world as narrated by the patient, (b)
the different ways the patient implicitly or explicitly characterized himself,
and (c) the themes of his story. When considering the characters we were
interested in both the number of characters and the nature of those characters. For instance, characters could also be actual persons or groups of
actual persons known directly by the narrator (e.g. six cousins living nearby),
abstract groups (women in general), actual persons not known directly (e.g. a
famous singer), imaginary (e.g. hallucinated ghosts), etc. When assessing the
ways in which the patient characterized himself, we were interested in the
various self-facets invoked (e.g. self-as-former-criminal, self-as-sexually-
frustrated, self-as-loving). To examine themes, we distilled into a brief para-
graph the basic plot of each session's narration. More detailed descriptions
of these methods have been presented elsewhere in an analysis of a smaller
portion of the early material of this case (Lysaker et al. 2003a).

A qualitative case analysis of narrative and dialogical transformation

Epoch 1: the first six months

Across the first six months of psychotherapy, Ralph revealed a landscape full of angst and suffering. Never an active agent in his life, he exerted little control beyond abstract forms of protest (e.g. wearing certain clothing to make a political point to others hundreds of miles away). He attended almost every session but repeatedly expressed doubts regarding his ability to talk about his life, often, either directly or indirectly, asking the therapist to tell his story for him. The characters populating his story were often abstract groups of persons (e.g. women in general), or substances like nicotine. Mention of other individuals he knew was also cursory and little detail was provided about their emotional states. The world as a whole seemed impersonal and empty and the position of the narrator was one of helplessness. As an example consider the following:

> Do I look like a cartoon character, have a big head like the character on your desk calendar? No I'm not worried about much now. Life is stagnant. I'm in between . . . not much other than caffeine and nicotine. I do have a major problem my social security cheque is late. Just caffeine and nicotine and not much of it . . . I'm catching a cold and ache all over. I get six to eight hours of sleep per night. Little energy and no gumption. Don't know what to do except take it slow. Nothing much for months. No sexual gratification. Just disappeared might be medicine or the voices getting over. Got a letter from my cousin. It was an order, court order I can't go there any more. It is meaningless.

As can be seen, if one considers that during this epoch, material such as the above examples was repeated over and over in session, Ralph's self-presentation was relatively monological. He spoke of himself primarily as a victim and alienated shade, who was forever on the verge of dying for lack of nurturance. There were few shifts we could detect in how the self was portrayed or in the voices that contributed to the story. Aspects of his story were also implausible during moments of therapy. For example, he told of how portions of his mind were being stolen and claimed that some people were really computers. Other themes common across sessions that did not appear in our excerpt, included a sense of heroism for resisting the injustices of mainstream life, as well as a sense of being entitled to revenge because of the involuntary hospitalizations, forced administration of antipsychotic medications, lengthy incarcerations, and physical assaults he suffered.

Epoch 2: the second six months

In the second half of the first year of psychotherapy Ralph's depiction of his life again involved lengthy descriptions of suffering that seemed to never abate. He still did not portray himself as an active agent, and while he still made almost every session, he remained doubtful about his ability to talk about his life. He directly discussed how previous therapists had chided and scolded him and implied that he missed their directiveness. He seemed to find it curious that the therapist was forever 'putting the ball back in my court'.

During this second segment, almost all the characters mentioned were real people he knew. There were considerably fewer references to either abstract groups or substances. Accounts of others remained cursory and generally one sided, however. Even with the presence of more persons, Ralph's self-presentation remained relatively monological. He again tended to present himself as an alienated victim with few resources living at the mercy of an uncaring world. His overall story became more plausible, and previously held delusional beliefs were a source of embarrassment, although they were not identified as aspects of his mental illness. The same themes of sexual frustration, revenge and heroism also remained present.

As an illustration, consider the following excerpt:

> Any time society sees someone as abnormal they look down on him and when you are six feet eight inches tall anyone looking down on five feet ten inches, it is difficult. So it is hard to fit in and go to parties to have friends . . . I am a recluse because of my outlook on society. I can see how it burns me up just to talk to girls in a coffee shop. They are coherent. They are about my basic manhood . . . maybe I sound like a teenager . . . it's the position I'm in life right now. How well we both know it's not healthy to stuff feelings . . . I'm fighting for a chance for my turn. Maybe they want, that the family who adopted me, for me to have my birthright somehow.

Epoch 3: the first six months of the second year

As the second year of therapy began, transcripts revealed a story in which the narrator was wracked with suffering and did not believe that he could recover. He continued to paint a world unresponsive to his wishes and actions, one in which he had little power. As in the second epoch, he continued to refer to a wide range of other real people. Unlike the second epoch, however, far more self-positions appeared in his self-presentations. In contrast to earlier sessions, when discussing events, he argued with himself, offering different sides and views, and directly vocalized conflicting aspects of himself, leaving little sense that his story was a product of an internal monologue. Moreover, Ralph's self-positions were more closely tied to interpersonal relations (e.g. friend, mother, father and grandfather) and were more attuned to the complexity of his situation. While the conversations earlier in therapy involved all or nothing issues (e.g. 'I am or am not worthless'), Ralph's reflections now seemed to entertain many more voices, and discuss more complex issues. During this time, there was both a sense of mourning tied to helplessness and hopelessness which was answered with the possibility that a twist of fate might bring about change, though this was explicitly not a twist that he could influence.

During this third epoch, Ralph increasingly mentioned hearing the voice of an angel who loved him and told him he was special and valuable. The description of this voice was far more articulate than previous mentions of hallucinated voices and Ralph stated how grateful for the love this figure gave him. Also themes of frustration, revenge and heroism remained, and he still did not regard positive symptoms as symptoms of mental illness. Strikingly, while Ralph attended the first three months of sessions during the second year, he suddenly stopped attending and offered no explanation.

Here is a brief excerpt from shortly before he took a break from therapy:

> I don't know if I'm financially or mentally stable enough to carry on with a relationship. I am not much of a problem solver or conversationalist. I am no good at arguing. I might be borderline inept when it comes to comforting or counselling her. I'm more simultaneous or spur of the moment. I might get tired of it if it became a crutch for the other person. That's part of my immaturity if I was in a relationship where I was always giving and not receiving comfort . . . maybe I've given up hope on something I've had my eye on for 25 years and never got close to . . . I know I can talk to girls easier now though . . . this society confuses me.

Epoch 4: the end of the second year

Just as Ralph did not attend therapy over the last three months of epoch 3 he also missed nearly every session during the first three months of epoch 4. During the few sessions he attended, however, the mystery was explained. Apparently, as Ralph felt 'better' he found himself better able to connect with others. This included forming what Ralph deemed a friendship with drug dealers, persons he viewed as having more social status than he possessed. He expressed feeling 'happier' than he had in years. Though now actively using illegal substances, losing weight and having more health problems, he felt more valuable as a person. Interestingly, despite considerable substance abuse, the severity of his hallucinations and delusions did not increase nor did he require hospitalization. When he returned to therapy, the content of sessions during this epoch involved a positively toned debate between the therapist and Ralph regarding the authenticity of his friendships and the destructiveness of the abuse.

As in epoch 3, Ralph's stories were populated with a number of different persons he knew and his internal conversations were far richer than those observed initially. Ralph retained the vision of himself as having been horribly wronged by others, and unable to influence his fate, though now he started to see himself a culprit as well. Entirely on his own prompting, he produced an outline of his life during a long weekend alone and as he recounted it in session, was shocked when he found little to support his view of himself as special. There was still much about revenge, frustration and implicit reference to his mourning. He did arrange near the end of epoch 4 a family meeting and re-established regular contact with parents and adult siblings.

Here is an excerpt from epoch 4:

> Just relaxing with my eyes shut . . . full of depression and apathy. Talked to the job counsellor told her the same stuff. No appetite. No sleep. Too much sleep. Nothing in balance. I'm tired of this city but I belong here. I was going to go to Kentucky, but Pat the kid was only in it for the money . . . and yes substances . . . cocaine. I've made a pact to my mother to lay off the stuff . . . now no cocaine or pot for two days . . . desire, habit, false sense of need, necessity. Talked to mom. She needs help too. I told her I'd help if I could get my act together. She staying with my cousin who's treating her awful just like I was treated, taking advantage of her . . . Mom's tired. She looking for an escape . . . I'm tired of this state of mind . . . Before I didn't have an outside perspective to see my finger on the button.

Epoch 5: the start of the third year

With the end of epoch 4 and the start of epoch 5, Ralph was in legal trouble and achieved abstinence periodically. His transcripts continued to involve many real characters with long stretches in which he debated and discussed matters with himself. Even more than in earlier sessions this involved the therapist listening while Ralph talked with himself. Ralph's conversations with himself deepened and included even more instances in which various aspects of self seemed to be in dialogue not about external matters but about his very identity. His narrative again seemed to change slightly here. He now described himself in detail as making poor decisions. He also talked about himself making bad decisions from different perspectives and broached the possibility that some of his experiences of being 'special' were not real but products of his illness and a wish to hide his problems from himself. This engendered much sadness and was linked to the losses of an adolescent dream of becoming a piano teacher. He was able to consider that he could control his fate in some part though he remained unsure about this. Here for the first time we see an impassioned conversation with Ralph talking with himself while the therapist listened:

I talk to people now . . . I keep that flowing every day, like taking a mask off and revealing a sense of humanity . . . humble and messed up but still humanity . . . I've come to grips with the problems of the voices that started years ago but I'm still dealing with the inferiority complex . . . if only I could work a couple hours, make minimum wage . . . I've never set goals since high school . . . I hoped to stay in the Armed Services for four years but lasted two . . . then I was incarcerated . . . but now I can see it with balance with a positive attitude.

Discussion

In response to the question what changes when narrative and dialogical transformation occurs in the psychotherapy of schizophrenia, we considered the transcripts of a single patient across two and a half years. In particular this examination was guided by three interrelated possibilities: first, content might shift with the emergence of themes of grief, agency and stigmatization, second, a generally narrativeless state might be replaced with a narrated life and/or a lost narrator might reappear, and third, dialogical exchanges among heterogeneous self-positions might occur more frequently as observable in the form of greater numbers of characters and self-positions, available to interact within the narrative.

Considering the first possibility, there were some constants and changes with regard to the content of Ralph's story. Throughout, Ralph remained someone insufficiently nurtured, often wronged and heroically protesting. Towards the end of the two-year period, however, Ralph began to present himself as an agent who had made some poor choices. He appeared saddened and seemed to lose a vision of himself as a hero and victim. At this point, his story also delved more deeply into his personal history. Grief thus did emerge as a theme, as did agency but quite late in the treatment. Stigma did not emerge as an issue. This might be because Ralph's strong rejection of identification and acceptance of the sick role.

Considering the second issue, a once lost narrator did not return. There was constant narration of life, though especially early on it was inordinately symbolic and implausible. There was no hint of an 'old' Ralph appearing or waking up. There was much mention of trauma but its resolution did not appear to be a focal point.

Regarding dialogical change we initially found relatively few self-positions available and relatively little reference to other actual people Ralph might interact with. During the second epoch there remained a paucity of self-positions in Ralph's commentary in psychotherapy. There was further little or no exchange between these limited self-positions nor development of their themes from a conversational point of view. By contrast, in the second year we found limited debate between adjacent self-positions. In the final epoch self-positions appeared throughout each session that occasionally contradicted or commented on previous positions adding internal complexity and dynamism to Ralph's self-presentation.

Concurrent outcomes

Since narrative change in a vacuum seems of little use, it lastly seems important to note other outcomes that happened during the course of psychotherapy. With regards to community tenure, Ralph had no admissions to the hospital. His symptom levels had fallen by the end of the third year to moderate levels of positive symptoms, and mild levels of negative symptoms, according to the Positive and Negative Syndrome Scale. There were lesser changes in cognitive symptoms. Concerning Ralph's behaviour, there was significant substance abuse, several changes of residence, and a period of homelessness during epoch 4. There were also legal problems in epochs 4 and 5. With regard to medication, Ralph was steadily prescribed both oral and depot typical antipsychotic medication with no obvious periods of noncompliance. During epoch 5 dosages of his typical antipsychotic medication were successfully reduced.

Summary and limitations

Assertions that transformed views of oneself contribute significantly to recovery from mental illness can be found long before terms such as schizophrenia were coined. In 1871, Maudsley, for instance, wrote of how the 'capability of self-formation . . . if it be only rightly developed' could be part of a 'cure' for some forms of 'insanity'. In this chapter we have attempted to refine this view by discussing what might change in the narratives of mentally ill persons undergoing psychotherapy, and what did change in a single case.

Accordingly, we found evidence that the dialogues and the themes of client's narrative in psychotherapy did change over time. Our analyses suggest the client's life story gained complexity, dynamism and subtlety. However, this did not seem to involve the creation of a new story, but the refinement of one he had been telling himself for some time. Rather than our observing an 'old' self reawaken, his narration struggled to keep pace with everything that had befallen him, evolving as he himself had evolved. His narrative began to reflect how complicated his life had become with transformations linked to the development of, and changes in the quality of internal conversations. To our minds, these changes in how the client narrated his life were much more striking than any changes in specifically what he had to say about himself.

In our analyses Ralph's improvement began when more real persons started to populate his narrative. His narration then evolved to include many more self-positions that debated multiple issues in the context of interpersonal relationships. Put another way, his gains seemed bound to a development of his capability for dialogical self-narration. More aspects of himself appeared or at least appeared distinct from others and in their conversation the narrative became more flexible and less monological. Indeed, with regard to his self-characterization, it was not that a positive view of himself replaced a negative view, but that various facets of himself were not only recognized but brought into conversation with one another.

Importantly, there are limitations. Only one case was examined and the rater was not blind. We are thus formulating hypotheses for larger projects that might employ the methods developed. There may also be many courses of narrative transformation in schizophrenia since changes in narrative constructions would seem to be as idiographic as any other variable in social science. Similarly, the integrative therapy offered Ralph may be dissimilar from other form of psychotherapy in ways not articulated here. It may be different transformations will be found when other cases are studied using psychotherapists with differing views.

While there was no cure here and there is still much to be learned, we suggest that the methods and concepts operative offer a starting point for studying the role of dialogical exchange in self-conception and mental health, particularly among those suffering from schizophrenia. Perhaps future studies of diverse individuals in diverse settings may reveal more of the hallmarks of narrative and dialogical transformation, and allow a greater understanding of the personal and social benefits such transformations hold in store for this disenfranchised group.

NOTE

1   Ralph's name has been changed and his personal characteristics and life history systematically altered to protect his confidentiality.

References

Amador, X.F., Flaum, M., Andreasen, N., Strauss, D.H., Yale, S.A., Clark, S.C. and Gorman, J.M. (1995). 'Awareness of illness in schizophrenia and mood disorders.' *Archives of General Psychiatry*, *51*, 826–836.
Bakhtin, M. (1981). *The Dialogic Imagination*. Trans. C. Emerson. Austin, TX: University of Texas Press.
Bakhtin, M. (1983). *Problems of Dostoevsky's Poetics*. Trans. C. Emerson. Minneapolis, MN: University of Minnesota Press.
Bell, M.D., Lysaker, P.H., Goulet, J.G., Milstein, R.M. and Lindenmayer, J.P. (1994). 'Five component model of schizophrenia: Factorial invariance of the Positive and Negative Syndrome Scale.' *Psychiatry Research*, *52*, 295–303.
Crossley, M.L. (2000). 'Narrative psychology, trauma and the study of identity.' *Theory and Psychology*, *10*, 527–546.
Danion, J.M., Gokalsing, E., Robert, P., Massin-Kraus, M. and Bacon, E. (2001).

'Defective relationship between subjective experience and behavior in schizophrenia.' *American Journal of Psychiatry, 158,* 2064–2066.

Davidson, L. and Strauss, J. (1992). 'Sense of self in recovery from mental illness.' *British Journal of Medical Psychology, 65,* 131–145.

Delis, D.C., Kramer, J.H., Kaplan, E. and Ober, B.A. (1987). *California Verbal Learning Test.* San Antonio, TX: Psychological Corporation.

Denzin, N.K. and Lincoln, Y.S. (2000). *Handbook of Qualitative Research.* Thousand Oaks, CA: Sage.

Drake, R.E. and Sederer, L.I. (1986). 'The adverse effects of intensive treatment of schizophrenia.' *Comprehensive Psychiatry, 27,* 313–326.

Duckworth, K., Nair, V., Patel, J.K. and Goldfinger, S. (1997). 'Lost time, found hope and sorrow, the search for self, connection and purpose during awakenings on the new antipsychotics.' *Harvard Review of Psychiatry, 5,* 227–233.

Fenton, W.S. (2000). 'Evolving perspectives on individual psychotherapy for schizophrenia.' *Schizophrenia Bulletin, 26,* 47–72.

Harding, C.M., Zubin, J. and Strauss, J. (1992). 'Chronicity in schizophrenia.' *British Journal of Psychiatry, 161* (supp. 18), 27–37.

Heaton, R.K., Chelune, G.J., Talley, J.L., Kay, G.G. and Curtiss, G. (1993). *Wisconsin Card Sorting Test Manual: Revised and Expanded.* Odessa, FL: Psychological Assessment Resources.

Hermans, H.J.M. (1996) 'Voicing the self: From information processing to dialogical interchange.' *Psychological Bulletin, 119,* 31–50.

Hermans, H.J.M., Rijks, T.I. and Kempen, H.J.G. (1993). 'Imaginal dialogues in the self: Theory and method.' *Journal of Personality, 61,* 207–236.

Holma, J. and Aaltonen, J. (1995). 'The self-narrative and acute psychosis.' *Contemporary Family Therapy, 17,* 307–316.

Holma, J. and Aaltonen, J. (1998). 'Narrative understanding and acute psychosis.' *Contemporary Family Therapy, 20,* 253–263.

Kleinman, A. (1988). *The Illness Narratives: Suffering, Healing and the Human Condition.* New York: Basic Books.

Lysaker, P.H. and France, C.M. (1999). 'Psychotherapy as an element in supported employment for persons with severe mental illness.' *Psychiatry, 62,* 209–222.

Lysaker, P.H. and Lysaker, J.T. (2001). 'Psychosis and the disintegration of dialogical self-structure: Problems posed by schizophrenia for the maintenance of dialogue.' *British Journal of Medical Psychology, 74,* 23–33.

Lysaker, P.H. and Lysaker, J.T. (2002). 'Narrative structure in psychosis: Schizophrenia and disruptions in the dialogical self.' *Theory and Psychology, 12,* 207–220.

Lysaker, P.H. and Lysaker, J.T. (2004) 'Schizophrenia as dialogue at the ends of its tether: The relationship of disruptions in identity with positive and negative symptoms.' *Journal of Constructivist Psychology, 17*(2), 105–119.

Lysaker, P.H., Lysaker, Judy T. and Lysaker, John T. (2001). 'Schizophrenia and the collapse of the dialogical self: Recovery, narrative and psychotherapy.' *Psychotherapy, 38,* 252–261.

Lysaker, P.H., Lancaster, R.S. and Lysaker, J.T. (2003a). 'Narrative transformation as an outcome in the psychotherapy of schizophrenia.' *Psychology and Psychotherapy, 76,* 285–300.

Lysaker, P.H., Wickett, A.M., Wilke, N. and Lysaker, J.T. (2003b). 'Narrative incoherence in schizophrenia: The absent protagonist, neurocognitive impairments and fear of audience.' *American Journal of Psychotherapy*, *57*, 153–166.

Martin, J.K., Pescosolido, B.A. and Tuch, S.A. (2000). 'Of fear and loathing: The role of "disturbing behavior," labels and causal attributions in shaping public attitudes toward persons with mental illness.' *Journal of Health and Social Behavior*, *41*(2), 208–233.

Maudsley, H. (1871). 'Insanity and its treatment.' *Journal of Mental Science*, *17*, 311–334.

Neimeyer, R.A. and Raskin, J.D. (eds) (2000). *Constructions of Disorder: Meaning-Making Frameworks for Psychotherapy*. Washington, DC: American Psychological Association.

Roe, D. and Ben-Yaskai, A.B. (1999). 'Exploring the relationship between the person and the disorder among individuals hospitalized for psychosis.' *Psychiatry*, *62*, 372–380.

Searles, H. (1965). *Collected Papers of Schizophrenia and Related Subjects*. New York: International Universities Press.

Seikkula, J., Alakare, B. and Aaltonen, J. (2001). 'Open dialogue in psychosis I: An introduction and case illustration.' *Journal of Constructivist Psychology*, *14*, 247–265.

Sensky, T., Turkington, D., Kingdom, D., Scott, J.L., Scott, J., Siddle, R., Carrol, M. and Barnes, T.R.E. (2000). 'A randomized controlled trial of cognitive behavioral therapy for persistent symptoms in schizophrenia resistant to medication.' *Archives of General Psychiatry*, *57*, 165–172.

Silver, A. (2002). 'A personal response to Gail Hornstein's To redeem one person is to redeem the world: The life of Frieda Fromm-Reichmann.' *Psychiatry*, *65*, 1–12.

Singer, M.T. and Wynne, L.C. (1966). 'Communication styles in parents of normals, neurotics and schizophrenics.' *Psychiatric Research Reports*, *20*, 25–38.

Warner, R., Taylor, D., Powers, M. and Hyman, R. (1989). 'Acceptance of the mental illness label by psychotic patients: Effects on functioning.' *American Journal of Orthopsychiatry*, *59*, 389–409.

Williams, C.C. and Collins, A.A. (1999). 'Defining new frameworks for psychosocial interventions.' *Psychiatry*, *62*, 61–78.

Wortham, S. (2001). *Narratives in Action: A Strategy for Research and Analysis*. New York: Teachers College Press.

Young, S.L. and Ensign, D.S. (1999). 'Exploring recovery from the perspective of persons with psychiatric disabilities.' *Psychosocial Rehabilitation Journal*, *22*, 219–231.

Chapter 14

A dialogical approach to patients with personality disorders

Antonio Semerari, Antonino Carcione, Giancarlo Dimaggio, Giuseppe Nicolò and Michele Procacci

For therapy to be successful, patients have to actively want this. If they are to change their point of view about the world, they need to start a dialogue with their therapist, listen to the latter's interpretations and suggestions and try to look at themselves from this new perspective.

When doing this, they start from their inner world and are likely to put together a picture of their therapist that is similar to the characters in their interior dialogues. The picture patients have of their therapist has an impact on the therapeutic alliance and on the outcome of their therapy (Safran and Muran 2000).

What operations do patients need to do in their minds in order to cultivate their tie with their therapist, share common goals and tasks, get involved in these in a constructive way and 'make their therapy therapeutic'? When do these operations encounter difficulties and what actions should a therapist take to overcome them?

As to the first question, Weiss (1993) suggests that patients test their therapists to find out how much the latter are compatible with their adaptive goals and to disprove the irrational beliefs that hamper their pursuit of them. The test takes the form of an anticipatory interior dialogue, such as 'If I let my therapist see my emotions, he'll think me despicable and reject me'. Patients put their therapists to the test and pay attention to even the smallest sign of rejection. The test is therefore a tool for checking the safety conditions necessary for patients to reveal themselves to their therapists; if the latter pass the test, patients can render themselves therapeutically operational.

Semerari (1991) initially used the analysis of psychotherapies involving 'neurotic' patients and came to the same conclusions. He hypothesized that when patients process therapists' verbal and non-verbal communication, they build a model of their mind and, in particular, a representation of the representation, that is a *metarepresentation*, that the therapists make of them. Luigi, for example, was a brilliant doctor but, just before specializing, he began to suffer panic attacks and periods of depression. He would feel tired, gloomy, unmotivated and doubtful about the path he was choosing in his profession (whereas until then he had been following it enthusiastically), and he was thinking about giving up specializing. All through his life he had felt he was lucky compared to his sister, who was severely mentally retarded. The pain and distress he felt for his sister were accompanied by guilt feelings about having had the chance to take up a job that was interesting and satisfying. When he got the offer of a university career, his guilt feelings were amply discussed during therapy. To start with, he was inclined to turn it down but, later on, he decided to accept because he held an interior dialogue, between one session and the next, in which he pictured his therapist saying to him that giving up his ambitions would only do harm to himself, without improving his sister's situation in any way.

If patients think that their therapist is supporting their objectives, this assists the therapeutic alliance and, if there is a good relationship between them, it is easier to agree on goals and tasks (Bordin 1979). In such circumstances patients see their therapists as being authoritative and reliable figures, trust them and use their character as a new perspective for observing their own problematic convictions and emotions.

Weiss focuses on the fact that patients have an unconscious, preformed plan when they put their therapist to the test. An example is a patient frightened of being criticized for what he or she says, who, as a result, speaks softly and vaguely. If the therapist asks questions patiently and without showing any irritation at the patient's almost unintelligible words, the latter will, without realizing it, relax. A change in the patient's facial expression and an ability to speak more freely are a sign that the therapist has passed the safety conditions test. Semerari focuses on the outcome of the testing operation on a conscious level: patients put together a representation of their therapist's way of thinking and then from this create a character that takes part in their imaginary dialogue.

Dialogical self theory (DST: Hermans 2003; see also Chapter 1 in this volume) provides a wider context in which to place both these models of the psychotherapeutic process. According to DST the creation of an imaginary dialogue with significant figures in our family, social and imaginary worlds is a constituent part of individuals' meaning-making activity. In their thoughts and in social relationships people continuously negotiate the meaning of what is occurring and the significance of events for their goals with characters that belong to the self's space. The tests described by Weiss (1993) and the building of a model of the therapist's mind, described by Semerari (1991), portray the process by which a patient puts the therapist in this space. The therapeutic relationship is in fact a particular example of the self-construction processes foreseen by DST.

Metarepresentation and imaginary dialogue with therapist

By the term 'metarepresentative function' we mean the ability to create representations of mental representations and thus to ascribe, both to oneself and to others, states of mind consisting of beliefs, desires, intentions and emotions (Sperber 2000). An example of mental representation is the thought: 'The beer is in the fridge'. A metarepresentation is 'Mark *believes* [that is, he represents to himself] that the beer is in the fridge'. The metarepresentative function has been studied by two different schools of research: metacognition (Flavell 1979; Nelson et al. 1999) and theory of mind (Baron-Cohen 1995; Leslie 2000). Metacognition studies how individuals monitor and control their cognitive functions, for example memory. Theory of mind investigates the understanding of the role of mental states in explaining and foreseeing others' behaviour. In fact, both are interested in how individuals create mental representations of mental representations and act on them. An example is: if I see Mark going towards the fridge and taking a beer (representation), I *deduce* that he does it because he *wants* a beer. This is a metarepresentation which has as its subject the other's mental state ('he wants'); that is I represent to myself Mark, who represents to himself the beer and wants it.

Increasing attention is being paid by clinicians from various backgrounds to patients' metarepresentative skills. They lay stress on two aspects in particular. First, individuals' ability to undertake complex operations involving their own and others' mental activities is an important factor for psychological health. If individuals lack these skills, they are probably suffering from a serious disorder (Carcione and Falcone 1999; Fonagy 1991; Semerari et al. 2003).

Second, the psychotherapeutic process reinforces a patient's metarepresentative functions and the latter are considered an essential factor for change. Stiles (1999) talks about a progressive increase in the ability to assimilate problematical experiences: individuals start out describing vague psychic and somatic sensations and gradually proceed to where they are capable of accurately identifying and mastering such states. Hermans (2003) talks about meta-position: a voice that acquires the ability to watch what is going on in the jockeying between other voices. Other authors talk about the Observing-I (Cooper, Chapter 4 in this volume; Leiman and Stiles 2001) to describe similar aspects of this phenomenon. These considerations give rise to one question: if metarepresentative functions are an important factor for change, what impact do imaginary dialogues with one's therapist have on them?

The fact that patients imagine what their therapist would say in a particular situation is, in itself, a metarepresentative action, in that it involves them putting together a representation of potential representations by the therapist (e.g. 'I imagine that you think I'm up to doing it'). This metarepresentation reinforces, in turn, patients' ability to understand and master their states of mind.

With less severe patients the dialogue can start right from the early stages of therapy, and its role is often one of soothing painful emotions and reassurance, linked to the recollection of specific comments by their therapist, as in this example from the third session with Maria, a 29-year-old patient, terrorized by haunting scenes in which she sees herself attack and injure her dear ones. Maria said:

> I felt less frightened because you were around. Whereas on the other occasions not being able to tell these thoughts to anybody and nobody reassuring me about them . . . made me more frightened. This time I felt more reassured because I was thinking: 'There you are; you must tell him about them' . . . *Anyway, you were around. I pictured myself telling you about them.*

As therapy progresses, patients get to use their imaginary dialogue with the therapist to describe their own inner state to themselves, so as to understand what is happening to them and put together mastery strategies. For example, Francesco, a 30-year-old man diagnosed for borderline personality disorder, suffered from jealousy with vivid fantasies in which he would imagine his girlfriend having sexual relations with her ex-boyfriends. This would provoke him into wild scenes of rage in which he smashed things to pieces or performed self-destructive acts. The following episode took place towards the end of the first year of therapy.

Francesco: I don't feel at all right. On Saturday I went for a stroll with Ada and we met her ex-boyfriend. Since I'd never seen him until then, I hadn't imagined any scenes of sex between him and Ada. At the time I felt quite calm; there was just a bit of embarrassment. But later I had a feeling of repulsion for Ada. I shut myself up like a clam.

T: What did you feel at that moment? Were you angry?

Francesco: Yes . . . I felt prostrated. I didn't feel like doing anything.

T: Did you feel confused?

Francesco: No. Not least because I kept repeating 'Keep calm!' and *thinking about you telling me again that it was my usual problem. I was telling you that it was my problem about suffering loss and you agreed.* I didn't argue and I didn't get angry.

Francesco has put together an imaginary dialogue with a metarepresentation of his therapist being critical about his emotional outbursts; he has made the latter's point of view his own and, thanks to this, has been able to modulate his emotions. There are instances in which the imaginary dialogue has a role in the understanding of others' states of mind and gets used to regulate relationships.

Anna, 37 years old, suffers from panic attacks. The initial part of her therapy is spent discussing her fear of anxiety. When she tells about the following episode, the symptoms have disappeared and Anna demonstrates that she has worked through the contents of her dialogue with the therapist and uses them in understanding and managing relationships. She said:

> At this dinner there was a friend of ours, who's recently separated from her husband and who's going through a very bad patch. She felt the need to talk about it. But there was a chill over the gathering. Everyone was embarrassed about taking up the subject. *I thought about what we've said about the fear of negative emotions.* And so I decided to tackle the subject. I saw she was relieved afterwards.

As can be seen from these examples, the role of the point of view emerging from an imaginary dialogue is, essentially, one of metarepresentation. It serves to identify and master one's own and others' states of mind.

Summing up, the cognitive processes used by patients to build a model of their therapist's mind take the form of therapeutic neo-structures and with these they ascribe new meanings to the world (Semerari 1991). In terms of DST, they get expressed in the form of an imaginary dialogue.

The metarepresentation paradox in patients with personality disorders

Thanks to psychotherapy patients can become better at understanding and regulating their states of mind. Nevertheless some individuals find it difficult to put together that multiplicity of characters in dialogue with each other, necessary to adapt to social relationships and achieve their goals. In particular patients suffering from personality disorders (PDs) generally have a problematical imaginal world, with characters experiencing under-modulated emotions, and the relationships between them rigid and stereotyped. It is unlikely that such patients will see their therapist as being authoritative and trustworthy; on the contrary, the latter often turns into an adversary. As a result, the therapeutic alliance is prone to ruptures and the therapist has to work hard to overcome them (Safran and Muran 2000). Our hypothesis is that such difficulties are a sign of underlying metarepresentative malfunctioning. There is a paradox as regards the processes involved in the therapeutic relationship. Their function is to increase patients' ability to metarepresent but, at the same time, the model presupposes that patients already possess well-developed metarepresentative skills: they need to be capable of using linguistic and paralinguistic communication to put together representations of representations by their therapist, integrate them and use them for therapeutic purposes.

Patients with PDs often have difficulties in performing metarepresentations and therefore in understanding both their therapist's mind and their own. As a result, they have problems in constructing an imaginary dialogue and there is an adverse impact on the stability and quality of the therapeutic alliance.

Our hypothesis is that metarepresentative skills are composed of a number of sub-functions, that is the ability: to monitor inner states and identify the emotions and thoughts in them; to reflect in an integrated manner on differences between states of mind and on transitions from one to another; and to use this knowledge to master one's states of mind, etc. (Semerari et al. 2003).

With certain patients only some of these skills are impaired and the types of problem they suffer from are directly linked to the type of impairment. Semerari and his colleagues identify the following among the various dysfunctional profiles: first, patients with a *monitoring* deficit, by which we mean difficulty in identifying the thoughts and emotions making up both their own and others' states of mind, and second, patients who find it hard to *decentre* from their own point of view and understand others' perspectives (Nicolò 1999).

These disorders result in particular problems for the construction of an imaginary dialogue with the therapist and for the unfolding of the therapeutic relationship, which we shall describe in this chapter. We shall then touch on the ways in which a therapist can regulate the relationship with a patient so as to reduce the impact any metarepresentative disorders might have and improve the related functions.

The interior dialogue with the therapist and monitoring problems

Some patients, in particular those diagnosed for avoidant or narcissistic PDs, find it difficult to identify their own emotions and their meaning. They are unable to say what they feel or think, and to link emotions to thoughts or both of them to life events. Their minds are opaque both for themselves and for others. Their narratives report principally facts.

Alessia, 32 years old, suffers from avoidant PD. She is pretty and intelligent and has a degree that could help her start a good career, but she is socially inhibited: she does not work, lives with her parents and keeps up only a few relationships, from which she, moreover, tends to withdraw.

Alessia:	My sister was insisting I go to a party with her . . . In the end I said yes. Then, at the last moment I didn't go.
T:	What were you thinking then?
Alessia:	Nothing. Maybe I didn't want to go.
T:	Do you recall what emotion you felt?

Alessia: I don't know . . . Last time you said that I ought to go. When it was time to get ready I called my sister and told her that I'd got a headache.

As is typical for monitoring disorders, it is impossible to define what thoughts and emotions trigger Alessia's behaviour. She refers to the previous session, in which her therapist tried to probe into her feelings of social inadequacy and fears about being judged critically. This conversation gets recalled in the form of instructions about what to do ('You said that I ought to . . . go out'). The imaginary therapist, even if present in her mind, does not carry out a dialogue helping to make sense of emotions and thoughts that are opaque, not least for the patient herself. Her difficulty in identifying thoughts and emotions makes her interior dialogue with her therapist abstract and without any impact on her state of mind.

This opaqueness as regards one's own inner state is, often, mirrored by opaqueness in the representation of others' minds ('Other people seem like Martians to me'). In such a situation we can see how she has a difficulty in forming a representation of her therapist's mind that can be turned into an interior therapeutic dialogue. Such patients often do not recall what their therapist has said or just remember single sentences (detached from what they were intended to communicate), taking the form of exhortations about what to do or critical judgements.

These problems are further aggravated by the type of interpersonal cycle (Safran and Muran 2000) that gets activated in patients with monitoring disorders. They cause therapists to enter states of boredom and alienation. Even after numerous sessions therapists find it difficult to keep a dialogue going when faced with a patient's laconic replies. In such a situation they tend to get distracted and back away from their obligation to provide therapy. They may find themselves thinking about their own personal matters, waiting impatiently for the session to end and putting questions just in order to fill up the time.

It is precisely patients presenting acute social withdrawal and feelings of interpersonal alienation that provoke an emotional detachment in their therapists, which, if enacted, becomes a confirmation during sessions of their isolation from relationships. Nevertheless, these states of malaise can turn out to be the starting point for actions improving their monitoring disorders and fostering the construction of an interior dialogue with their therapist.

Therapists have to help such patients to grasp what they have in mind with appropriate forms of self-disclosure (Dimaggio and Semerari 2004; Semerari et al. 2000). For example, this was how the therapist proceeded in Alessia's case:

T: I found myself in a situation that made me think about the problem of not belonging, and I'd like to tell you about it. I was invited to the inauguration of a law firm and, of course, since almost all the guests were lawyers, they knew each other well, while I knew hardly anyone.

Alessia: (smiling) A situation I know well.

T: I know. I have to say that I felt embarrassed and didn't know where to hide myself. This is how we feel when we are among people who share something from which we instead are excluded. I was struck by the fact that, even if, thinking rationally, we know that we are being totally ignored, we nevertheless feel that we stick out.

Alessia: It's the fact of being a stranger. The fact of not belonging to the group makes one stick out. Everyone can see that we are the only stranger.

T: That's exactly it! Probably it's a sort of recollection of how our ancestors must have felt when they found themselves in the midst of a different tribe.

The active manner in which Alessia takes part in this conversation is a marker of the change occurring in her state of mind. To encourage this shift, the therapist starts with a self-disclosure and stresses the experiences he shares with Alessia. Starting out from common experiences seems to make it easier for patients to understand their therapist's mind. As her therapy proceeds, these topics often get recollected in the form of a dialogue with her therapist, and help to make the thoughts and emotions underlying detachment intelligible and controllable. Currently Alessia is working and has managed to put together a network of relationships by choosing to mix in circles in which she feels she had something to share with others.

In case of monitoring disorders, discussing common experiences is particularly profitable: if, during their problematical states of mind, patients can recall that their therapist has revealed that he or she has had similar experiences, this helps them to make sense of what they are feeling.

Problematical interpersonal cycles are valuable for identifying the common parts of experience to be related to a patient. The inner discipline of therapists (Safran and Segal 1990) starts with an awareness of their feeling of detachment during sessions. When they have acquired this awareness, they can ask themselves if this is not similar to what their patients experience in relationships. When they consider they have achieved a shared condition, therapists can then switch from a problematical position (boredom or detachment) to an empathetic one. At this point they are in a position to reveal that they share an experience with the patient.

The interior dialogue with one's therapist and decentring disorder

Other patients are able to identify and interpret the emotional and conceptual contents of their states of mind. They can also grasp the signals sent out by others and, through these, comprehend their emotions. Nevertheless, they read others' minds in a rigid, stereotyped fashion, always with the same kind of interpretation and meaning, to the extent that their ability to regulate interpersonal relationships is seriously impaired. Such patients generally suffer from paranoid PD.

They are capable of understanding if another is, for example, anxious or calm. Where they fail, almost systematically, is in understanding the reasons for another having that particular emotion: they are unable to adopt another's mental perspective or decentre from their own point of view and expectations. They can only therefore ascribe goals and intentions that are part of their own meaning system, which is concentrated on mistrust, suspicion and deception, to others. Believing they are being deceived, they are constantly looking to protect themselves from others' malicious intentions. As a result they are never ready to consider the variety of states of mind providing colour to human experience. They withdraw from relationships and, in isolating themselves from society, lose any opportunities to practise decentring.

In such a situation, the interior dialogue with one's therapist concentrates on trying to unmask his or her trickery and bad faith. Every detail of a session gets recalled and analysed from a mistrusting stance. Furthermore, the difficulties in decentring prevent patients from perceiving that the therapist's intention is to help them. Such a condition gets aggravated by interpersonal cycles involving mutual mistrust, which often arise with such patients: therapists feel that they are being continuously examined and evaluated, and as if they were treading on eggs. Any action whatever is capable of being misunderstood and interpreted as proof of their dishonesty and deceit. The relationship is a precarious one, and even something insignificant can lead to a rupture, without it being possible to understand which part of the dialogue or element in the interaction has been absorbed into the patient's dysfunctional perspective. There are occasions when these patients can be frightening. Not being able to foresee how the patient will react to their actions, therapists tend to start up an interior dialogue in which their wish is that the latter cancel the appointment, move to another town or refuse to come (even if perhaps feeling ashamed for such thoughts). The therapists' interior dialogue therefore gets filled with horrifying fantasies in which the patient becomes a dangerous and scary character.

Such a state of mind has a negative impact on the therapeutic relationship, with therapists concerned about not getting attacked, not upsetting patients' sensitivities and hurting their feelings, or the therapeutic dialogue not provoking patients' 'paranoia'. Therapists become ever more wary, adopt a strictly non-contentious style and keep communication to a minimum. However, by doing this, they deprive the patient even more of information about what they are thinking, thus encouraging his or her suspiciousness: 'What's he trying to hide from me?' is the patient's reaction. And this interpersonal cycle tends therefore, if enacted, to increase the difficulties that patients with decentring problems have in comprehending their therapist's perspective.

In such a situation it is unlikely that treatment will alter the way in which such patients picture others to themselves (deceitful and untrustworthy). Therapy will need to aim at prompting alternative narratives to those a patient uses in a stereotyped manner. In this instance too, self-disclosure operations and a statement of the common aspects of experience shared by therapist and patient can ameliorate the metarepresentative deficit. They do not, of course, guarantee that the therapist will not be constructed as threatening. Nevertheless, what is certain is that if others are opaque, patients can only ascribe their own habitual thoughts to them: consequently, if a therapist does not disclose him- or herself, a patient will construct the therapist as a persecutory character.

With such patients these sharing operations requires careful regulation. First, a therapist needs to really be able to identify any common aspects, and this is not easy to achieve with patients consumed by fears of persecution. Second, if they are to be receptive to the meaning of what the therapist shares with them, such patients need to be in a state of mind that is not excessively mistrustful. For these reasons, the therapist should, right from the earliest sessions, look for shared experiences involving common interests not touching on the most emotionally heated topics or the patient's persecutory fears.

Giovanni, 42 years old, works as a terminal operator in a firm. He has never been married and does not mix with anyone except for a few close relatives. He is convinced that people in the street give him strange looks and laugh at him behind his back. He has turned up in therapy after being charged for assault. After the first session he wants to sue his therapist because, in his opinion, his fees are too high. But instead he carries on with treatment for about two years. In the following extract we can see the therapist concentrating on topics of common interest.

T: So you take photos for a hobby. What sort of camera have you got?
Giovanni: Why? Do you know about photography?
T: I like taking photos too, even if I'm a complete amateur.
Giovanni: I've got an old Leika that my father left me. It's totally manual. When I pull it out, people think I must be a beggar with such an ancient camera. I can see from how people look at me.

T:	Is it by chance one of those models with which, if you want to rewind the film, you need to do three turns precisely?
Giovanni:	Exactly. What camera do you have?
T:	A semi-automatic Nikon, but it's ten years old. Before that I had a Zeiss but it got stolen in Naples. You can imagine how I cursed those scoundrels! It still hurts me when I think about it.
Giovanni:	I'm fonder of my camera than of my own mother. The other day in the park I felt like sending someone to hell, because they were looking at me with a disdainful expression, just because I was taking more time than usual to focus.

When a dialogue on topics of common interest gets going, the therapist notices that there is a switch from a precarious situation in which everything risks being misinterpreted, so that he has to be wary and prudent, to a relaxed one. He notices that tension drops, and is less concerned about becoming part of the patient's persecution theme. Starting with these dialogues about non-contentious topics, the therapist proposes new narratives and new perspectives from which to see reality.

T:	What do you mean by a disdainful expression?
Giovanni:	He was staring at me with an idiotic expression, as if he was disgusted by my camera.
T:	Perhaps he was just curious. In fact, a camera like yours attracts attention and you certainly don't see one often, like when a big limousine or an old Fiat 500 goes past: everyone turns round and is astonished and perhaps a bit envious when they see it.
Giovanni:	No, believe me, I'm sure that he was looking at me askance.
T:	How can you distinguish between someone looking at you enviously and someone looking at you in disgust? If I'd been there, I'd probably have looked at you with a strange, surprised expression and not a disgusted one. You're a photographer too and you know well how the expressions others have in photos can seem to be all sorts of things. It depends on us and what we think.
Giovanni:	That's true but there and then it seemed as if he was looking at me askance. Now you've got me confused and I'm not so sure.

In this instance the therapist exploits a dialogue about a common interest to provoke two therapeutic actions: first, encourage the patient to stand back critically from his representation of the world, by emphasizing that what one thinks is not necessarily a mirror image of reality; second, foster decentring operations by supplying direct information on what he himself would have thought in such circumstances and thus preparing the ground for the introduction of a new character in the patient's dialogues, which is interested rather than ill-intentioned.

The timing of the action is regulated by the therapist's emotional marker, consisting of a transition from a state of relational alarm to a more relaxed one, which is a sign that a non-paranoiac dialogue is unfolding.

Starting with topics that they know well and live through with less intense negative emotions, patients find it easier to develop new narratives, in which the dialogue can be with characters which understand them instead of threatening them.

With such patients each session should follow the same structure: first, therapists should initially press for a discussion about topics of common interest; second, if they register a change in their interior state, from a situation in which they see the therapeutic relationship to be at risk to one in which they feel more relaxed and the patient converses in a more flowing manner, they can, at this point, attempt to tackle problematical topics, running a limited risk that they become part of the patient's persecution theme. The access to these topics is made easier by the discussion previously, in which the therapist gets seen as a person to be trusted and with whom one can have a mutual understanding; finally, when discussing being threatened or derided, as in the above example with Giovanni's reflections on the person looking at him while he was taking some photographs, the therapist should propose a new point of view. If this operation is successful, then, when away from their therapist and during their imaginary dialogues with him or her, patients will recall the dialogues from their sessions and the sharing atmosphere in which they took place.

It may, of course, occur that patients reject alternative interpretations of events as they consider them to be proof of the therapist's bad faith. In such a situation therapists can resort to self-disclosure and reveal what they think about what has taken place, what they themselves would have done in such a situation and what they are feeling at that precise moment in the session, at which they are aware of the patient's mistrust. Self-disclosure should refer to situations that have already been shared with the patient during non-contentious dialogues, as in the following extract.

Giovanni: You can't understand me either. Perhaps it's better if I stop coming. All you're doing is stealing money off me.

T: I don't understand what's annoyed you.

Giovanni: Every time you tell me that it isn't true that my section head is taking the mickey out of me and doing all he can to get me rattled, essentially you're on his side.

T: I've never said that. I reckon that in your position, rather than punching my boss I'd have invited him to the bar for a coffee, and maybe afterwards I'd have punched him just the same if I'd realized he really was taking the mickey out of me. But the question is similar to when we were talking about photography: if you switch suddenly from a low sensitivity 50 ISO film to a 1000 ISO one, the high intensity of the light blinds you and everything you see is the same, without any differences or contrast. Earlier, when we were talking about photography, everything was fine, and you seemed like an old friend and were using the right film. Now we're talking about your workplace and I'm your worst enemy. In these instances even I – and I know you well – don't know what to do with you, let alone other people.

Giovanni: Sorry, don't take it badly. Maybe I exaggerate a bit, but in the end we understand each other.

In this sequence the therapist uses a shared metaphor (the sensitivity of a film) to recall how they were in tune with each other shortly before. He expounds his point of view, discloses his state of mind and, in this way, helps the patient to stand back critically. At the end it is the patient who seeks a new chance to be in tune. From now on this patient uses the photography metaphor constantly in his imaginary dialogues with the therapist, and it comes to symbolize the possibility of altering one's point of view and perspective about reality and relationships.

Conclusion

The theory about the psychotherapeutic process that we have been expounding in this chapter is, first, a cognitive-constructivist one, which sees the person as an active constructor of reality; it makes it possible to enter into the detailed aspects of how this construction occurs within a therapeutic relationship. According to DST a change in meaning-making processes, when performed voluntarily and during psychotherapy, occurs, through, among other things, the introduction of characters with new points of view into the scenario in which patients' inner dialogues take place. In their narrative landscape the latter give the therapist the role of a figure with whom they are in dialogue and discuss the meaning of the events that make them suffer. To do this patients need to have a certain degree of metarepresentative skills, as with these they manage to understand how the therapist thinks *vis-à-vis* themselves. At this point they are able to internalize him or her as a new character with whom to hold a dialogue, with the aim of constructing new meanings.

Second, the theory allows a bridging of the gap between the concept of metarepresentation and the meaning-making processes foreseen by DST, by showing how metarapresentative functions can influence and be influenced by dialogical processes. A metarepresentation disorder is an obstacle in the process of self-reconstruction that takes place during psychotherapy, in that it prevents the inclusion in a positive way of the therapist figure among the characters with which one is in dialogue. The nature of the obstacle depends on the type of subfunction damaged.

Third, as regards clinical theory, it is possible to distinguish between different metarepresentative disorders and identify the specific impact each one has on the therapeutic relationship. The assumption in clinical theory, according to which patients with PDs have problems carrying out metarepresentation, leads to the technical principle by which therapists should help them in the task of getting to know their therapist's own thoughts and applying this knowledge to their own states of mind. Self-disclosure and experience-sharing operations are useful tools in this respect.

References

Baron-Cohen, S. (1995). *Mindblindness*. Cambridge, MA: MIT Press.

Bordin, E.S. (1979). 'The generalizability of the psychoanalytic concept of working alliance.' *Psychotherapy, 16*, 252–260.

Carcione, A. and Falcone, M. (1999) 'Il concetto di metacognizione come costrutto clinico fondamentale per la psicoterapia.' In A. Semerari (ed.) *Psicoterapia cognitiva del paziente grave: Metacognizione e relazione terapeutica* (pp. 9–42). Milan: Cortina.

Dimaggio, G. and Semerari, A. (2004). 'Disorganized narratives: The psychological condition and its treatment. How to achieve a metacognitive point of view restoring order to chaos.' In L. Angus and J. McLeod (eds) *Handbook of Narrative Psychotherapy: Practice, Theory, and Research* (pp. 263–282). Thousand Oaks, CA: Sage.

Flavell, J.H. (1979). 'Metacognition and metacognitive monitoring: A new area of cognitive-developmental inquiry.' *American Psychologist, 34*, 906–911.

Fonagy, P. (1991). 'Thinking about thinking: Some clinical and theoretical considerations in the treatment of a borderline patient.' *International Journal of Psychoanalysis, 72*, 639–656.

Hermans, H.J.M. (2003). 'The construction and reconstruction of a dialogical self.' *Journal of Constructivist Psychology, 16*(2), 89–130.

Leiman, M. and Stiles, W.B. (2001). 'Dialogical sequence analysis and the Zone of Proximal Development as conceptual enhancements to the assimilation model: The case of Jan revisited.' *Psychotherapy Research, 11*, 311–330.

Leslie, A.M. (2000). ' "Theory of Mind" as a mechanism of selective attention.' In M.S. Gazzaniga (ed.) *The New Cognitive Neurosciences*. Cambridge, MA: MIT Press.

Nelson, T.O., Stuart, R.B., Howard, C. and Crowley, M. (1999). 'Metacognition and clinical psychology: A preliminary framework for research and practice.' *Clinical Psychology and Psychotherapy, 6*, 73–79.

Nicolò, G. (1999). 'Deficit di decentramento e ideazione delirante.' In A. Semerari (ed.) *Psicoterapia cognitiva del paziente grave: Metacognizione e relazione terapeutica* (pp. 281–312). Milan: Cortina.

Safran, J.D. and Muran, J.C. (2000). *Negotiating the Therapeutic Alliance: A Relational Treatment Guide*. New York: Guilford.

Safran, J.D. and Segal, Z.V. (1990). *Interpersonal Process in Cognitive Therapy*. New York. Basic Books.

Semerari, A. (1991). *I processi cognitivi nella relazione terapeutica*. Rome: Carocci.

Semerari, A., Carcione, A. and Nicolò, G. (2000). 'Metacogniciòn y relaciòn terapéutica en el tratamiento de pacientes con Trastornos de la Personalidad.' *Revista Argentina de Clinica Psicologica*, *9*, 257–270.

Semerari, A., Carcione, A., Dimaggio, G., Falcone, M., Nicolò, G., Procacci, M. and Alleva, G. (2003). 'How to evaluate metacognitive functioning in psychotherapy? The Metacognition Assessment Scale and its applications.' *Clinical Psychology and Psychotherapy*, *10*(4), 238–261.

Sperber, D. (ed.) (2000). *Metarepresentation*. Oxford: Oxford University Press.

Stiles, W.B. (1999). 'Signs and voices in psychotherapy.' *Psychotherapy Research*, *9*, 1–21.

Weiss, J. (1993). *How Psychotherapy Works: Process and Technique*. New York: Guilford.

Part IV

Methodological issues in the psychotherapeutic process

Chapter 15

Hearing voices

Methodological issues in measuring internal multiplicity

Katerine Osatuke, Michael A. Gray, Meredith J. Glick, William B. Stiles and Michael Barkham

Clients in therapy convey psychological meaning through the sounds of their speech as well as their words. Words used in therapy are always embodied in a rich interpersonal and non-verbal context shared by the client and therapist. Therapy transcripts represent only the verbal text. Text-based research has proved useful, but many authors have lamented the restricted view it offers. In this chapter, we consider what may be learned by attending not only to the verbal content, but also to the speech sounds of clients in psychotherapy. To understand the relationship between content and sound, we used a theory of internal multiplicity called the *assimilation model* (Stiles 2002; Stiles et al. 1990). In this chapter, we review the assimilation model's account of multiplicity and report a study in which we systematically examined internal multiplicity as manifested by content and sound in a therapy session.

People's multiple internal parts and their expression in psychotherapy have been an object of much theoretical interest to us and others, both recently (e.g. contributors to this volume) and historically (as reflected in such popular terms as internal objects, automatic thoughts, inner critic, false self, ideal self, etc.). A few other investigators have gone on to distinguish internal voices empirically using verbal content. Leiman (Chapter 16 in this volume) used the dialogical sequence analysis to uncover the ongoing dialogue between the parts of self. Muntigl (2003) applied functional linguistic analysis to track changes in clients' dialogical positioning of themselves *vis-à-vis* important others, as reflected in utterances throughout couples therapy. Hermans (2003) offered a method of assessing change in personal position repertoire using a grid format and combining qualitative and quantitative procedures. Verhofstadt-Denève (2003) illustrated an application of a phenomenological-dialectical personality model to psychodramatic group therapy through a five-phase semi-structured protocol. She suggested techniques of client engagement in an exploration of theoretically relevant personality aspects, and thus related theoretical concepts of the model to clinical observations and prompts for action.

Whereas studies of internal multiplicity in therapy have relied mainly on content analysis, studies examining sounds of people's speech have focused on comparing different people rather than different internal parts within people. A connection between the *voice sound* and the speaker's personality has been recognized since antiquity (Scherer 1986). Scherer and colleagues (1984) examined how personality traits are inferred from speech sounds by comparing personality ratings based on transcribed interviews with ratings based on audiorecords as well. They found that vocal cues were much more important than verbal content for forming impressions about personality. The relationship between content and sound was mutually complementary for some types of affect and parallel for other types.

Raters can reliably decode emotions from speech sounds (for a review, see Scherer and Bergmann 1990). Not only are the sounds of speech used to infer particular emotions, but also particular emotions influence sounds of speech (see e.g. Fonagy 1976; Williams and Stevens 1972). Attention to voice sounds has been acknowledged as specifically important in understanding the process of psychotherapy (e.g. Bady and Lachmann 1985; Sullivan 1954). Rice and Kerr (1986), looking for interpersonal similarities between vocal patterns of different clients in therapy, used audiotape ratings and instructed raters to ignore speech content. They found four vocal patterns across clients, independent of content cues. These patterns had sufficient stability within clients to predict therapy outcomes from the first session, but enough variability across sessions that these patterns could be used as a measure of therapy process.

In this chapter, we first review the assimilation model (Stiles 2002; Stiles et al. 1990), focusing on the theoretical relation of different aspects of internal multiplicity such as voice content and voice sounds. We then report a study of one psychotherapy session where we compared the information about internal voices yielded by transcripts with the information yielded by the audiorecord.

Assimilation model of internal multiplicity: theory and methods

Like other models discussed in this volume, the assimilation model (Honos-Webb and Stiles 1998; Stiles 1997a, 2002; Stiles et al. 1990) postulates that the self is multifaceted. Its multiple parts, metaphorically described as *voices*, are traces of a person's prior experiences. The voices of these experiences are active agents within a person that strive for expression, wanting to speak or act when they are addressed. Theoretically, a person's speech proceeds from traces of whole experience as lived in the moment, so that both the original experience and subsequent expressions of it encompass motor activity, bodily reactions, motives and affect, as well as sights, sounds and thoughts (see Stiles et al., Chapter 6 in this volume). For example, when talking about the loss of a loved one, we may feel sad, cry and speak in a quivering voice. Expressions of voices reflect aspects of the original experiences that formed them. Since voices are multiple, any personality can be understood as a *community of voices*, negotiating a shared understanding of their experiences through active dialogic interactions with each other (or other people). Through this mutual two-sided process, called *assimilation*, voices develop connections to each other, and their differences become resources – a reservoir of inner richness and diversity, rather than a source of internal conflict. Facilitating assimilation between internal voices is seen as the main task of psychotherapy, independently of a particular therapy approach (see Stiles et al., Chapter 6 in this volume).

This understanding of personality implies that voices are unique for every person, as they are traces of personal experiences rather than psychological functions or structures typical of people in general. The uniqueness poses a measurement puzzle: how can one describe in standard terms something that is unique for each individual? How this puzzle is solved depends on the purposes of measurement.

In most previous assimilation research, voices have been examined using the qualitative method of text analysis called assimilation analysis (Stiles 2002; Stiles and Angus 2001). The data for assimilation analysis usually consisted of transcribed psychotherapy sessions, although there has been some initial attention to the non-verbal communications embodied in speech sounds (Stiles 1999; Osatuke et al. 2003). It turned out that clients' multiple voices were characterized by features that could be distinguished in the text and used to identify and track these voices throughout the therapy dialogue. The method has been used to describe psychotherapy cases and explicate process-outcome relationships by following clients' progress in assimilating problematic voices (see Stiles (2002), for a list of assimilation studies and findings). The main interest was in identifying voices that were unassimilated (experienced as problematic by clients), and tracking these voices' evolution across therapy. This was done in order to build an account of the assimilative process that applies to a broad variety of cases, clients, and psychological conditions.

The richly nuanced data accessible to clinicians far exceeds what is available in a session transcript. These data include not only what clients say, but also how they say it, accompanying gestures, tone of speech, etc. We suggest that acoustic differences between voices can help guide clinical applications. If voices can be distinguished on a moment-to-moment basis using such information, this would greatly enhance the usefulness of the assimilation model to practising clinicians. As practising clinicians, we try to identify internal voices that are problematic or unacceptable to the client, and facilitate their emergence and therapeutic dialogue with the client's community of voices. Through this dialogue, problematic voices may eventually become accepted and assimilated into the community.

Internal voices sound different from each other

If speech sounds are relevant to understanding personality, as linguistic research suggests, and if personality consists of multiple voices, as the assimilation model suggests, then intrapersonal differences in clients' speech sounds may point to different internal voices within that client.

The metaphor of voice made salient to us the possibility that a person's multiple internal parts might express themselves with recognizably different vocal qualities. We have heard striking differences both in our research and in our clinical work. For an example, listen to the dramatic shift that we think illustrates the interruption of one internal voice by another in a passage from the case of Debbie (transcription in Stiles 1999: 15; audiofile used with client's permission) at these websites: http://www.users.muohio.edu/stileswb/debbie-1a.htm, or http://www.psychotherapyresearch.org/journal/pr/pr9-1.html

The idea that different voices may literally sound differently has theoretical plausibility. Prior assimilation research showed that different voices could be identified from the client's words (naming of topics, attitudes, objects). Thus, *word use* appears to reflect systematic intrapersonal differences pointing to different voices. In so far as voices reflect not only cognitive but also affective, motoric, physiological and other traces of the original experience (Stiles 1997b, 2002; Stiles et al., Chapter 6 in this volume), differences between voices should be manifested in many modalities. In particular, when a person is speaking from a different voice, one might observe differences not only in content and phrasing, but also in the way the voice sounds.

To explore this hypothesis, we have systematically compared vocal manifestations of internal voices in audiorecords with their written manifestations in therapy transcripts (Osatuke 2003; Osatuke et al. 2003). We developed methods of identifying voices that use phonetic characteristics of speech sounds. Our observations have raised some theoretical and methodological issues that are intriguing on their own. In this chapter, we examine these issues through a case study: a combined transcript-plus-audio analysis of one client's voices in one session of psychotherapy.

The case we chose was one of a set of seventeen cases that had been already subjected to a voice analysis based on transcripts only (Osatuke 2003). In the case study reported here, we used transcript-plus-audio qualitative analyses of voices in one of these seventeen clients, to examine the relationship between what she said (verbal content) and how she said it (speech sounds). We generated a description of the client's voices, taking into account both verbal and vocal cues. We then considered whether the transcript-only and transcript-plus-audio parts of this account paralleled, contradicted or complemented each other.

Method of combined transcript-plus-audio analysis

Case study

We studied one session from the psychotherapy of Sally (a pseudonym), a 43-year-old severely depressed female manager whose initial presenting problems had to do with stress and coping difficulties at work. Later in therapy, she realized the importance of family and self-concept issues as well. Sally participated in the Second Sheffield Psychotherapy Project, a clinical trial comparing two contrasting brief therapies for depression (Shapiro et al. 1994). Sally received sixteen sessions of cognitive-behaviour therapy (CBT), had a good outcome on standard measures (see Shapiro et al. 1994) and was considered one of the most successful cases in the project. As part of the project design, all sessions were recorded on audiotape.

We studied Sally's eighth session. Only one session was used because this study focused on detailed description of client voices, rather than on tracking them through therapy. The eighth session was the best or most impactful according to Sally's therapist and her own post-session ratings. Sally's therapist was a male Caucasian clinical psychologist in his thirties, newly qualified at the onset of the project, with five years of postdoctoral experience providing CBT.

Investigators

The transcript-plus-audio analysis (to which we subsequently refer as *audio*) was done by three assimilation researchers, doctoral students in clinical psychology, designated KO, MJG and MAG, who are three of the authors of this chapter. Two of them (KO and MJG) had participated in a previous transcript-only rating procedure of a set of seventeen cases that included Sally (Osatuke 2003). The fourth author (WBS) participated in designing the project, and he served as a consultant and auditor of the research process. The fifth author (MB) was a member of the Sheffield Project team and was Sally's therapist.

Prior transcript-only analysis of the case

In the previous transcript-only rating procedure, three doctoral students in clinical psychology (including KO and MJG) read through transcripts of one high-impact session from each of seventeen Sheffield Project clients. They then generated a set of consensual, mutually agreed-upon voice characterizations. Through several iterations, they each examined voice descriptions produced by the others, and were encouraged to borrow the strengths of each other's drafts en route to building a sophisticated group characterization of clients' voices (Osatuke 2003). This final product of their work is shown in Table 15.1. They also identified 89 *exemplar passages* from the transcript,

Table 15.1 Description of voices based on transcripts only, versus on transcripts and audio

Voice	Transcript-only description	Number of exemplar passages and lines	Audio-and-transcript-based description of voices in the same exemplar passages, with vocal features
1	VICTIM, PERSECUTED, PARANOID	9 passages 46 lines	WHINY, 'BAD THINGS HAPPENED TO ME', A BIT HYSTERICAL, MELODRAMATIC, REACTIVE, PREACHING, MORALLY SELF-RIGHTEOUS, LASHING OUT, INDIGNANT, 'BITCH, BITCH, BITCH' Loudest and widest range of all voices, strong and sudden emphasis on certain words, vacillating intonation (peaks and valleys)
2	Believes in self, asserts/fulfils own needs, does something constructive and positive for self	29 passages 100 lines	Confident, thoughtful, steady pace, straightforward and matter-of-fact, competent, reasonable, assertive without being aggressive Less emotionally expressive than voice 1, slower and not as held back as voice 3, punchier than voice 4
1 & 2			BLEND OF 1 AND 2: CONFIDENTLY ASSERTIVE, BUT MEETS OWN NEEDS WITH HOSTILITY AND AGGRESSION TOWARDS OTHERS
3	Healthy anger, 'It's ridiculous', 'I've got rights', taking charge and fighting back, angry, opposes/fights against someone or something	22 passages 67 lines	Hostile, repressed but intensely aggressive, seething anger, snarling as if through clenched teeth, sinister laughter, venomous Lowest and most restricted range of all voices; rushed, eruptive, hissing
2 & 3			Blend of 2 and 3: voice of healthy anger
1 & 3			BLEND OF 1 AND 3: DRAMATIC ANGER, MILDLY PUNCHY AND SOMEWHAT DEMONSTRATIVE. HOSTILE LIKE VOICE 3, BUT UNRESTRAINED IN ITS EXPRESSION LIKE VOICE 1. ANGER IS THE STRONGEST EMOTION, BUT NOT THE ONLY ONE

4	Depressed, unworthy, disbelief that someone cares, disoriented, doesn't know how to respond to attacks or stand up for self	29 passages 72 lines	Wants to be taken care of, incredulous, stumbling, resigned, disoriented and confused, morose, malaised Flattest range of all voices; low, sometimes whispery, slower pace and sighing quality, fades away at the end
1 & 4			BLEND OF 1 AND 4: CRUSHED AND COMPLAINING
2 & 4			Blend of 2 and 4: tentative, cautiously optimistic

Note: From the exemplar passages previously selected from transcripts, all but four were consistent with one of the voices described based on speech sound (passages were consistent with one of the four main voices, or their blends — see Table 15.2 for numbers). The four passages deemed inconsistent were too fast spoken and brief (less than one line), and therefore were insufficiently distinctive to be classified.

Different fonts (consistent with Table 15.1) represent ratings of passage segments into voices, based on audiorecords (column 3) and on transcripts (column 4):

voice 1: VICTIM, PARANOID, PERSECUTED
voice 2: *confident, thoughtful, reasonable, assertive*
voice 3: **hostile, repressed but intensely angry**
voice 4: wants to be taken care of, resigned, disoriented
blend 1–2: *MEETS HER NEEDS, WITH HOSTILITY TO OTHERS*
blend 2–3: *voice of healthy anger*
blend 1–3: **DRAMATIC ANGER**
blend 1–4: CRUSHED AND COMPLAINING
blend 2–4: *tentative, cautiously optimistic*

considered as clearly exemplifying each voice (Table 15.1, column 3, shows the number of passages representing each voice).

Materials

Researchers on the present project had access to (a) the consensually agreed upon voice descriptions for Sally from previous research (i.e. Table 15.1) – derived solely from transcripts; (b) the 89 passages considered to be exemplars of these voices – also derived only from transcripts; (c) audiorecords of these 89 passages, excerpted from the full audiorecord of the therapy session with Sally; (d) the complete verbatim transcript of the session; (e) the full audiorecord of the session.

Procedure

The three researchers met weekly over the course of two months, for 90 minutes each time, to work on their consensual descriptions of the voices. The procedure may be described in three phases:

1   *Familiarization:* one of the investigators (KO) had listened to the entire audiorecord of the session and to the audiorecorded passages before the other investigators did, and shared with the other two investigators her preliminary impressions about patterns of divergences between audio and transcript data. Then, the other two investigators listened to the whole audiorecord of the session. Their tasks were to become familiar with the contents and Sally's vocal range, and to form preliminary impressions of how Sally's internal voices were expressed through speech sounds (impressions already formed by KO). Subsequently, all three investigators read the descriptions of voices from the previous transcript-based analyses. Looking at these descriptions, they listened together to the audiorecords of the 89 exemplar passages that had been selected from transcripts, one voice at a time. Their initial focus was to consider the passages that had been classified as the same voice based on transcripts, and decide how homogenous they sounded.

2   *Describing voices and reclassifying passages into voices:* after they became thoroughly familiar with the passages, the investigators began distinguishing between voices based on their sound, describing systematic vocal differences between them, and reclassifying the previously selected exemplar passages, this time accounting for the sound of these passages as well the content and phrasing. These tasks were accomplished consensually. The investigators listened to the passages together, stated their opinions of what voices they were, and exchanged and discussed their perceptions and reasoning whenever they disagreed. Passages were relistened to as many times as needed to reach consensus. In the course of

this process, the investigators formulated a description of each voice in terms of its vocal characteristics. These built upon and slightly modified the descriptions of voices from the previous study based on transcripts only (see Table 15.1 for a comparison).

3   *Analysis of discrepancies between transcripts and audio:* the investigators paid particular attention to discrepancies and attempted to describe their patterns. To this end, the investigators repeatedly compared the verbal content with the audiorecord, rereading the transcript and replaying the exemplar audio passages. They used session transcripts that displayed how Sally's voices had been classified based on transcripts. On this same transcript, they superimposed a marking system to indicate their audio-based classification of Sally's voices (differently sounding voices marked in different colours). This allowed for a direct comparison between the two classifications.

During this process of rereading and relistening, audio-based descriptions of voices became more precise, as did the classification of exemplar passages. Patterns of convergence and divergence between transcript and audio were identified and labelled. In a final round, the investigators relistened to all the passages as a final check of their consensus on the audio-based descriptions and classifications of exemplar passages.

Besides asking how voices identified in transcripts sounded, we also asked how voices that sound different looked in transcripts. Having completed the ratings of audiorecorded segments, we proceeded to listen to the entire session, noting exemplar passages where Sally sounded vocally distinctive, and comparing them to the transcript. This was done independently, with subsequent comparison of notes and observations. The purpose was to check if the voices identified from transcripts (and confirmed in the audio analysis) still seemed accurately descriptive of the client's personality, based on the audiorecord of her whole session.

Results

Voices identified by vocal characteristics

Reaching consensus in classifying voices based on their sound was easier than anticipated. Each of the four voices that had been identified in the transcript (1 – VICTIM, PERSECUTED, PARANOID; 2 – *Believing in Self, Asserting/Fulfilling Own Needs*; 3 – **Healthy Anger, Fighting Back**; 4 – Depressed, Unworthy, Disbelief that Someone Cares) also had a distinctive vocal profile (see Table 15.1, column 2). These descriptions, conversely, offered recognizable indicators of each voice that could be used to classify other segments of the client's speech. That is, a back-translation from these descriptions to speech sounds worked as well.

The sound-based descriptions were conceptually consistent with the descriptions based on verbal content (cf. columns 2 and 4 in Table 15.1). However, the description of voices based on their sound (column 4) elaborated the transcript-only descriptions (column 2). Listening also allowed us to identify voices that sounded like combinations of the four primary voices, as noted in some cells of column 4.

As we listened to the session to check the transcript-based classifications of Sally's voices, each of us at a separate table, taking our own notes, we could not help noticing how often we reacted similarly to particular segments. The obvious incongruence between the content and sound in mismatching passages, or an excellent prototypical example of the main voices often prompted a shared laughter or exclamation from all the three of us at the same time. That is, in our experience of the rating process, the data spoke for themselves. Comparing our notes later added to this impression. We cannot show all of these data to the reader due to space limitations, but we have included a few examples as a sampler of what made us feel confident in our conclusions.

Matches, mismatches, shifts, blends and mixtures

The passages represented a range from excellent to good to less good examples of each voice. Even though all but four passages could be categorized, some passages were more vocally distinctive and thus better exemplars, and several passages were so distinctive that we called them prototypical illustrations of particular voices.

Some passages were considered *matches* (n = 38). For these, the whole passage was classified as the same voice in both transcript and audio ratings, with no parts of the passage being excluded.

Other passages were considered *mismatches* (n = 10). Hearing them completely changed our classification. The transcript and audio categorizations were different, with no part of the passage being labelled as the same voice. These instances are discussed later in more detail.

Many passages, however, were partial matches (n = 37). Hearing them did not completely confirm or completely change the transcript-based classification. Instead, the vocal information prompted us to divide the passage into several parts (usually from two to four), and classify each part as a different voice. There were sudden and subtle shifts in the client's voices that were not noticeable from transcripts, but obvious in audio. We distinguished three types of partial matches: *shifts* between voices, *blends* of voices, and *mixtures*.

In *shifts*, we heard distinct turn-taking between two different voices, though only one of these two voices had been identified in the transcript. It is noteworthy that the other voice (the one missed in transcripts but identified in the audio) was almost always one of the other four described in this client (i.e. it was seldom an unidentified voice). For example (see Table 15.2, shifts), one

Table 15.2 Classification of passages into voices: transcripts versus audio ratings

Relation of transcript to audio ratings	Number of passages and lines	Audio ratings of exemplar passages previously selected from transcripts	Transcript ratings of same passages
Match	38 passages 98 lines	JUST NOW, THEY'RE CONDUCTING THIS GREAT INVESTIGATION, GOD KNOWS WHAT HE'S SAID TO THEM, BUT I CAN UNDERSTAND NOW HOW THE PEOPLE IN HOLLYWOOD FELT DURING THE McCARTHY WITCH HUNTS.	VOICE 1
		Then I started to think things through which of course, is one of the things that I've never been able to do before. Um, and I started to look more positively at myself.	*Voice 2*
		I've certainly given a lot more than I've received. A hell of a lot more.	**Voice 3**
		And . . . well (signs), oh I don't know.	Voice 4
Mismatch	9 passages 21 lines	NOT JUST CLERICAL WORK, I MEAN I'VE DONE ALL KINDS OF THINGS	*Voice 2*
		YEAH, THIS IS IT, WHY HAVEN'T THEY TOLD ME WHAT HE'S ACCUSED ME OF?	**Voice 3**
		I've got the . . . I've got the right to do that.	**Voice 3**
Partial match – blend	8 passages 29 lines	(Sally discusses her work performance:) *BUT I MUST HAVE BEEN DOING TO . . . TO THE EXTENT THAT . . . THAT THE EXAMINING BOARDS MUST HAVE THOUGHT THAT IT WAS ABOVE AND BEYOND THE CALL.*	*Voice 2*
Partial match – shift	11 passages 50 lines	*I . . . I . . . I never expected it at all. I* MEAN I KNOW *I did wrong authorizing 20 pounds without getting a, you know, proper signature from somebody, but, I* WAS SO DESPERATE AT *that time. And I . . . I* MEAN I WASN'T THINKING THINGS THROUGH *and I never even realized,* AND THEN I FORGOT ALL ABOUT IT.	*Voice 4*

Partial match – mixture	18 passages 86 lines	IT'S BECAUSE HE HOLDS A FAR HIGHER POSITION THAN I'LL EVER HOLD. **THAT'S WHAT IT IS.**	VOICE I
		I've started doing the books already, *so I'm not back at square one, you're quite right*	*Voice 2*
		I shall go back with a copy of Telly's 'Employment Law' strapped under my arm I think (laughing). MAKE SURE THEY KNOW THAT I KNOW.	**Voice 3**
		I MEAN, IT'S REALLY, IT'S SHOCKED ME, IT REALLY HAS. IN FACT, HE'S EVEN GONE SO FAR AS TO ER, BRING ABOUT A MEETING BETWEEN ME AND E., YOU KNOW, THE MIDDLE SON.	*Voice 4*

Note: Different fonts (consistent with Table 15.1) represent ratings of passage segments into voices, based on audiorecords (column 2) and on transcripts (column 4):

voice 1: VICTIM, PARANOID, PERSECUTED
voice 2: *confident, thoughtful, reasonable, assertive*
voice 3: **hostile, repressed but intensely angry**
voice 4: wants to be taken care of, resigned, disoriented
blend 1–2: *MEETS HER NEEDS, WITH HOSTILITY TO OTHERS*
blend 2–3: *voice of healthy anger*
blend 1–3: **DRAMATIC ANGER**
blend 1–4: CRUSHED AND COMPLAINING
blend 2–4: *tentative, cautiously optimistic*

passage rated in transcripts as voice 4 (depressed, disoriented) sounded like a rapid crossfire between voice 4 and voice 1 (VICTIM, PERSECUTED, PARANOID). Only four instances of shifts involved passages where the other voice was unclassifiable (see Note for Table 15.1).

In *blends*, two voices seemed to be simultaneously present in the audiorecord. In passages rated as blends, we could simultaneously hear vocal features belonging to two main voices, whereas in the transcript, only one of these voices had been noted. For example (see Table 15.2, blends), a blend of voice 1 (WHINY, HYSTERICAL, INDIGNANT) and voice 2 (*confident, steady, assertive*) presented with strong emphasis on certain words, like that of voice 1, but in a steady unrushed pace, like that of voice 2. Importantly, these blended voices appeared to be not only blends of sound, but also blends in the content and feeling they expressed. That is, psychological characteristics of blends (see Table 15.1 for descriptions) seemed intermediate between those of the respective main voices.

Finally, *mixtures* combined the audio features of shifts and blends. In mixtures, we heard more than one distinctive voice shifting in a passage, and one of these voices was a blend while the other was pure. These passages had been classified into only one voice in transcript ratings, but they seemed far more complex when we listened to them. A few examples of mixtures are given in Table 15.2.

Audio-based categorization of the entire session

Armed with our audio-based voice categories (Table 15.1, column 4) we returned to the audiorecord of the entire session. Recall that the categories had been based only on the 89 passages selected previously in the transcript-based analysis. In this section, we report our observations based on subsequent listening to the full audiorecord.

1   Our understanding of Sally's voices based on the whole audiorecorded session was generally consistent with the prior understanding based on transcripts. That is, we did not hear any speech segments that sounded distinct enough to be classified as new voices. However, we did make some slight modifications. Some segments, although they sounded consistent with voices already identified, had vocal qualities that we had not heard before, when rating passages. For example, voice 1 sometimes had a more high-pitched screeching quality to its whine than previously noted. Similarly, we found new shades of voice 3, in its occasional evenly spaced, very low-pitched, almost subvocal presentation.

2   Across the entire session, Sally spoke by far most frequently with voice 4 (depressed). This preponderance had not been clear from reading the transcript; without the audio information, large portions of the session could not be confidently classified into any particular voice.

3   Listening to the session also revealed an additional number of good or excellent examples for each voice, though particularly voice 4.

4   Vocal differences of voice 4 from the other voices were the largest: voice 4 was usually found in a pure (non-blended) form. In contrast, voice 2 (*positive-assertive*) was only rarely encountered in a non-blended form, and then only in short segments.

5   Voices 2 and 4 participated in the largest number of mismatches. Frequently, the content could be interpreted as voice 2 (*positive-assertive*), but the sound suggested voice 4 (depressed). For example (Sally, who faces a disciplinary procedure at work, plans a defence strategy, with her therapist's active coaching):

> Right. I know that the first thing is contact the union. Find out what I'm charged with, and get them to . . . to work for me rather than the other way around, for a bit. Yes.

Such segments (assertive content, depressed sound) were classified as voice 2 in the transcript analysis but as voice 4 in the audio analysis.

6   There were also a number of partial matches where the content suggested voice 2 (*positive-assertive*), but the sound included both voices 2 and 1 (PERSECUTED-PARANOID). The following example was classified as voice 2 in transcripts, whereas the audio analysis indicated a shift between voices 2 and 1:

> Therapist: And you need also to find out whether they are compelled to tell you or whether (Sally: *Yeah*), or what the time frame of that is, and stuff like that, so it's all, you know . . .
>
> Sally: *Yeah. Yeah, because it's all laid down. I know there is a procedure written down somewhere*, AND I WANT A COPY OF IT. *And if I don't get it*, I'LL TAKE IT FURTHER.

(See also Table 15.2 for an example of a blend between voices 1 and 2, which had been classified as voice 2 in transcripts.)

7   Voices 1 (PERSECUTED-PARANOID) and 3 (**angry**) seemed the closest in sound and location, and often appeared in shifts and blends. This is an example of a shift:

> Sally: . . . AND I THOUGHT THE UNION FELLOW WOULD HAVE, YOU KNOW, JUMPED IN. NOT A WORD. AND I THOUGHT: '**Oh, great**.' I'M GOING TO TAKE N. WITH ME NEXT TIME ANYWAY BECAUSE HE IS FAR BETTER AT THIS KIND OF THING . . . SO, HE . . . **He'd be far better than some union** . . .

In the transcript analysis, the first half of this example had received a matching classification (voice 1). The portion starting from 'I'm going to . . .' was left unclassified. Without hearing the segment, it was unclear whether it was voice 1 (PERSECUTED-PARANOID) or voice 2 (*assertive*).

Discussion

The convergence of Sally's verbal content with her vocality was shown by the similarity of voice descriptions and by the high frequency of passage classifications matched in the transcript and audio analyses. When Sally's voices spoke, their verbal content, affect and manner of vocal presentation tended to convey similar messages. As a result, our understanding of Sally was generally similar (see Table 15.1) whether it was based on a transcript analysis of what she said, or a combined analysis taking into account how she sounded when saying this.

Although the broad pattern was one of convergence, the match between transcript and audio-based classifications was far from perfect. The main differences seemed to reflect an improved precision, or metaphorically, a finer resolution in distinguishing the voices. The transcript alone gave a relatively blurry picture, less elaborated and distorted in details, although recognizable overall. Adding auditory information allowed for a closer look, and led to discovering new shades. Hearing a voice was a more direct, evocative experience to us than reading its words, and it resulted in more specific and therefore more subtle understandings of the client (cf. columns 2 and 4 in Table 15.1). Thus, mismatches and partial matches may reflect psychological complexity, as when vocal aspects elaborate on the content rather than simply restating it (cf. Scherer et al. 1984).

As an illustration, mismatches where Sally's assertive content had a depressed sound may point to these different coexisting perspectives on her experience. That is, co-present voices may be negotiating their respective positions as the client speaks (see Table 15.2 for examples of mismatches; see also Stiles et al., Chapter 6 in this volume, for more theoretical discussion). The notion of co-presence of several voices has been recognized and theoretically explored in many models of internal multiplicity (e.g. Bakhtin 1986; Cooper 2003; Hermans 2002; Hermans and Hermans-Jansen 1995; Valsiner 2002; Verhofstadt-Denève 2003; see also Leiman, Chapter 16 in this volume).

Mismatches and partial matches illustrate how new observations, at first seemingly contradicting our theory about internal voices, could be understood as consistent with it. This is because they helped uncover a further layer of complexity (e.g. not only separate voices but also co-present voices), yielding a more sophisticated understanding of Sally. Such elaborations of the theory support its *catalytic validity* (Lather 1986; Stiles 1993), showing that it can change to encompass new observations while retaining its conceptual integrity.

We felt confident in our identifications of matches, mismatches and shifts; these could be easily and reliably classified by all three investigators. We felt more tentative about classifying blends and mixtures – partly, because blends, by definition, have a less well-defined character than pure or shifting voices. This makes their rating more impressionistic; for example, we occasionally wondered whether a blend was instead a not-so-good instance of one of the main voices. Nevertheless, we did not consider the blends as previously unidentified voices, because they had clearly recognizable features of the main voices.

Listening to the session showed that the depressed voice 4 was by far the most prominent, frequent and distinct. This was not obvious from the transcript where voice 2 (*positive-assertive*) appeared equally or more prominent. Sally's vocal presentation thus was more consistent with her presenting problem and diagnosis of severe depression than was the content of her speech.

Speculations based on the assimilation model

We speculate that inconsistencies between content and sound may point to co-presence of voices. As they encounter each other, they are both addressed and both try to respond at the same time. When experiences expressed by each voice are too discrepant, they are difficult to put together: this would result in conflict, discomfort, or pain, and this may prompt moving away to a different voice (*shift*), or combining a problematic voice with a more acceptable one, to make it more palatable (*blend*). Further discussion of this process is offered by Stiles et al. (Chapter 6 in this volume).

Also, vocal distinctiveness may reflect the extent of assimilation between voices. Unassimilated voices are likely to contradict or interrupt each other. A sharp change in speech sounds, whether consistent with content or not, may point to the shift in the experience that the client expresses (a different internal voice). Thus, we speculate that relatively assimilated voices sound more alike. More research is needed to explore this possibility.

Conclusion

We have found that distinguishing internal voices based on the sound of clients' speech is possible, and generally consistent with an understanding based on content of speech. We suggest that voices are more than a metaphorical description of internal multiplicity: they can be literally heard in a person's speech. This underscores the physicality of psychological self. Voices – traces of experience – talk, smell, sound, want or demand certain things. Experience is more than its cognitive representation: it is embodied. A client coming to therapy brings a community of voices, multiple and not necessarily internally consistent. Each of these voices may be expressed at some point in therapy. Recognizing who speaks now is thus an important task for a psychotherapist. We suggest that listening to how clients speak, in addition to listening to what they say, may help address this task.

References

Bady, S.L. and Lachmann, M. (1985). 'The voice as a curative factor in psychotherapy.' *Psychological Review, 72*, 479–490.

Bakhtin, M.M. (1986). *Speech Genres and Other Late Essays*. Austin, TX: University of Texas Press.

Cooper, M. (2003). ' "I–I" and "I–Me": Transposing Buber's interpersonal attitudes to the intrapersonal plane.' *Journal of Constructivist Psychology, 16*, 131–154.

Fonagy, I. (1976). 'La mimique buccale: Aspect radiologique de la vive voix.' *Phonica, 33*, 31–44.

Hermans, H.J.M. (2002). 'The dialogical self as a society of mind.' *Theory and Psychology, 12*, 147–160.

Hermans, H.J.M. (2003). 'The construction and reconstruction of a dialogical self.' *Journal of Constructivist Psychology, 16*, 89–130.

Hermans, H.J.M. and Hermans-Jansen, E. (1995). *Self-narratives: The Construction of Meaning in Psychotherapy*. New York: Guilford.

Honos-Webb, L. and Stiles, W.B. (1998). 'Reformulation of assimilation analysis in terms of voices.' *Psychotherapy, 35*, 23–33.

Lather, P. (1986). 'Research as praxis.' *Harvard Educational Review*, *56*, 257–277.

Muntigl, P. (2003). 'Systemic functional linguistics: A model for mapping out clients' semiotic development during therapy.' In P. Muntigl (moderator) *Language, Culture, and Client Change*. Panel presented at the Thirty-Fourth Meeting of the Society for Psychotherapy Research, Weimar, Germany.

Osatuke, K. (2003). 'Hearing voices: Verbal and vocal cues of internal multiplicity.' Doctoral dissertation in preparation, Miami University, Oxford, Ohio.

Osatuke, K., Humphreys, C.L., Glick, M.J., Graff-Reed, R.L., McKenzie Mack, L. and Stiles, W.B. (2003). *Vocal Manifestations of Internal Multiplicity: Mary's Voices*. Manuscript submitted for publication.

Rice, L.N. and Kerr, G.P. (1986). Measures of client and therapist vocal quality. In L.S. Greenberg and W.M. Pinsof (eds) *The Psychotherapeutic Process: A Research Handbook* (pp. 73–105). New York: Guilford.

Scherer, K.R. (1986). 'Vocal affect expression: A review and a model for future research.' *Psychological Bulletin*, *99*, 143–165.

Scherer, K.R. and Bergmann, G. (1990). 'Vocal communication.' *German Journal of Psychology*, *8*, 57–90.

Scherer, K.R., Ladd, D.R. and Silverman, K.E.A. (1984). 'Vocal cues to speaker affect: Testing two models.' *Journal of the Acoustical Society of America*, *76*, 1346–1356.

Shapiro, D.A., Barkham, M., Rees, A., Hardy, G.E., Reynolds, S. and Startup, M. (1994). 'Effects of treatment duration and severity of depression on the effectiveness of cognitive-behavioural and psychodynamic-interpersonal psychotherapy.' *Journal of Consulting and Clinical Psychology*, *62*, 522–534.

Stiles, W.B. (1993). 'Quality control in qualitative research.' *Clinical Psychology Review*, *13*, 593–618.

Stiles, W.B. (1997a). 'Signs and voices: Joining a conversation in progress.' *British Journal of Medical Psychology*, *70*, 169–176.

Stiles, W.B. (1997b). 'Multiple voices in psychotherapy clients.' *Journal of Psychotherapy Integration*, *7*, 177–180.

Stiles, W.B. (1999). 'Signs and voices in psychotherapy.' *Psychotherapy Research*, *9*, 1–21.

Stiles, W.B. (2002). 'Assimilation of problematic experiences.' In J.C. Norcross (ed.) *Psychotherapy Relationships that Work: Therapist Contributions and Responsiveness to Patients* (pp. 357–365). New York: Oxford University Press.

Stiles, W.B. and Angus, L. (2001). 'Qualitative research on clients' assimilation of problematic experiences in psychotherapy.' In J. Frommer and D.L. Rennie (eds) *Qualitative Psychotherapy Research: Methods and Methodology* (pp. 111–126). Lengerich, Germany: Pabst Science Publishers. Also in *Psychologische Beiträge*, *43*, 570–585.

Stiles, W.B., Elliott, R., Llewelyn, S.P., Firth-Cozens, J.A., Margison, F.R., Shapiro, D.A. and Hardy, G. (1990). 'Assimilation of problematic experiences by clients in psychotherapy.' *Psychotherapy*, *27*, 411–420.

Sullivan, H.S. (1954). *The Psychiatric Interview*. New York: Norton.

Valsiner, J. (2002). 'Forms of dialogical relations and semiotic autoregulation within the self.' *Theory and Psychology*, *12*, 251–265.

Verhofstadt-Denève, L.M.F. (2003). 'The psychodramatic "Social Atom Method":

Dialogical self in dialectical action.' *Journal of Constructivist Psychology*, *16*, 183–212.

Williams, C.E. and Stevens, K.N. (1972). 'Emotions and speech: Some acoustical correlates.' *Journal of the Acoustical Society of America*, *52*, 1238–1250.

Chapter 16

Dialogical sequence analysis

Mikael Leiman

What follows is an introduction to dialogical sequence analysis (DSA) as a concept-based procedure for analysing client and therapist utterances. The methodological basis of such an approach differs greatly from the discourse-oriented research techniques that are currently used in psychotherapy process research. DSA is based on employing a set of theoretical concepts to articulate the dialogical patterns that are embedded in the utterances. These concepts are quite complex. Hence, the technique requires a good command of the meaning of the concepts, which includes their history and the broader theoretical tradition to which they belong. In addition, because the concepts articulate relational configurations rather than particular features or elements, the progress and complexity of analysis will vary depending on the material that is examined. Consequently, it is not possible to generate straightforward methodical rules or procedures by which the analysis can be carried out in all cases. I will however include a DSA of the opening discourse from a psychotherapy assessment interview to illustrate how it works with a particular case.

DSA evolved in the context of supervising and teaching cognitive analytic therapy (CAT) (Leiman 1994a; Ryle 1990; Ryle and Kerr 2002). Psychotherapy trainees under my supervision taped their sessions. In addition to the customary session report they also prepared transcripts from passages that they found either problematic or particularly important. Gradually, the interplay between client utterances and therapist's responses became the main focus of the supervision.[1] Being familiar with the Bakhtinian concept of the sign (Bakhtin 1986; Leiman 1992, 2002; Voloshinov 1986) as well as Bakhtin's theory of utterance (Bakhtin 1984, 1986), I found myself repeatedly using his concepts of *addressee, personal stance* to the object or to the other, and *responsive understanding* as the structuring devices in making sense of the discourse.

The structural units of utterance

Mikhail Bakhtin's (1981, 1984, 1986) theory of utterance evolved alongside Valentin Voloshinov's (1986) early studies on language and discourse. The analytic concepts of DSA are an offspring, although not a direct derivation, of this theory. In addition to their origin in the Bakhtinian theory of utterance, they have collected new meanings by their application to the psychotherapeutic discourse.

Any utterance is composed of three structural and three expressive aspects. The three structural aspects are *the author, the addressee* and *the referential content*. What, by whom and to whom, encapsulates the essence of any utterance. The three expressive aspects, namely *intonation, composition* and *stylistic devices*, are the means by which utterances are expressed (cf. Osatuke et al., Chapter 15 in this volume). They signpost the ever-changing dialogic positions and movements of the structural aspects and are therefore very important indicators in the practice of DSA. Because of space limitations, only the structural aspects will be addressed in the following.

Multiple addressees

We commonly think that people tell stories because they want us to know their content. The narrative, the events that are described and the people that are included in the story become the main focus of our attention as listeners. This common-sense view recognizes the speaker and the content as the salient features of utterances.

Voloshinov and Bakhtin transformed this view by emphasizing that the addressee, or the recipient, is the basic structural aspect of utterances. They frequently claimed that the anticipated response of the addressee affects every aspect of the utterance, including its content. The speaker's speech plan does not evolve in a vacuum. It takes shape in the shared intersubjective space, created by the interlocutors. In all human discourse, every utterance is addressed and expects a response. This feature is so salient that Bakhtin defines the boundaries of any utterance by the possibility of formulating a response, of responding to it by another utterance.

This structural aspect of utterances forms the starting point of analysing psychotherapeutic discourse. In order to understand herself the client needs the therapist as a responsive other. The fundamental role of the other as an addressee represents an early finding of psychoanalysis. Freud discovered the role of transference by noticing that his patients' free associations were frequently disturbed by his presence. Because he believed that those associations arose from unconscious sources, he first regarded transference as a form of resistance. Only later did he realize that the addressivity of the patients' utterances forms the main dynamics on which the curative effects of psychoanalysis rests (Freud 1914/1958).

Matters are made more complex by the fact that there are usually other addressees that are invisibly present besides the listener to whom the speaker seems to talk (Bollas 1987). In accounts involving other people it very often happens that the speaker directs her words at those very persons about whom she is talking. The listener's position then changes. He becomes a potential ally, a witness, a helpless spectator, etc.

Clients frequently make addressees of different aspects of themselves. Again Freud's early observations can be used as an illustration. When treating depressed patients he noticed that they seemed to relate to 'a critical instance' in their mind (Freud 1917/1958). It appeared as if this instance acted like an internalized figure, judging their thoughts and expressions. This instance was clearly active, responding to and commenting on the patient's wishes, thoughts and actions. In such cases, an explicit self-dialogue could be observed. But even when the patient's self-criticisms did not take an openly dialogic form, her ways of relating to herself revealed the presence of a judgemental addressee. Inanimate objects, natural phenomena and even such abstract things as values or social symbols can become important addressees. We baptize our boats, curse the weather, cherish our country and salute our flag as if true others. Voloshinov (1976) emphasized the potential to personify any object or activity as a fundamental feature of human beings.

To summarize, every utterance has an addressee. In DSA, it is the fundamental structural unit that guides the researcher. 'To whom is the person speaking?' is the starting point of analysing utterances. The listener represents only the immediately observable addressee but, more often than not, the addressee is a complex web of invisible others whose presence can be traced in the content, the flow and the expressive aspects of the utterance.

Referential object – the topic

Every utterance is about something. It can be an account of an event or a personal comment on the meaning of some experience. It can be a remark concerning some observation or an elaborate description of a person. It can be expressed as a command or a warning but then too it has a referential object; it warns about something or it encourages the other to do something.

The referential aspect of utterances has had an important role in the history of philosophy and epistemology. It has been so fundamental that it has overshadowed the other structural aspects of utterances and reduced them to statements about matters and facts. As self-contained propositions their truth or falseness, as well as the conditions by which truth can be ascertained, have occupied philosophers for centuries. The current debates around postmodern epistemologies still revolve around issues of veracity, but the conditions for true statements are mainly sought in the structure of language and in the social practices that shape language use (Gergen 1994).

The Bakhtinian theory of utterance can be regarded as semi-postmodern in the sense that utterances emerge in social practice and communication. However, the referential object is not reduced to a linguistically constructed object whose meaning is defined by a never-ending chain of other linguistic signifiers. For Voloshinov (1986) and Bakhtin (1981), every sign refers to something outside itself. Communication represents a vital area of social practice by which the meaning of signifiers is established but there are additional, equally important, ways of creating meaningful signs that refer to an object. In fact, there are two kinds of semiotic activity, instrumental actions and communication. Alongside communication, instrumental actions represent a fundamental mode of creating referential links between objects and their signifiers. Vygotsky's (1978) example of tying a knot in a handkerchief in order to remind oneself of something illustrates this mode of generating meaning. The referential object is clearly something external to the person as well as to the knot, but the object is, literally, tied to the knot through the concrete action. Now looking at the knot, the person remembers what he or she had to do.

There are two important aspects that characterize the speaker's relationship to the referential object which is established through the utterance. The first of these is our already mentioned tendency to personify the referential object about which we are talking. When this happens, the 'about which' becomes a 'you', in other words, one of the addressees. This phenomenon has a semiotic origin. According to Bakhtin (1986) and Voloshinov (1986), the sign of an object is not simply a representation. Because signs are formed by actions with objects, those objects are semiotically present in related, later activities. This is called the epiphanic quality of signs (Leiman 2002). They seem to put us in touch with the things that they pass on.

Second, every utterance positions the speaker with regard to the referential object as well as the addressee. The speaker unwittingly knows that whatever she says will put her, in the listener's eyes, into a certain position. When there is more than one addressee, the speaker's task becomes challenging. The listener may be benign but an 'internalized judge' may be very critical. Such tensions usually generate so-called loopholes in the utterance. The speaker modulates her expression in order to avoid the potential of becoming embarrassed, humiliated, dismissed, ridiculed and so on.

Bakhtin (1984) gives a vivid illustration by way of Dostoevsky's Makar Devushkin in *Poor Folk*. Devushkin describes his room to Varenka in a letter and, being afraid of the impression she might get, his account of this room, which in fact is a niche behind the kitchen, is filled with internal dialogic by which he tries to escape the humiliated position into which his own opinion about it seems to put him.

The referential object, the niche in the kitchen, positions him unfavourably both in his own eyes as well as, potentially, in Varenka's mind. He tries to undo the risk by inserting all sorts of responsive comments into his description. The letter is populated with additional addressees who are there to compensate for Varenka's imminent ridicule. Thus, the referential object as it is expressed in the utterance becomes a complex fabrication, indeed a 'linguistic construction of reality'. Yet, Bakhtin maintains the view that referential objects have an independent existence. There is a dialectical tension between the thing in itself and the thing for us. Although Makar constructs a winding story, it is still an account of the niche in the kitchen.

In summary, any utterance may involve several positions and positional shifts concerning the referential object. This internal movement is generated by the constant interplay between object and addressee in the speaker's mind. The speaker is carrying out an internal dialogue in the course of expressing herself. The positional switches in relation to the object are *replies* to the anticipated responses of the addressee(s) within a single utterance. While giving accounts of something, we have an elaborate store of rhetorical devices that we may use in order to convey our evaluative stance to the referential object of our account. We can use figurative expressions, play with selected details, or portray the object by framing it in different ways. When describing events with people we may repeat their actual words or paraphrase them adding stylistic overtones that reveal our personal response to the event described. The expressive aspects of utterances are thus inseparably linked with their content.

Polypositioned author

There are no utterances without authors, but as is the case with addressees, authorship is also complex. As already stated, the basic function of the speaker is to express her specific evaluative stance, or semiotic position (Leiman 2002; Shotter 1993) regarding the referential object.

Voloshinov emphasized that the very act of expression serves to position the person both with regard to the object and to the addressee. The client's evaluative stance, or position, regarding the referential object is usually our primary interest when listening to her account in psychotherapy. As already argued, the matter is complicated by the fact that the client's stance to an object is not only determined by the client's past and present experiences with it,[2] but also by the fact that she is describing her experiences to the therapist. The addressee thus mediates the speaker's evaluative stance to the object.

Because of the presence of one or more addressees, the utterance positions the author into one or more locations. They usually form a sequence, but sometimes we may observe simultaneous presence of two or more positions, affected by the addressees. When writing his letter to Varenka, Makar Devushkin's authorship is divided into the *expresser* and the *commenter*, the latter trying to fend off Varenka's potentially negative responses to his account. For a psychotherapist, it is important to recognize that Devushkin addresses the Varenka-in-his-mind as much as the real Varenka. His internalized Varenka is perhaps much more critical and dismissing that the young woman who is not much better off than Makar himself. Thus Makar's evaluative stance regarding his 'room' is powerfully mediated by a double-faceted addressee that is a blend of the real and the imagined Varenka.

Self-reflection is a particular instance of double-voiced speech. As a discourse mode it lies at the heart of psychotherapy. The client makes an aspect of self – a memory, a feeling, a thought, etc. – as the referential object of her utterance. All the above-mentioned structural aspects and complexities apply to these self-referring utterances as well as to ordinary accounts of things and events. In addition, the author occupies a specific position in relation to the experiencing self.

As with every utterance, even self-reflective utterances articulate the speaker's evaluative stance to the referential object, in this case, some aspect of herself. For instance, by making a remark on her looks she positions herself by the evaluative comment she makes. Thus, the act of self-reflection brings the speaker into an *observer position* regarding her appearance (the referential object of her speech).

The speaker may also comment on her thoughts, actions, and feelings with similar evaluative statements. Such habitual patterns of self-reflection can be viewed as the personal quality of her observer position. It is often this which plays an important role in the client's problems. If every remark concerning the self is critical and disappointed, or blaming and demeaning, then the client's central problem seems to be that whatever she does is not good enough. She may do her utmost to the verge of exhaustion and yet still feel miserable and inadequate. Listening to her self-critical reflections, the therapist recognizes that she tends to position herself unfavourably in almost every respect and this must be addressed in therapy.

When the personal characteristics of self-reflection are explored, an important aspect of authorship may become apparent. The therapist may get an impression that the client is portraying herself through somebody else's eyes when describing her experiences, actions and thoughts. Is it her mother, father, primary school teacher, a friend, or a partner? Or is it 'people in general' as it so often seems to be in cases of social anxiety? In such instances, the authorship is double-voiced in an additional sense. There is the voice of someone else that blends with the client's voice while she reflects on her experiences. The observer position is occupied by another.

In the British psychoanalytic object relations theory, such internalized evaluative stances of others are addressed as internal objects (Fairbairn 1944; Klein 1946/1984). Following Freud, the object relations theory assumes that such objects are formed through processes of early identification. In psychotherapy, such identifications become manifest through the positioning that the client adopts with regard to herself and others. They create dialogic relationships within self-reflective utterances. The client responds to her own statements, for instance, by justifying her stance in face of a self-reproach that arises from identifying with a critical other. An illustration of this will be shown in the case to follow.

The dual, and sometimes even a multiple, authorship of expressions needs to be considered when performing a dialogical analysis of client utterances. In addition to this, there is still one further complicating aspect of authorship. It too has been addressed in the psychoanalytic object relations theory, mainly through the concept of projective identification (Klein 1946/1984).

We habitually assume that the authorship rests in the person who is speaking. Even when we allow for a multivoiced utterance we tend to assign its authors to the speaker. The situation is, however, not so straightforward. Melanie Klein (1926) noticed quite early that the author of an utterance can be displaced in dyadic relationships. In child analysis it frequently happens that the child invests the therapist with their own destructive and persecutory fantasies. Later on Klein (1946) called this phenomenon *projective identification*. The concept is not without problems (Leiman 1994b; Ryle 1994), but it serves to bring forth the idea that dyadic authorship is a frequently occurring phenomenon in psychotherapeutic discourse. The therapist may indeed 'speak with the client's mouth' as if accepting the role that the client assigns to him. Ryle (1997) has named this phenomenon as an identifying countertransference.

From the viewpoint of the Bakhtinian theory of utterance, identifying countertransference represents a specific mode of responsive understanding (Bakhtin 1986). It is an adequate response to the client's specific mode of projective communication. Projective identification is problematic because the authorship, or the true subject position regarding one's actions, seems to stay with the therapist. Self–other distinction is distorted and confusion ensues, if the therapist does not recognize what has happened. By 'voicing the client's experience', the therapist accepts this indirect mode of communication and uses it in order to foster joint reflection. He adopts a temporary authorship aimed at helping the client to own it in due course.

To sum up, the question of who is speaking is not a straightforward issue in psychotherapeutic discourse. Utterances are multivoiced, because the speaker's 'I' is formed by identifying with others. In addition, the formative centre of utterances does not reside exclusively in the client's mind. Sometimes she may speak through the therapist. Then the author of utterances is a truly dyadic subject.

The organizing concepts of cognitive analytic therapy

Bakhtinian theory of utterance has contributed to the basic concepts with which client and therapist utterances can be studied. The multilayered dialogic phenomena *in utterances* point towards mental processes that share the same features. There is a two-way connection between mental processes and their expression. Psychotherapy is a process where a joint understanding is sought through utterances. The therapist attempts to make sense of the client's problems by receiving the wealth of meanings embedded in the client's accounts and expressions. His responsive understanding is mediated by concepts that describe human action, its development and its maladaptive patterns that may account for the client's problems. The process of change occurs along similar lines. Psychotherapy mends through talking.

Cognitive analytic therapy is currently based on the Semiotic Object Relations Model (SORT) as its organizing conceptual device (Ryle and Kerr 2002). It uses three concepts to describe dialogically structured action sequences and recurring experiential states. The concepts of *dialogical pattern*, *dialogical sequence* and *self state* will be briefly introduced.[3]

Addressees and referential objects are counterpositioned

When the speaker expresses her evaluative stance to an object, the object is assigned a reciprocal position. The same is true for the speaker's relation to the addressee. When Devushkin writes his letter to Varenka, he adopts an embarrassed and submissively deferential position to a potentially scornful and dismissive addressee. The dialogic relations in an utterance will not be comprehensively covered unless these counterpositions are spelled out. This aspect is perhaps not explicitly stated in Bakhtin's theory of utterance. Its salience in DSA stems from CAT.

The importance of the counterpositioned other was recognized in CAT quite early. It was mainly affected by British psychoanalytic object relations theory, but it also had a connection to G.H. Mead's theory of symbolic interaction. Our relationships with others are reciprocally patterned. In being a traveller to a ticket-collector or a patient to a doctor we regard the other, and expect to be regarded by the other, largely in terms defined by the reciprocal roles (Ryle 1975).

Although less obvious, we relate to ourselves in the same way. Everyday accounts of people one knows are full of phrases such as 'he's hard on himself', 'he's self-indulgent', 'he's sorry for himself', 'he drives himself', 'he admires himself', 'he neglects himself' (Ryle 1975). In such descriptions the person is seen as divided, one part treating the other in a specific manner or adopting a specific position to the other part.

In social relationships the other is expected to respond according to the position defined by the reciprocal roles. This responsiveness also applies to intrapersonal phenomena. The 'other part' responds to the 'first part' from the position into which it has been placed. Thus in reciprocal relationships every positioning invokes a counterposition that is uniquely related to it.

In DSA, this notion of the reciprocating other is extended to include the referential objects of utterances in addition to its addressees. Hence, it is more appropriate to use the term *dialogical pattern* instead of reciprocal roles which denote inter- and intrapersonal relationships. When a person speaks about something, it is positioned and can be seen as reciprocally related to the speaker's stance.

Dialogical sequences

The course of any action proceeds through a series of responsive positions with regard to the object of action. It is possible to distinguish object-oriented actions from communication. In the former, the object and the addressee coincide:[4] object-oriented actions aim to transform the object in some ways, for instance when the potter moulds lumps of clay into jars and plates. In communication the person generates or reproduces the object by semiotic means in order to convey an aspect of it that is relevant for her as well as to the other participants. The structure of communication is ostensibly dialogical because of the manifold relations of objects and addressees in utterances. However, even object-oriented actions share the positional nature of our activity. When trying to create a vase that stretches the limits of clay as a raw material, the potter goes through a speedy sequence of different positions, ranging from excitement of success to the frustrations and disappointments caused by the limitations. Later on, when telling about her experience, she portrays it by reproducing those experiential positions in words. However, her listener, as the addressee, adds the extra dimension into the account.

The idea that all action is positioned permits us to explore unfolding actions as dialogically structured. They are described as chains of dialogical patterns. In any moment of the sequence the acting person identifies temporarily with a position and assigns the relevant counterposition to the object, as in the example of the potter making a vase.

Action sequences are infinitely variable because they mirror the infinite variability of objects and the contexts in which we act. Human activity is adaptable. Problems ensue when this is not so. Psychological disorders can be described as action patterns that have become repetitive, inefficient and even harmful to self and others. One of the first observations in the history of psychotherapy was the patients' tendency to repeat and re-enact past traumatic events. Even now, when we listen to our clients we tend to pay attention to recurring themes and inflexible patterns. In DSA, extracting the dialogical sequences constitutes the second step in organizing the material of client utterances.

Self states

Mental integration is a clinically important viewpoint in CAT (Ryle 1997). The basic therapeutic strategy depends on whether or not dissociative phenomena characterize the client's experience and action. When relatively integrated, the client's general sense of self is coherent and there are not abrupt shifts in her way of describing herself and her daily experiences. The main focus of therapy then becomes the repetitive, unmodified action patterns, in other words the problematic dialogical sequences. If the client's sense of self and the world is discontinuous, achieving integration is the key aim of therapy.

To support this clinically important distinction, the concept of *self state* evolved in psychotherapy conducted with personality disordered clients (Ryle 1997). The phenomenon of self states has a long history in psychotherapy. Both Freud and Janet began their psychotherapeutic career by treating hysterical patients. In CAT, the self state seems to be more closely allied with the Janetian concept of dissociation than with the Freudian repression. The self state is described by a dissociated dialogical pattern (reciprocal role in CAT terminology) that accounts for the specific quality of experience and action. Usually the client is identified with one role position and the shift to another is marked by discontinuity of experience and difficulty in recognizing the shift. Hence, self-reflection is also largely state dependent.

By focusing on dissociative phenomena, the concept of self state is not relevant in all cases. In the case presented here, it seems to be useful. The client describes two quite different experiential modes. The shift from an everyday sense of self to an altered state of consciousness is quite abrupt. Relation to others and to self is different in the two states. The altered state appears embarrassing to the client when she tries to describe it from her 'normal' observer position. The discontinuity in experiencing the self is one of the most important criteria when deciding to use the concept of self state to organize the dialogic multiplicity in client utterances.

A case illustration

The following vignette is a transcribed excerpt of the client's first account in an initial interview with the therapist.[5] The client was a woman in her late twenties who suffered from depression and had recently been discharged from the hospital after a major depressive episode. Her father had died when she was very young and she had lived a rather lonely childhood with a possessive mother. The woman met the therapist for a single assessment interview when considering her options after the hospital treatment. The therapist opened the dialogue by making a general question about the client's situation.

C: This situation?
T: Yes.
C: It is a sum of so many things that, then, got me into such a bad shape that I had to stop working . . . for a while . . . and it's quite a big thing to me, because it is the only place to earn money . . . /// And it's so . . ., so, especially a, like an eating disorder that has been going on for years, and . . . then . . . like . . . a depression that got worse . . . on the top. That's like . . .

T: And right now, what's the situation just now?

C: Well, rather chaotic, frankly (chuckle) . . . you just get out of hospital and you get back home, and you're able to calm down, but . . . but everyday life is still quite a . . . Well, of course my work is very demanding . . . and I must always be extremely careful not tooverstrain myself. And then my mates get cross and demanding . . .that I hang out with them . . . then you feel guilty, and you feel like such a bad person . . . and . . . it's such a foolish whirlpool.

T: You feel that your everyday life is demanding . . .

C: Yes. Yes . . . and then, when it . . . when it gets too much like that, then comes the self-destructive urge that I've had since . . . since quite early on, and I don't understand what has caused it, but . . . it is bizarre.

T: How did it express itself then?

C: Well, it is totally . . . it's like I took . . . like . . . mum's sleeping pills and . . . red wine . . . Then there's been like some minor self-cutting then.

The analysis begins by examining the expressive style of the client. Although much is lost in translation and transcription, some characteristic patterns remain. A recurring feature is the client's use of the passive voice.[6] 'I' and 'you' alternate in her expressions. This may indicate a shifting attitude within the observer position. At times she clearly identifies with the 'experiencing I' but that is soon replaced with a more distancing observer position. The client's use of the passive form seems to affect the therapist's way of phrasing even her questions by omitting direct reference to the client.

Another expressive feature is the constant interruptions in the account. The client seems to swallow her own expression and instead continues with a commentary statement. This can also be seen as an indicator of the dialogue between the experiencing and observing positions that are quite distinctly voiced from different locations.

There is also a recurring intonation, marked here by underlining the transcript, which has a conspicuously convincing quality as if she were addressing someone who either does not believe, or listen to, her. The therapist is obviously the client's primary addressee, but her intonation hints at somebody else who is not at all as attentive as the therapist. This extra addressee seems to be present especially in those passages where the client speaks about her attempts to cope alone and without support in face of difficulties and demands.

The client's first account is divided into two parts (marked textually by ///) that differ with respect to the observer position. In the opening part she describes a sequence of events that led to hospitalization. She emphasizes that helplessness implies loss of financial support. There is nobody to lend her a hand. We may assume that becoming vulnerable and helpless implies being abandoned. Helplessness can be provisionally named as the feared, perhaps even the worst, position to be in.

The client's mode of expression changes in the second part of her first utterance. It becomes an impersonal account of her long-standing predicament, framed in medical terms. The distancing from the experiential mode is obvious. It may be seen as a response to the feared position that was evoked by the first statement.

When studying utterances, we are able to make hypotheses about the client's positions to referential objects and addressees from the start. However, we should be aware of the fact that, as researchers, we do not get the client's responses to our descriptions that would validate them. We will need several instances of positioning in order to claim that a specific pattern is typical for the client. Even then it is worth remembering that human utterances are semiotically multilayered. Any expressive act involves several aspects of the client's personal life and history. When we recognize a recurring pattern, we cannot claim to have exhausted the possible variations of meaning that it may have. As Bakhtin said, 'the word is bottomless' (Bakhtin 1986: 127).

In her next utterance, the client describes a sequence of events that leads into a turning point at which the 'self-destructive urge' appears. Here we have a sign of a possible state shift. When the destructive urge takes over, another mode of experience and action seems to set in involving self-injury. Self-cutting and taking pills with wine can be seen as intrapersonal dialogic patterns in which one part deliberately harms the other part.

The sequence of events that leads to the destructive self state also involves dialogical patterns. The first can be recognized in her way of describing her work and her mates. Both are 'demanding' and she responds by trying to cope by compliantly meeting the demands. Feeling not able to cope makes her feel guilty. The counterposition to her guilty position is clearly located, involving her mates' response to her failing. They get cross and probably critical.

An intrapersonal repetition of this cross-guilty pattern can be seen in the client's next remark describing the event sequence: 'You feel like such a bad person.' Here we have an instance of a self-referential statement that has an implicit dialogical structure. A 'bad person' is voiced from the disapproving position while 'you feel' indicates the quality of experience when failing to meet the demands.

At some point in this intrapersonal dialogue a state shift occurs and the dialogical pattern obtains a sadistic tone. We may assume that the 'bad person' is worthless, foolish and deserves punishment. However, such an assumption goes well beyond the available material. Self-harming behaviour can have many meanings, for instance, it may be an attempt to escape, to find a fresh start after a failure, or even an act of purification. The client has no idea of what may be involved and in her current state she regards it as a weird phenomenon. A little before she described the sequence leading to the self-harming state as a 'foolish whirlpool'. This indicates a dismissive quality in her self-observations. Does this hint at the ways by which she has been met when feeling weak and vulnerable? We do not yet know, but it is worth noticing. It may represent the first explicit response by the hidden addressee that could be discerned in the client's peculiar intonation.

Conclusion

The case illustration shows that even in a relatively short utterance it contains dialogical phenomena, providing potentially useful hypotheses about the client's recurring problematic positions and action sequences. DSA can indeed be used as a clinical tool in brief psychotherapy to focus the therapist's listening and thinking during the initial encounters.

DSA can also be used in psychotherapy research to generate very early formulations about the client's predicament. Leiman and Stiles (2001) analysed the first session of a successful process-experiential therapy case and showed that the problematic patterns, which later became the main focus in the therapy, were already present in the client's first utterances.

DSA was developed as a micro-analytic method to examine the dialogical organization of client and therapist utterances in psychotherapeutic discourse. The dialogical self (DS) is a general theory of human experience and personality. It is appropriate to ask at what level do they meet.

It seems that the concept of position has somewhat different meanings in DSA and DS, although both are inspired by Bakhtinian dialogic. DS emphasizes the multivoiced nature of personality derived from Bakhtin's conception of the polyphonic novel (Hermans 2003). The self is described as a multiplicity of I-positions.

DSA has its origin in Bakhtin's theory of utterance. Whereas the idea of I-positions employs the polyphonic novel as its root metaphor, DSA starts from the dialogic structure of utterances. It means that, in DSA, the position is defined by *the act of expression* in relation to the addressee and to the referential object. In DS, the position is mainly defined by the stance that each of the voices adopt in the polyphonic configuration of the self. Thus, both views converge in the emphasis that the position articulates the speaker's personal stance, but the meaning of stance seems to be different because of the root metaphors from which the two conceptions stem. To explore the divergences and convergences of DSA in relation to DS will remain a task for the future.

NOTES

1   Throughout the presentation the client (or the speaker) will be denoted as 'she' and the therapist (or the listener) as 'he'.
2   The relevance of this aspect in psychotherapy process research was emphasized in

the assimilation model (Stiles et al. 1990, 1992). The client's problematic experiences were identified by cataloguing all instances of 'an attitude to an object'.
3   In the SORT the terms of the two first concepts are different. Reciprocal roles stands for dialogical patterns and procedures for dialogical sequences. In DSA they are modified in order to be conceptually more compatible with the Bakhtinian theory of utterance. For instance, reciprocal roles refer mainly to interpersonal configurations, while the dialogical pattern applies to any referential object. The person relates dialogically to other people but also to inanimate things, events, etc.
4   This is, in fact, another way of understanding our tendency to personify the referential objects.
5   The original language is Finnish. Some of the nuances of expression are obviously lost in translation.
6   Finnish language permits an easy use of the passive voice. It might be more correctly translated as 'one' instead of 'I' though here it is translated by the colloquial English usage of 'you' to preserve the flavour of the encounter.

References

Bakhtin, M.M. (1981). 'Discourse in the novel.' In M. Holquist (ed.) *The Dialogic Imagination: Four Essays by M.M. Bakhtin* (pp. 258–422). Austin, TX: University of Texas Press.

Bakhtin, M.M. (1984). *Problems of Dostoevsky's Poetics*. Manchester: Manchester University Press.

Bakhtin, M.M. (1986). 'The problem of speech genres.' In C. Emerson and M. Holquist (eds) *Speech Genres and Other Late Essays* (pp. 60–102). Austin, TX: University of Texas Press.

Bakhtin, M.M. (1986). 'The problem of the text in linguistics, philology, and the human sciences: An experiment in philosophical analysis.' In C. Emerson and M. Holquist (eds) *Speech Genres and Other Late Essays* (pp. 103–131). Austin, TX: University of Texas Press.

Bollas, C. (1987). *The Shadow of the Object*. London: Free Association.

Fairbairn, W.R.D. (1944). 'Endopsychic structure considered in terms of object-relationships.' In W.R.D. Fairbairn (1992). *Psychoanalytic Studies of the Personality* (pp. 82–132). London: Routledge.

Freud, S. (1914/1958). 'Remembering, repeating and working-through.' *Standard Edition*, Vol. 12 (pp. 147–156). London: Hogarth Press.

Freud, S. (1917/1958). 'Mourning and melancholia.' *Standard Edition*, Vol. 14 (pp. 243–258). London: Hogarth Press.

Gergen, K. (1994). 'Exploring the postmodern: Perils or potentials?' *American Psychologist*, 49, 412–416.

Hermans, H.J.M. (2003). 'The construction and reconstruction of a dialogical self.' *Journal of Constructivist Psychology*, 16, 89–130.

Klein, M. (1926). 'The psychological principles of early analysis.' In R.E. Money-Kyrle (ed.) *Love, Guilt and Reparation and Other Works 1921–1945* (pp. 128–138). London: Hogarth Press.

Klein, M. (1946/1984). 'Notes on some schizoid mechanisms.' In R.E. Money-Kyrle (ed.) *Envy and Gratitude and Other Works 1946–1963 by Melanie Klein* (pp. 1–24). London: Hogarth Press.

Leiman, M. (1992). 'The concept of sign in the work of Vygotsky, Winnicott and Bakhtin: Further integration of object relations theory and activity theory.' *British Journal of Medical Psychology*, *65*, 209–221.

Leiman, M. (1994a). 'The development of Cognitive Analytic Therapy.' *International Journal of Short Term Psychotherapy*, *9*, 67–81.

Leiman, M. (1994b). 'Projective identification as early joint action sequences: A Vygotskian addendum to the Procedural Sequence Object Relations Model.' *British Journal of Medical Psychology*, *67*, 97–106.

Leiman, M. (2002). 'Toward semiotic dialogism.' *Theory and Psychology*, *12*, 221–235.

Leiman, M. and Stiles, W.B. (2001). 'Dialogical sequence analysis and the Zone of Proximal Development as conceptual enhancements to the assimilation model: The case of Jan revisited.' *Psychotherapy Research*, *11*, 311–330.

Ryle, A. (1975). 'Self-to-self and self-to-other.' *New Psychiatry*, 24 April, 12–13.

Ryle, A. (1990). *Cognitive-Analytic Therapy: Active Participation in Change. A New Integration in Brief Psychotherapy*. Chichester: John Wiley.

Ryle, A. (1994). 'Projective identification: A particular form of reciprocal role procedures.' *British Journal of Medical Psychology*, *67*, 107–114.

Ryle, A. (1997). *Cognitive Analytic Therapy and Borderline Personality Disorder*. Chichester: John Wiley.

Ryle, A. and Kerr, I. (2002). *Introducing Cognitive Analytic Therapy: Principles and Practice*. Chichester: John Wiley.

Shotter, J. (1993). 'Vygotsky: The social negotiation of semiotic mediation.' *New Ideas in Psychology*, *11*, 61–75.

Stiles, W.B., Elliott, R., Llewelyn, S.P., Firth-Cozens, J.A., Margison, F.R., Shapiro, D.A. and Hardy, G. (1990). 'Assimilation of problematic experiences by clients in psychotherapy.' *Psychotherapy*, *27*, 411–420.

Stiles, W.B., Meshot, C.M., Anderson, T.M. and Sloan, W.W., Jr (1992). 'Assimilation of problematic experiences: The case of John Jones.' *Psychotherapy Research*, *2*, 81–101.

Voloshinov, V.N. (1976). *Freudianism: A Marxist Critique*. New York: Academic Press.

Voloshinov, V.N. (1986). *Marxism and the Philosophy of Language*. Cambridge, MA: Harvard University Press.

Vygotsky, L.S. (1978). *Mind in Society*. Edited by M. Cole, V. John-Steiner, S. Scribner and E. Souberman. Boston, MA: Harvard University Press.

Index